AN ASTONISHING LOOK AT
THE WOR[...]
NEW YOR[...] W9-BFE-639
THEIR COAST-TO-COAST RIVALS

THE BRONX ZOO

Sparky Lyle
and
Peter Golenbock

A Dell Book

To my wife, Mary, whom I can always count on in the clutch, and to my two sons, Dane and Shane, who mean so much to me.

A.L.

To Grandma Ray and Aunt Shirley, may you be with us forever, and to Rhonda, my friend and lover, lover and friend.

P.G.

Published by
Dell Publishing Co., Inc.
1 Dag Hammarskjold Plaza
New York, New York 10017

Dell ® TM 681510, Dell Publishing Co., Inc.

ISBN: 0-440-10764-4

Reprinted by arrangement with Crown Publishers, Inc.
Printed in the United States of America
First Dell printing—March 1980
Second Dell printing—March 1980
Third Dell printing—April 1980

THE
BRONX
ZOO

Preface

When I was approached to write a book with Sparky Lyle, I must admit that at first such a prospect didn't particularly excite me. I had known a few things about him. Behind the Daliesque, funky mustache, Lyle was an athlete seemingly without a nervous system. He'd go into the game with the bases loaded, and with uncanny regularity, he'd get out of the inning without the other team scoring. Over the last ten years, no relief pitcher did it better. It can be argued, in fact, that no relief *ever* did it better. And on those days when with the bases loaded, the batter got lucky and blooped one in for a two-run single that won the game, if you looked at Sparky's face, you'd never guess that he had just lost. Kipling once said that it's a rare man who can treat winning and losing as the same. Sparky Lyle has been one man who can do that. There was one other thing I knew about Sparky: he enjoyed sitting nude on teammates' birthday cakes. I figured, that's gotta tell you something.

Still, a skilled athlete doesn't necessarily produce compelling reading. After having been weaned on soporific books like *How to Throw the Spitball* and *The Joe Shlobotnick Story*, I did not want to write such a book. Sparky had always kept such a low public profile. I wondered whether he would have something special to say.

Sparky himself had had reservations about writing a book, I later found out. However, his agent, Doug Newton, who knew both of us, was a persistent cuss, and he convinced us to meet in Fort Lauderdale during spring training to talk about it. I figured that at worst it would be a vacation I could write off my taxes.

To my surprise and delight, Sparky had no intention of writing the ordinary jock book, and after long discussion we decided to give the fans an inside look at baseball by recounting the 1978 season as it was happening. With personalities like Billy Martin, Reggie Jackson, Thurman Munson, Lou Piniella, Mickey Rivers, and Graig Nettles on the team and with George Steinbrenner at the helm, we reasoned that the project had an excellent chance of turning out to be a unique and memorable one.

I underestimated how memorable. Something else I had underestimated: the perspicacity and insight of Sparky Lyle. He's a keen observer with an excellent memory, and he has the ability to tell a story and make it come out funny and right. At the beginning, moreover, he had given me his word that if some of what he had to say was controversial, he wouldn't play safe and chop the manuscript to ribbons at the end, and he didn't. If this book was to be the true representation of his feelings, actions, and observations, he, too, wanted the honesty to come through.

When Crown, Sparky, and I sat down to sign the contract for the book, the Yankees were mired in third place, eight and a half games behind the Boston Red Sox. Some of the other publishers had asked, "How's it going to end?" and decided not to bid on it. By this time I had been working with Sparky for several months, and my answer was "If we make the first two-hundred and-fifty pages interesting and exciting, no one'll care how it ends." Crown, to its credit, didn't care either.

As it turned out, the how-to-end-it problem never arose. Whether by magic, Dame Fortune, or destiny, the Yankees made up the deficit and won the Division title, pennant, and World Series. Oh, ye of little faith! For me, watching Graig Nettles sitting under Yaz's pop-up in the bottom of the ninth on the last day at Fenway was one of those memorable moments. When he caught the ball, giving the Yankees the Division title, I was sitting in front of the TV set wondering how the Yankees had managed to overcome it all with the divisive animosities and the oppressive pressure and the injuries. I also couldn't help but feel that whatever the quirks in personality of the players, the guys in Steinbrenner's zoo were nevertheless a very special collection of ballplayers. The 1978 Yankees were a team that will be remembered throughout baseball history along with the 1914 Miracle Boston Braves and with the 1951 New York Giants, pennant winners after the Miracle of Coogan's Bluff.

I would like to take this opportunity to acknowledge the contributions of the following: Mary Lyle, Mrs. Sparky, for bearing with us while we spent all those hours locked up with our tape recorder. Her encouragement and hot coffee were greatly appreciated. I'd again like to thank Doug Newton for initiating this project and giving his valuable advice so freely. My thanks, too, to my estimable literary agent, Jay Acton, for recognizing the worthiness of the project and of encouraging me to pursue it, and to Frank Coffey and Tom Biracree for their sound advice and for bringing me to Jay. My gratitude also goes to Drew Hart, who scouted the book for Crown, and to editor Larry Freundlich of Crown, a man of sensibility and taste. It was his masterstroke to name the book *The Bronx Zoo*. I wish to acknowledge Amy Heller and Alexa Pierce, who typed long hours to enable me to complete the book on time.

Also, I'd like to express my gratitude for the guidance of the late Dr. Joseph R. Kidd, who instilled in me the love of writing, and thank journalists Robert Sumner, Rich Duffy, and Albert Winslow for working on and hopefully improving whatever writing skills I may have. Finally, to Vivienne, Keith, and Sandy Sohn, Rich Hershenson, Jim and Paula, and to Barry and Sharon Halper and their little Yankee, Jason, thanks for your special friendship.

PETER GOLENBOCK

Englewood, New Jersey

October 25, 1977   Demarest, New Jersey

A group of businessmen and I were discussing whether I should invest some money in a shopping center in Kentucky when the phone in my New Jersey home rang. I picked it up and answered it, something I don't usually do, but I was hoping it was Jack Lang, the president of the baseball writers. It was. "Sparky," he said, "may I offer you my congratulations. You have won the Cy Young Award."

I couldn't say a thing. I was dumbfounded. The writers had voted me, a relief pitcher, the best pitcher in the American League.

I knew I had had as good a year as possible. I pitched in 72 games, had a 13-5 record, a 2.17 ERA, and had 26 saves. Every game I relieved in, I finished. But never in a million years did I even secretly believe that the writers would give me the award, because it's so rare for a relief pitcher to get it. Mike Marshall won it once with the Dodgers, but he had been the only one. I thought for sure the Orioles' Jim Palmer would win it. He won 20 games, he's a great pitcher, and, besides, every year he campaigns for the thing. No one can blow his own horn the way Jim Palmer can.

I thanked Lang for calling, hung up, and that was the end of the business meeting. The shopping center could wait. My wife, Mary, and I got out the Dewar's and we started hollering and yelling and carrying on, and then the phone started ringing. I couldn't believe how many people and reporters called.

One reporter called and asked me what I'm going to do with the plaque when I get it. "I'm going to build a glass case on my front lawn with a big spotlight and display it," I told him. "But I'm only going to leave it out there for ten years." He wasn't sure whether to believe me or not.

I'm not the emotional type, and I've had so many ups and downs during my career that by next week this thing will be history to me, but I feel that on this one day, at least, I can be excited and proud and even fart in public if I want. I was on a team that won the pennant and the World Series, despite enough crap to last an entire career, and now that I've won the Cy Young Award everyone can say that Sparky Lyle was an important part of that team.

I don't remember any one pitch or any one game during the regular season. It was the season in general. Billy Martin's having enough confidence in me to pitch me in all those games, usually in critical situations with men on base and the game close, and me proving once again what I've been saying ever since I came up to the majors in '67: if you let me pitch often enough and make me the big guy in the bullpen, I'll do the job for you. I'll come in when it counts and get them out.

The best thing that happened to me was finishing the final two games of the play-offs against Kansas City and right after that winning the first game of the World Series against the Dodgers. The Royals were leading us in the play-offs, two games to one, and they needed only one more game to win. In the fourth game we were ahead 4–0 real quick, but in the fourth Reggie Jackson screwed up a couple of balls in the outfield, the Royals scored two runs, and with two outs and a runner on, Billy brought me in. Ordinarily the fourth inning is much too early to bring me into a game. I'm a short relief pitcher. I pitch in the eighth and ninth when there's a lead that has to be protected. I'm the last resort, the guy who has to put his finger in the dike every night. But I guess Billy was desperate, so he brought me in in the fourth.

As I was warming up in the bullpen, Fred Stanley, our backup shortstop, was catching me, and when pitching coach Art Fowler called from the dugout and asked how I looked, Fred told him, "Sparky ain't got nothin', Art."

Billy brought me in anyway, and when I got out to the mound and threw my warm-up pitches, my slider suddenly started to work right, and for the next five innings, it was the Royals who didn't have nothin'. I faced 16 batters and got 15 outs.

I knew that the Royals weren't going to beat me. I had told Mary, "I can't pitch in games when we're real far behind or ahead. I'm just not into the game." In fact, when Ralph Houk was the Yankee manager, I had once come into a game with men on and the score tied, got out of the inning, and after we scored about eight runs, even though I had another inning to go, I asked him to take me out of the game.

The best time for me to pitch is when we're ahead by a run or the score is tied. When the game is on the line. Against the Royals I was ahead by a run, and Mary was telling me that she was sitting in the stands watching me, and when everybody was hollering for the Yankees to score a few more runs, she was thinking, "No. I don't want them to score more runs." Later she told me, "I knew you weren't going to lose that game. You only had a one-run lead." And she was right.

After the game, the writers asked me, "Can you pitch again tomorrow?" I said, "Only four or five innings. After that, I might start getting tired." They laughed. They must have figured I was joking. We were losing 3–2 going into the top of the ninth of the final game. Paul Blair singled, Roy White walked, and Mickey Rivers singled up the middle to drive in a run to tie it. Willie Randolph drove in Roy with a long fly to put us ahead, and after we scored a fifth run, Billy brought me in to pitch the bottom of the ninth and end it.

I got the first guy out real quick, then the next guy up got a base hit. We were in Kansas City and with Freddie Patek, their shortstop, up, everybody in the stands was ranting and raving and going crazy. Thurman dropped the sign down, I threw Patek a slider, and he hit a nice one-hopper to Graig Nettles at third, and that was it. A perfect double-play ball. Graig didn't even have to move. He caught it chest high, threw to Randolph at second, and bang, bang, it was over. All I remember is raising my arms high and jumping straight up in the air. Thurman started hugging me, and then there was a big pile of players around me. It was a great feeling, because we had battled our asses off to win that pennant. Goddamn it, we battled hard, played better than they did, and deserved to win. All season long, we never gave up.

I had pitched good again, and because we were on national television, people were beginning to notice me. They were saying, "Goddamn, this son of a bitch *can* pitch every day if he has to."

Also, what was important to me about our winning that game was that if we had lost, I am convinced that George Steinbrenner, who owns the Yankees, would have fired Billy. There had been talk the last couple of weeks, yet despite the talk, Billy still benched Reggie Jackson in the final game, because the Royals were throwing a tough left-handed pitcher, Paul Splittorff, and Reggie doesn't hit the tough lefties. Billy knows that, too, and he decided to play Blair instead. Ordinarily it's no big deal when a manager does something like that, but last winter George had paid Reggie $2,930,000 to play for the Yankees, and George wasn't paying Reggie all that money to sit on the bench. When we heard Reggie wasn't going to start, we thought, "This guy"—meaning Billy—"has some balls." But then again, Billy and George had been fighting all year, usually after a fight between Billy and Reggie. And talk that Billy was going to get fired had popped up so often that after a while we stopped paying any attention to it. It was getting in the way of our playing. When Billy benched Reggie against Splittorff, my only reaction was "We'll be a stronger team with someone else playing right field and with someone else batting fourth against the guy." With him or without him, I knew the Royals weren't going to beat us.

I wasn't particularly proud of how I won the first World Series game, but on the other hand, I won't give it back either. We were ahead by a run in the ninth when I came in, and I gave up a hit to tie it, but still I pitched pretty well, holding the Dodgers through the twelfth inning when Randolph doubled, and Blair, a defensive replacement for Reggie, singled through short to win it. I know the statistics show that Blair hit only .200 this year, but to me that doesn't mean squat. I'll bet he won ten games for us in the late innings.

We split the next four games, with Catfish Hunter and

Don Gullett, both sore-armed, getting bombed. Mike Torrez and Ron Guidry got the wins, and again Reggie caused a lot of crap by complaining he wouldn't play unless the Dodgers gave him better tickets for his friends, and by criticizing Billy for not playing him against Splittorff and for pitching Cat in the second World Series game. With all the talk of Billy getting fired, George and general manager Gabe Paul called a press conference right after the sixth game and announced that Billy would be back in '78 as manager. George agreed not to interfere with Billy so much next year, and Billy said he wouldn't say bad things about George in the newspapers. I understand Reggie went to George and told him he wouldn't play if Billy was allowed to manage another year, but apparently George didn't believe him.

With that out of the way, all Reggie did was put on one of the greatest exhibitions of hitting in baseball history. Reggie hit three home runs on three consecutive pitches off three different pitchers, and we won 8–4. I was in the clubhouse watching the game on TV when Reggie hit the final one. What a display of raw power! When a batter hits a home run, he usually hits the ball when it's out in front of him a little bit. On his third home run, when Reggie made contact, the ball was almost even with his body. You should have seen it in slow motion. Charlie Hough, a knuckleball pitcher, floated the ball in, and when it was almost past him, Reggie swung his bat so hard and quick I couldn't believe it. He powered that ball into the center-field bleachers. If he had hit the ball another inch or so in front of him, he would have hit that son of a bitch right out of Yankee Stadium. It was like he knew the pitch was coming. He swung so fast, and wham, he threw his bat down, and he just knew it was gone.

At the ticker-tape parade down Broadway a few days after the Series, George came up to me and asked me to drop by his office when I had a chance. A couple of days after the parade I drove to the Stadium to see him, and when I got there he said he wanted to reward me for my outstanding season by extending my contract another year at my $135,000-a-year salary. Plus, he said, he was going to give me a $35,000 bonus—if it was OK with me. I told him, "I didn't come here to negotiate my contract.

Whatever you say is fine with me. Whatever you feel like doing is just fine."

I was ecstatic. George had made me feel so good, because it had been so unexpected. What a guy he is! What a great thing for him to do! I just couldn't believe it.

On top of all this, now I've won the Cy Young Award. I've got to pinch myself to know this isn't a dream.

I wonder what Ben Shingledecker thinks of my winning the Cy Young. Shingledecker, who had never played any sports in his life, was the manager of my hometown teener league team. I tried out for the team when I was thirteen, and after the tryout, Ben, a little butterball with thinning hair and glasses, told me, "You can't throw hard enough to be a pitcher."

That sorta crushed me because I wanted to play so bad. Then again, I thought, "Damn, maybe he's right," so I said, "Screw it," and for the next few years I just played pickup around the neighborhood. Sometimes we played in my backyard, and if we hit the ball into the yard of our neighbor Tom Patterson, he'd raise hell and take the ball. To get him back, I'd cut his cabbage plants.

My hometown, Reynoldsville, Pennsylvania, is a nice little town of about 2,700 people. I'm glad I grew up there. It's maybe three blocks long, and it's got two stoplights. On each corner there's a gas station. At one time, it had a very nice business district, small but still nice, but a lot of the stores are no longer in business.

Reynoldsville is about 100 miles northeast of Pittsburgh in the northwest corner of the state. It was a coal mining town, and at one time almost everybody worked in the mines. All of them are closed now except one. Our next-door neighbor, Cooney Fye, worked in the mines. I used to see him come home at night all pitch-black. And this guy who lives on the other side, Matt McKinley, he worked in the mines all his life, and he was bent over working in there. It was terrible to see. And boy, they worked their asses off for not a hell of a lot of money, I'm telling you.

I remember when the picture show burned down. The fire damn near took the whole town. The theater had been closed, reopened, closed, and reopened. When it burned down, we had to go to the next town, Dubois, about nine miles away.

Reynoldsville High didn't field a baseball team. I played football and basketball there, but there was no baseball team. Instead, we had a local Legion ball league. It was open to anyone who wanted to play. The spring of my junior year in high school I started pitching for the Dubois team of the Legion league 'cause not only did Reynoldsville not have a picture house, it didn't field a Legion team either.

The Dubois coach was a guy who did the news on the local radio. We had to practice in a swamp. Games were on Sunday, and then afterward we'd pile into a couple cars with our uni's on and go to a Legion Post. It was kinda fun 'cause I pitched most every Sunday. When you're a kid, that gives you something to look forward to.

When I pitched for Dubois, I was always striking out 16 or 17 batters, and losing. I never won many games. There was one pitcher by the name of Fred Sherkel I could never beat. He was so good. Every time I'd pitch, it seemed, I'd be pitching against the son of a bitch. He had played minor league ball, and he could change speeds, and he had great control, which I didn't. I'd be striking out a lot of guys, and he'd just be up there pinpointing. I don't think I ever beat him, and I never could understand it. I was a kid, and all I could think was "Goddamn, that guy's not throwing hard enough to hurt you." And yet he'd give up only five hits and never be in trouble and win.

I was still making headlines because of all the batters I'd strike out. In one game that summer I struck out 31. It was a 17-inning game, but the funny thing about it, I only pitched 14 innings. In the middle of the game I played first base for three innings. To this day I feel it was as a result of that game that I got to sign a pro contract because nobody outside the area ever heard about me before that. I threw a fastball and a curve ball, which I threw with my thumb up in the air. Everyone knew it was coming. In that game I walked eight or nine, I always did, but that was something. I remember how exciting it was when we kept playing extra innings, and I kept striking out all these guys and I kept wondering, "Jesus Christ,

how long will this go on?" Maybe I was throwing harder
that day or had a better curve ball. I don't know. But
after the game, the next day it was in the papers, with
big headlines, and some scouts started coming to watch
me pitch.

By the next summer I was getting a lot of recognition.
I switched teams and played with Dubois's rival, Curwens-
ville. I felt I could learn more because they were a better
team with a better organization. A lot of local people
were kinda pissed off about that, though some continued
to take an interest in my career. Rube Haggerty, a great
big guy, had had some minor league experience as a
pitcher, and he told me, "Let me tell you something. There's
only two things that can ruin a baseball player, alcohol
and pussy." I'm young and listening to this stuff, and he
says, "To keep yourself from being ruined, every time
you think you want some pussy, jack off, and then take
a dollar and put it in the trunk of your car and forget
about it. You'll keep your fastball, and you'll have a lot
of money at the end of the season." So now I had to
find a car with a very small trunk—or no trunk at all.

A bird dog from Pittsburgh, Socco McCarrey, wanted
to sign me. Socco told my dad, "If they get a look at your
son, I'm sure they'll be interested in him." I went to
Forbes Field for a tryout, and I remember I was throwing just as hard as I could, and they asked me if I had
anything else. I said, "Yeah, I have this curve ball." This
coach says, "Let me see it." I threw a couple of curves,
and he said, "Son, you can stick that up your ass. You
ain't gonna make it." He didn't even give me a chance
to finish throwing. They told me, "See you later, son." Of
course, I was heartbroken.

I talked to a lot of clubs. Ray Mueller from the Cleveland organization came to see me pitch one day. I struck
out 19. I was so happy because I figured, "Damn, I
pitched good when he saw me and I won." I couldn't wait
to talk to Mueller. After the game was over, I walked over
to him and I was all excited, and the first thing out of
his mouth was "I'd like to see you pitch again." I went,
"Arrrrrrrrrrrrrrgh." I said to my dad, "What the hell can
I do? I can't pitch any better than I pitched today." I

said, "Screw it," and I went to work at the pottery. Tim
Thompson, a scout for the Dodgers, looked at me and
told my dad he wanted to sign me, but he wanted me
to pitch one more year of Legion ball. That just sounded
ridiculous to me.

The guy who finally signed me was George Stoller, a
scout for the Baltimore Orioles. He came to see me pitch,
and afterward he called the house and said, "I'd like to
come over tomorrow and sign Sparky to a professional
baseball contract." My dad said, "Yeah." Stoller said,
"Your son does want to play professional baseball?" Dad
said, "Oh, yeah." Dad put me on the phone, and I said,
"Yes sir, I do." Stoller said, "OK, I'll be down tomorrow
at three P.M."

When the time came, I figured, "This is going to be
the same old crap. He isn't going to sign me," so when
he came, I wasn't even home. I had gone down to the
ball field to play basketball, so my dad had to come after
me and tell me that the Baltimore scout was at the house.
I went home, and son of a bitch, he really was there.
It didn't take fifteen minutes for me to sign, and the very
next day I left for Bluefield, West Virginia. Before I signed,
Stoller told my dad, "I want you to know one thing. Once
he puts his name on that contract, you lose a son. The
Orioles own him, lock, stock, and barrel."

That's one thing that always stuck in my mind up until
this day. I think that has a lot to do with why I don't get
upset when a club would try to do something to you, like
trading you or telling you how horseshit you are or doing
things to you just because they feel like it. I always thought
back to what Stoller said. Sometimes I didn't think it fair
or didn't think it right, but I always went along because
I even started playing this game. Stoller gave me fair
warning.

You might be interested in knowing how big a bonus
I got to sign. Well, it was *nada*. Nothing. Zero. Zip. I
didn't get a cent. When Stoller said he wanted to sign
me, my dad said, "Well, you know we'd like to have a
little money." Stoller started hemming and hawing, and
I got nervous and I said, "Screw it, man, where do I

sign? Let's go." Stoller told me later that we could have gotten maybe $10,000, which at the time would have been a lot of money for us, but, dumb old me, I was too anxious. I wanted to sign. When I got to the minors, I found out that almost everybody got $8,000. That was the standard bonus. It was giveaway money, and when I saw some of the guys in the minors who were pitching and had gotten their $8,000, I was so mad I couldn't stand it. Hardly any of them are playing today or even played long afterward for that matter. I found out, too, that how much money you got had a lot to do with how you were treated. In the minors the first couple years it didn't matter which pitcher was better. What counted was how much money was invested in you.

I had never been away from home before going to Bluefield. I was twenty. I lived in a lady's house with another guy, Bob Patrillo, and he and I didn't get along. I don't know why, but for some reason he just didn't like me. He had taken his bonus money and bought himself a Corvette. We lived in the same room, and he'd drive to the park without me.

In Bluefield the park is down in a valley, and there are beautiful meadows all around. It's real pretty, with big hills in the background. We'd take a bus to go on road trips, and we'd get about halfway up one of the hills, and that son of a bitch wouldn't go any farther. We'd have to pile out of the bus sometimes for it to keep going. It was the lowest rung of the minors, and things would happen, and yet when you looked back on it, it was fun because everybody's so Goddamn happy to be there, they'd have put up with anything.

At Bluefield, when I wasn't at the park, I rarely went out. I didn't eat in the lady's house, so after the game I'd either go and get something to eat or I'd come home and go to bed. I was getting $400 a month, which isn't very much, but I wasn't doing anything. I wasn't even putting the dollar bills in the trunk. I didn't care about anything else except playing. I was putting forth every bit of effort I could because I had told my dad that I was giving it four years. If I didn't get my shot at the majors by then, I was going back to the Reynoldsville china factory. I felt that, hey, this is fun and you're mak-

ing some money, but to play in the minors for ten years
was getting nowhere. I didn't want one job in the summer-
time and another job in the wintertime. That wasn't for
me. As much as I loved the game, I didn't want that. I
would have rather worked at the pottery factory and
played Legion ball on Sundays.

I pitched well enough at Bluefield so that after a couple
of months the Orioles moved me up to A ball at Appleton, Wisconsin, which was funny because my mom and
dad, my Uncle Walter, and some friends were driving
down from Reynoldsville to see me play at Bluefield, and
as they were driving, I got sent up. They got to Bluefield,
and I had already left. My manager at Appleton was
Billy DeMars, who is now a coach with the Philadelphia
Phillies. I thought he was tough. He had a frightening
glare, was a disciplinarian, and didn't stand for any bullshit, which I liked. He was a baseball man, and I admired
that because I was there to learn.

I remember the first game I started at Appleton. We
were playing against Rich Reichardt and Tom Egan, two
bonus babies signed by the Angels. Reichardt had gotten
a $200,000 bonus, which was tremendous for 1964, and
he was one big son of a bitch. I struck Reichardt out
four times and Egan three times. And I was so happy because I had been unsure about how good I really was.
When Reichardt came to the plate the first time, I thought,
"It doesn't matter what I throw because this guy is going
to hit the ball very, very far." But when I saw that he
couldn't hit my curve ball, he didn't see anything else. I
just kept striking him out. I felt so good after the game
was over. From that time on, there was no stopping me.
It's not that I knew I was going to make the major leagues.
However, when I saw what the other kids from around the
country looked like, I knew I had a chance. I discovered
then and there that everyone has something he can't hit,
and it was up to me to find out what it was.

I was in the Oriole chain for about five months. I started
six or seven games for Bluefield and about a half-dozen
for Appleton, won about half of them, and after that I
was drafted by the Red Sox organization. Some of the
pitchers the Orioles had signed had been paid $30,000
or $40,000 as bonuses, and they had to be protected, and

the only way they could do that was to put them on the major league 40-man roster. A team can draft a player only if it promotes the player to the next rung on the minor league ladder, so if you're a major leaguer, there's no higher rank and you can't be drafted. The Orioles told me they were going to do the best they could for me, which was to put me on a Triple-A roster. I was wild, but I had pitched well. Still, I hadn't cost them anything, and they couldn't protect me and not protect one of their big bonus boys, so they felt they had no choice. They also said that they didn't feel that any club would draft me and sign me to a major league contract. They were wrong. The Red Sox took me.

After I came home at the end of my first year in the minors, I was still getting advice from the older athletes. Art Benny, the most knowledgeable guy about sports in Reynoldsville, called me and said he had a solution to my control problems. He said, "I'll tell you what to do if you want to get your control. Go buy a heavy hammer, paint a mark on a tree, and you go out and hit that mark every day with that hammer. Take that hammer and keep pounding that mark, and you'll find that your control will get better." So I bought a heavy hammer, and all winter I hammered trees. My control never got any better, but I killed 450 maple trees.

Because the Red Sox had drafted me onto their major league roster, I went to my first major league camp in 1965, when I was twenty-one. It was held in Scottsdale, Arizona. The Red Sox sent me back down to the minors, of course. I started my second year of pro ball at Winston-Salem, North Carolina, at the Double-A level. It was my toughest year in baseball. It was the first year I was pitching in relief, and I wasn't doing the job. It was so hard for me because my control was so bad, and I'd end up walking runs in and getting no one out. It was terribly frustrating. At the ball park there was this old guy who used to sit up on a hill behind third base and holler at me all the time. Every day. "Hey, rabbit ears," he used to call me. And every now and then I'd say stuff to him. This one night I got shelled, and the manager came out to the mound to take me out, and as I was walking off, this old guy yelled, "I see you did it again. Another fine job." Boy, my ears got red. I made a hard right turn and went right up the hill after him. I was going to choke that old bastard to death. As I charged up there, a group of old guys were picking up their lawn chairs, ready to hit me with them. Fortunately, Kenny Wright and Bob Montgomery, who were out in the bullpen, tackled me before I could reach him, and we rolled back down the hill. That was the last time I lost my temper on the field.

You see some crazy things in the minors. At Winston-Salem our trainer was a guy by the name of John Dennai. He used to be an Olympic walker, and on special nights Dennai would stand at first base in his Olympic uni, and the other team would pick anyone they wanted, and Dennai would heal-toe it from first while the other guy would start at home and run the bases as fast as he could. I never saw Dennai get beat.

One night Wright's elbow swelled up, and he went to Dennai. "Boy, my elbow's killing me," he said, and John grabbed it and fiddled around with it a little bit and said, "Yep, looks like a case of tenderitis." Wright said, "You mean tendonitis, don't you?" Dennai said, "Well, it's either tenderitis or tendonitis, one of those two." I said to myself, "That guy is never going to touch my arm."

The lowest I'd ever been in my entire life was at Winston-Salem. We weren't playing real well, and I wasn't pitching good, and from out of the blue Bill Slack, my manager who I despised, put me on the disabled list. My arm wasn't hurt. I couldn't understand why he had done that. I said to myself, "I'll be a son of a bitch, being on the disabled list for no reason at all." I wanted to play so badly, and for fifteen days I couldn't. When they do a thing like that to you, especially when you're young, you say to yourself, "What the hell am I doing here? Why am I bothering to do this?" I was so disappointed, and it was frustrating because it was totally out of my control. It was the longest fifteen days I ever spent.

After a 5-5 season at Winston-Salem, the next year I went to Ocala, Florida, for spring training. Ted Williams was a coach there, and it was he who changed my life. He watched me pitch one afternoon, and afterward he

asked me what I thought was the best pitch in baseball.
I told him I didn't know. Williams said, "The slider. You
know why?" I said no. He said, "Because it was the only
pitch I couldn't hit consistently even when I knew it was
coming." I was in awe of Williams. He had been a lifetime
three-forty-something hitter, and he knew more about hitting than anyone alive. When Ted Williams told me something, I listened, because he knew so much about the
pitchers he faced. All Williams did was tell me how the
slider broke and what the ball was supposed to do. He
gave me the incentive to find things out for myself. He
taught me to be inquisitive and to be precise about my
pitching. He told me that the ball should come in at a
right-handed batter and drop down. He did not tell me
how to accomplish this. It was up to me to figure out how
to throw the ball to make it spin the right way *and* break.
Making it spin isn't too tough. Making it break is. It was
difficult, like walking into a strange room with the lights
off. I didn't know what the hell I was going to run into.

For three-quarters of a season the slider was on my
mind constantly. I was always practicing, experimenting
with different ways of holding the ball, different ways of
releasing it. I never got any help with it from anybody.
Our pitching coaches were good, but they taught you how
to pitch like they had back in the forties. Their era is
gone. Baseball keeps changing. Pitchers no longer throw
the roundhouse curve, the emery ball, or the spitter, except maybe Gaylord Perry. Whenever I told one of these
coaches I wanted to practice my slider, they'd say, "You
don't want to learn that pitch, son, because it'll hurt your
arm." The way it had been taught, you had to throw the
ball across your body and snap your wrist, which did
hurt the arm. I didn't learn to throw mine that way. I
always thought that the "you can hurt your arm throwing
the slider" line was a bunch of bullshit. You can hurt your
arm jacking off. If you learn to throw the pitch right,
you're going to be all right.

In 1966 I was playing for Pittsfield, Massachusetts. We
were at home, and it was June, and one night about three
in the morning I was lying in bed mulling over how I
should grip the ball to make it break and drop. Suddenly,
and I can't explain why this was, I felt I knew. I had to

get out of bed and try it, and I went outside under the streetlamp and started throwing it against my house. The ball broke a little bit. The next day when I got to the park I told my catcher, Bob Montgomery, about it. I'll never forget the first time I threw it in a game. It went in on the batter and fell right off. I said, "Well, Jesus Christ, will you look at that."

Eddie Popowski was the manager of Pittsfield. He had ulcers, used to get real sick, and he had an alarm watch that was always going off to remind him to take his medicine. One night he was coaching third base waving runs around when the alarm went off. You could hear the "ding-a-ling-a-ling" all the way in the dugout as he waved the runners in. It looked like a Chinese fire drill.

Popowski was one of those managers who would give a baseball to the elevator operator and tell him, "Whoever comes in after two o'clock in the morning, have them sign it." We had one guy who used to stay out late, but Eddie could never catch him. Eddie used to sit in the lobby after the game and watch the guys go out, and he'd be there waiting for them to come in. This one guy he never saw come in again, even though Eddie would be sitting there way after bed check, yet when Eddie checked this guy's room, he'd always be there. Popowski couldn't figure out how this guy was doing it.

Eventually Popowski noticed that the only thing coming through the lobby late at night was the laundry cart. The next night when the cart came through, Eddie ran after it, and just as the cart was being wheeled into the elevator, he caught up with it and started pulling all the towels and sheets out. Sure enough, on the bottom was the player. "I caught you, you son of a bitch," Popowski yelled at him, and right there he fined him.

Eddie used to get on my ass a lot because I would carry miniature slot cars on road trips with me. I was a big slot car buff back when they were the rage, and there were tracks in a lot of the towns we played in. Pop would say, "If you'd stop carrying those little, funny cars around and concentrate on your pitching instead, you'd be a better pitcher." To me stuff like that was silly, because if you're doing your job, then damn it, he should just leave you alone. Managers are always wanting you to be thinking about baseball twenty-four hours a day, but damnit, if you have to be thinking about baseball every minute you're awake in order to play well, then you might as well not bother.

It's funny what I remember. We had a guy by the name of Dick Cratz. I have never seen anybody sweat like him. He would get into his uniform, go out through the runway, and before he'd reach the dugout he'd be soaking wet. Another one of my teammates at Pittsfield was Carmen Fanzone. He played the trumpet, and I used to love to go with him to places where he played his horn. We'd go on the road, and we'd find a little club where they played jazz, and he was so good that he'd go in and sit with them. I remember one year in Sarasota, Florida, when we were playing winter ball together, we stayed at a big hotel, and he used to go upstairs to this big auditorium and practice. He'd be going up and down the scale. He said, "If I ever reach double high C, I'll be able to make it. I'll be able to play for a living." I don't know whether he ever did or not. He was a good steady ballplayer, stronger than hell. His hands were so strong he could grab you and bring you to your knees. Kenny Wright and Paul Dowd used to agitate him all the time. Carmen had a rubber ball that he was always squeezing. You never saw him without it. And he'd always say to Wright and Dowd, "Don't be messing with my ball." One night we took it and cut it into little pieces and stuffed the pieces inside a rubber that we filled with water. We hung it on his doorknob before he came back. Carmen came in, and he saw his ball cut up and the next thing I knew, Dowd was screaming, "No Carmen. No Carmen. Pleeeease no." We ran into the room, and we saw that Carmen had picked up one end of Dowd's mattress and made a sandwich with Dowd in the middle of it. He was jumping on him and yelling, "You gotta buy me a new ball. You gotta buy me a new ball."

I started my fourth year in baseball at Toronto in the International League. It was the highest classification in the Red Sox chain, but to be honest, Toronto was a terrible experience. I was there in 1967, and Torontonians didn't dig baseball that much then. It was hard to find a place to live, you had a hard time getting your money exchanged, and customs wasn't fun either. Our clubhouse guy, his name was Smitty, used to get out of the bus and give the customs agents some autographed baseballs, and they'd let us go through without checking our baggage. That was a big help, because most of our bus trips were about eighteen hours long, and any time that could be saved getting home was a plus. One night, though, Smitty got out, handed over the signed balls, but the guy at customs, instead of being thankful, got pissed. Maybe he had bet on us the night before. He told Smitty, "Take those baseballs and shove them up your ass." We knew we were gonna be there all night.

The worst part about it was that no one showed up to watch the games in Toronto. A team normally plays better at home than on the road, but none of the guys on the Toronto team looked forward to going back home. There were more pigeons than fans. Things were so disorganized that on opening day, an hour before the game, they didn't even have a pitcher's mound.

The year 1967 was when I got called up to the Red Sox. A few weeks before I got to Boston, the checks of the Toronto players all bounced. The club went bankrupt. The Red Sox, a class organization, took care of everything, though.

By the time I got to Toronto, the slider was working real well. I had good control over it, that was the biggest thing. Finally I had good control. At Toronto I was having a good year. My earned-run average was under two. When Dennis Bennett got hurt I got my shot with the Red Sox. Dick Williams was the Red Sox manager. He told me, "You're going to be number two behind John Wyatt. If you can't do that, we'll send you back. If you can, we'll see." That's all he said to me.

I remember the first time with the Red Sox when I warmed up to go into a game. I threw the first two pitches right out of the bullpen. Wyatt, who was nice and easygoing, said, "Hey, man, you just want to get loose. There's no sense throwing hard in the bullpen. Just throw it like me." I listened and took that in, and that's the way I've been doing it ever since. I see young kids come up and they do exactly the same thing as I did. When they get up to throw, they want to throw as hard as they can, even though they can get ready at half speed. Wyatt taught me. You learn from other guys.

When I was with the Sox, I was mostly by myself. I never ran around, never drilled holes in hotel doors, didn't go beaver shooting. I didn't feel I had been around long enough to be carrying around a pair of binoculars with me. When we stayed in New York, I used to go into Grand Central Station at about three, four in the morning. In the middle of the terminal I'd drop a dollar bill on the floor and pretend I didn't know I had dropped it and I'd watch the winos try to creep over and get it. They'd be lying around like they were sleeping, and even though that dollar bill didn't make any noise when it fell, as soon as it hit they'd start to stir. They knew where it came from, and they'd walk by me and try to slide it away from me with their feet without my seeing them, or they'd drop a newspaper on the ground on top of it to get it.

I stopped doing that when guests at the hotel started getting held up. A group of muggers would go up to the second or third floor, wait for the up elevator, get on, and rob the guests. They had been pulling these robberies about the time when I was getting in, and that scared me a little. I had a .25 then, and I would ride up the elevator with my gun pointed, waiting for them when the door opened. If the door had opened and I had seen another person with a gun pointing at me, I had a little surprise waiting for him.

My first year with the Red Sox we won the American League pennant. That was the year Carl Yastrzemski was walking on water. Almost singlehandedly he carried us to victory. In the field he was always making spectacular running and diving catches or he'd be throwing runners out at home. He played left field in Fenway like he built the place. At bat he'd always get the hit in the ninth to win it. Yaz used to call his shots. We'd be losing, and he'd say, "You get on, and I'll hit one, and we can go home," and he'd do it. Yaz was so spectacular that year it was unbelievable, and though he was exhausted at the end of the season, he never let down, not even once. One reason we won that year was that we had absolutely nothing to lose. The year before we had finished ninth in a ten-team league—only the Yankees had been worse—and we didn't have any idea that we could actually win the thing until about the first week in September. Right up to the final day of the season, we didn't feel any pressure. The fans were hollering and yelling and going crazy because the team hadn't won a pennant for a long time, but when we played the last couple of games against the Twins, it was nothing. And even after we won the final game, we didn't crack the champagne because we had to wait to see whether the Tigers would win or not. Detroit was playing a doubleheader against the Angels, and the Tigers had to win both to tie us. I remember watching the second game on the TV in our clubhouse. The Tigers had won the first game, but the Angels won the second. Our whole team was watching the tube, and when Jim Fregosi, the Angel shortstop, turned over a double play to end the game, all hell broke loose. I brought a bottle of champagne with me outside the stadium, stood in the middle of the crowd, and popped the cork. Then I shared the champagne with them. It drove them nuts. Around Boston, fans were overturning cars and stuff. It was insanity.

I couldn't pitch in the World Series because with two weeks to go in the season, I hurt my arm. Not being able to pitch just killed me. I didn't even stay to sit in the dugout and watch it. I went home. I won one game and had five saves that year, my small contribution. Dick Williams, the manager, was a tough son of a bitch, but he was fair. I remember I had just been called up from Toronto, and we were playing in Kansas City when Williams brought me into a game in relief. It was the thick of the pennant race. Ellie Howard, who the Sox bought from the Yankees to beef up their catching for the pennant drive, was behind the plate. He called for a fastball, and I shook him off and threw a slider for a ball. He called for a fastball, and again I shook him off, and again I threw a ball. I ended up walking the batter, and right then and there Dick Williams took me out of the game. We won, finally, and after the game Yaz cornered me in the locker room and said, "I want to know one thing. How can a guy who's been in the big leagues two weeks shake off a guy who's been catching fourteen years?" I said nothing. Then Williams gave me hell. He said, "Every time you shake him off from now on it's going to cost you fifty dollars."

Elston heard that, and he came over and said, "Screw that. From now on, if I give you a sign that you don't want, don't start your windup right away, and I'll flash you another sign. Nobody'll ever know." And that's what we did. Nobody ever did know, not even Dick Williams. Especially Dick Williams. Ellie was great to throw to. He blocked the low balls real well, and I'll tell you, he stung the ball well too. He should be in the Hall of Fame. They had a special day in Chicago where pennants were put on the roof indicating where balls went out of the park. Ellie's got one up there. That son of a bitch, I'll tell you what, was hit, 'cause it went over the roof in left center about 500 feet from the plate.

The owner of the team was Tom Yawkey, who was such a nice person. If you got your ass kicked the night before, he'd come over and say, "Don't worry about it, just come back and get 'em the next time." He really made you feel good. He wasn't like George Steinbrenner, the Yankee owner. George would say, "What the hell were you doing last night? Jesus Christ! You looked like a monkey trying to fuck a football out there." Mr. Yawkey would pat you on the shoulder and say, "Don't worry about it. You can't win them all."

When I was with the Red Sox, everybody was saying how the team didn't win as much as it should because Mr. Yawkey paid the players so much money. But the thing was, the people making the big money were having good years. The high salaries had nothing to do with our not winning the pennant after '67. We just didn't have a team that was good enough, plain and simple. You can't tell me that Carl Yastrzemski wasn't worth $100,000. The difference with our club was that our younger players were making more than the younger players on other teams, but still that didn't have anything to do with winning pennants. No way. If you were supposedly making that much more money than everybody else, just imagine what we would have been making if we had been winning. The incentive was still there. If incentive is so important, then Rod Carew should be hitting .800, because he ain't getting crap compared to how much he should be getting. But you don't hear about how cheap Calvin Griffith of the Twins is or Gabe Paul of the Indians. You only hear about the owners who pay their players well.

We didn't win again. The other teams got better. We didn't. Denny McLain won 31 games to lead the Tigers in '68, and the next three years the Orioles won with their great pitchers, and with the "brothers" Robinson, Frank and Brooks. People blame Jim Lonborg for our not repeating. He was 22 and 9 in '67, but that winter he had a skiing accident and hurt his leg. The next year he was 6 and 10. The Red Sox management tried to convince everyone that the skiing accident was the cause of Lonborg's problems, but it wasn't. Jim was throwing, and he hurt his shoulder, and after that he didn't have his good curve ball anymore. What hurt us, too, is that Dick Williams got fired with about ten games to go in '69. I don't really know why. Part of it may have been that he wanted more control over the ball club, and management didn't want to give it to him. Everyone thought that Yaz got him fired, but I don't believe that.

Eddie Kasko was hired to manage the team in 1970. Kasko was the only big league manager I ever played for who I didn't like. Kasko lost total confidence in me, which is a terrible thing to happen between a manager and a ballplayer. He didn't think I could get left-handers out after Boog Powell, who is left-handed, beat me up in Boston on two consecutive nights. The second night Boog hit a little pop-up that landed right on the left-field foul line. It was in the newspapers the next day: "KASKO: LYLE CAN'T GET LEFTIES OUT." Kasko didn't like me much anyway because of my life-style. He wanted Sunday school-type ballplayers, and he wanted me to curtail my staying up late, which I had been doing since I'm old enough to remember. I just can't fall asleep at one in the morning. It's too early for me.

If you were in a bar after a game, you could talk with him, but he acted like he was noticing how many drinks you were having. Plus, he didn't want you talking about pussy. He wanted you talking baseball, and I'm just not that way. To me, when the game is over, it's over. Talking about it isn't going to change it.

But what really burned my ass was a meeting Kasko held in spring training in '72. He said, "If you have anything to say to me, come to my office and say it to my face. Don't talk behind my back." A couple of days later, Kasko fined me for being overweight and gave the clubhouse boy the message to give to me. The clubhouse boy was having drinking problems and forgot to give it to me, so when I went into the clubhouse the next day, he said, "I forgot to give you this." It was the message from Kasko that he had fined me. I went bananas. I stormed into Kasko's office yelling and carrying on, and I reminded him of his speech about saying things to guys' faces. I said, "You don't have enough respect for me to tell me about this fine to my face? I have to find out from the clubhouse boy?"

That night I went to the racetrack with Red Sox pitcher Ray Culp, and while we were there, we ran into Kasko, Eddie Popowski, who was a coach, and trainer Buddy Le Roux, and they didn't talk to me. Culp said, "Uh oh, something's up. There's a trade brewing." I said, "Yeah, they sure are acting funny."

The next day the Red Sox traded me to the Yankees for first baseman Danny Cater. Before the trade, Yankee manager Ralph Houk would come over and say, "Don't let them hurt that arm, now. It's your bread and butter." I'd tell him, "Don't worry. I won't." Then he'd say, "This winter I'm going to try and get you. If I have the chance, I'm going to." I thought he had been kidding around, but then it actually happened, and it was the biggest break of my career. I had done well in Boston, averaging about 16 saves over the last three years, but it was still the left-hander, right-hander thing. Most managers like to bring in a left-handed pitcher from the bullpen to face a left-

handed batter and like to bring in a righty to face the
righty batter—not so much because it's tough to hit the
breaking ball, but because they don't face them that often.
However, there are a number of relief pitchers in the
major leagues who have the ability to pitch to both lefty
and righty batters and get them both out. Rollie Fingers
is a pitcher like that, so is Mike Marshall, and so is Rich
Gossage. You roll those guys out every day and just let
them pitch, no matter who the batter is. By the time I
came to the Yankees, I figured I was that type of pitcher,
too, and in spring training I said to Ralph, "Goddamn it,
let me take this thing over. Give me the chance for a
couple of weeks. If I don't do the job, you can do whatever you want with me."

Ralph gave me that chance, and whether I was successful or not, it wouldn't have mattered. It was great for
my peace of mind just to know I was getting the chance.
I caught a break, a break a lot of major leaguers don't
get, and I took advantage of it. In '72 I was 9 and 5,
with a 1.92 ERA. I pitched in 59 games and recorded
35 saves. Under Ralph the next year, I had 27 saves.
They were my best years in the majors until this year.

Tuesday, November 22   Albuquerque, New Mexico

Mary and I were traveling through New Mexico in our
customized van, driving from Fred Stanley's home in
Phoenix to my home in New Jersey, when a newscaster
announced on the radio that the Yankees had signed
Rich Gossage to a six-year, $2,750,000 contract. Gossage,
who played with the Pirates last year before becoming a
free agent, was probably the best relief pitcher in the
National League. "I'll be a son of a bitch," I said aloud.
Mary understood what it meant too. She started to cry.
She was hurt for me because of what I had done for the
Yankees this year and for the past six years, and for them
to just go and dump on me like that—she couldn't understand why they did that. As the tears were running
down her cheeks, I told her. "That's baseball. They can
do with you anything they want." But she just kept crying.
It's kinda tough for her to understand.

While I was driving, I was staring out at the highway, thinking to myself that George knew all along that he was going to sign Gossage and that that was why he extended my contract and gave me a bonus. He was trying to appease me, because he knew how pissed I would be when I heard about Gossage. Oh, I can understand why George bought Gossage. I've had a lot of great years, but the way George thinks, I'm thirty-four, and he feels I'm getting up there in age, that one day I'm going to get old right on the pitcher's mound and that's going to be it, I'm never going to be able to play again. Which is ridiculous. Modern-day players are performing until they're thirty-eight and thirty-nine before they start going downhill, where they didn't do that before. We're bigger and stronger. But George, he thinks a lot about age. When you get past thirty, he starts worrying. That's one reason he got Gossage, who's in his midtwenties.

Intellectually I know George was right in getting the guy. Hell, yeah. When will they have another chance to get a free agent like this guy? In three years when my contract runs out? No. Never. But now that George has gotten Gossage, he has no choice but to get rid of me. George is thinking, "Now I have the best bullpen in the majors with Lyle from the left side and Gossage from the right." He's figuring on a two-man system, me pitching against lefties and Goose pitching against righties, but hell, that just won't work. Both Goose and I need a lot of work to be effective, a lot of work, and with both of us there, if we split the work, neither of us will be able to stay sharp.

If Billy alternates us the entire season, we might be able to stay sharp. But it won't work that way. Oh, maybe for a month or two. But then when he has a choice between a guy who throws a 100-mile-an-hour heater, as Goose does, and an 80-mile-an-hour slider, you'll see, it'll be Goose in there, not me. Forget the Cy Young Award. Forget my 200 career saves. When a manager has a 100-mile-an-hour flame thrower as good as Goose, he's the guy who's going to get the call. Then what? They can't make me a long man. Our starting pitchers are so good that I'd only get in one or two games a week, and without enough work, I'll be ineffective. I wouldn't allow them to make me a long man anyway. I'm not at my best pitching the middle innings. It's hard for me to do, and I won't do it.

It's not the first time I've wanted to be traded by the Yankees. After Ralph Houk quit at the end of the 1974 season, George hired Bill Virdon as manager. In '74 I was 9 and 3, with 15 saves and a 1.66 ERA. That year the Yankees finished second, only two games behind Baltimore. The next year Virdon didn't pitch me very much. I had a half-dozen saves at the All-Star break, nothing great, but I could have had a lot more if he had pitched me. I messed up the first three games I pitched after the break, and damn it, that was it for me. Virdon said, "Lyle's burned out," and he just buried me. About every ten days I'd go in and get my ass kicked. At the end of the season, I said, "I'm not going through this again."

Virdon was a very nice guy, but he was one of those managers who didn't know anything about pitching. He'd be the first to admit it. Whitey Ford was the pitching coach, and he'd ask Whitey for advice, Whitey would give him an answer, and he'd do the opposite. Virdon always said, "I don't know squat about pitching." He didn't have to tell us that.

What hurt him most as manager was that he had managed the Pittsburgh Pirates the year before, when they had some real horses, Roberto Clemente, Willie Stargell, Al Oliver, to name a few. He came over here, and even though we didn't have the sluggers Pittsburgh had, he managed like we did. He didn't bunt, didn't hit and run, didn't move the runners. We'd lose games by a run, or the other team would break the game wide open because we were waiting for the home run that never came. After a while we took matters into our own hands. For weeks everybody was saying, "Let's do something," and finally all the players met secretly in my hotel room in Texas. Everyone was there—me, Nettles, Tidrow, Chambliss, Piniella, Roy White, Bobby Murcer. I don't like to do something like that, but there was so much talk, I felt it was the only way to put a stop to it and get us going. There was so much pissing and moaning because we weren't winning, and everyone felt we could have won games if we had moved a runner or two over, which is the manager's prerogative.

But I wouldn't have wanted to be the one, or even one of three or four of us, to go in to Bill and say, "We talked it over with the rest of the guys, and we think we have to start moving runners over." Maybe that was the right thing to do, but he was such a nice guy, we didn't want to hurt his feelings. At the time I didn't feel this was going behind his back, even though that's exactly what it sounds like. At the meeting we all agreed that whenever a bunt was in order and there was no sign, we'd lay the ball down, give ourselves up. I got up and said, "This is one of the worst things we could do, but if we're going to do this, we can't have one guy sit here and agree and when his time comes not do it. 'Cause eventually The Man is going to know what's going on. You can't have one guy do it and the next guy not do it because it's going to defeat everything." So everyone agreed to go along.

The first night we started moving runners on our own, we lost, but then we won two or three games, and after a while Virdon knew what was going on. He just stood there, smiling. It could have been an ugly mess, but Virdon just smiled, which was a nice thing for him to do.

Virdon took his losses as hard as anyone. When something bad would happen in a game, you could see his veins come busting out of his neck. You could almost see his stomach knotting up. We used to call him The Milkshake Man, Mr. Milkshake, because everybody thought he was a health nut. It wasn't that. The Yankees threw a party one night, and I went, and I got to talking with him. He was standing there with a drink in his hand. He said, "Ya know, everybody thinks I drink milkshakes all the time because I like them. The truth is, I hate them. I'll tell you why I drink milkshakes. My stomach is so damn bad, I can't drink."

One of Virdon's flaws was his lack of diplomacy. He was too honest with the players. If you asked him why you weren't playing, he'd say, "You're just not that good," and he'd tell you why. Roy White went into his office once to complain, and Bill told him, "Roy, you look real good when you stand in your batting stance, real good.

And when you start your swing until you get to the half-way point, you really look good. But just at the height of your swing, when you pop your wrist," he said, "nothing happens." And he said, "That's from both sides." Roy went, "Ahhhhhhhhhhhhhhh, fuck." I mean, what can you say to that? Bill told him, "Nothing happens. From either side!" I told Roy, "Boy, that's a good one."

Virdon was always flexing his pipes. He'd wear short-sleeved shirts, and he'd scratch his head and flex his muscles at the same time. We used to make jokes about it. Every time Virdon would do it, Bill Sudakis, who had tremendous arms, would stand in the corner doing it too.

Virdon was such a good guy. I liked him, and he enjoyed our fooling around. I remember one day before a game, Virdon called a team meeting to go over the hitters. We were playing Baltimore, and Fred Stanley had gotten a casket from a guy in the business, an economy one with white silk, silver sprayed. It was finished inside, and Fred was going to make a bar out of it for his van. When he got it, he brought it into the clubhouse and kept it there until he could ship it home. It was sitting on a hand truck in the middle of the room. Well, I had gotten a surgical mask from a friend of mine. It had a hood that fit over your head, and all you could see were your eyes. I got lampblack and put it around my eyes and made them real black. Before the meeting started, I laid down inside the casket and shut it. I was listening, and Bill was going over the Baltimore lineup, and all of a sudden I lifted the top of the casket and sat up and said, "How dooooooo yooooooo pitch to Brooks Ro-beenson?" Virdon started hollering, "Somebody tie that bastard in there. Tie him up."

The front office once bought him a director's chair with his name on the back, and I took a hacksaw and cut that baby in half. I left it lying in a heap. Bill held a meeting and he said, "I got a birthday present today. And I really liked it. It was a chair with my name on it. Which somebody cut in half. And I have a pretty good idea who did it." And he looked at me. But I had hung the hacksaw in Rudy May's locker, which is where Virdon always stood when he held a meeting. After looking at me, he turned back and noticed the hacksaw hanging

in Rudy's locker. Rudy saw it too. Rudy jumped up and
yelled, "It wasn't me. It wasn't me. I know who did it,
but I can't tell ya." Bill said, "I'm getting another chair,
and that son of a bitch better not be cut." He did get
another one, but he didn't dare assemble it.

Another thing I remember about Virdon was that he
had this coach, Mel Wright, who always went with him
wherever he managed. He told Bill everything that went
on. In Detroit one day I figured I'd test Mel out. Virdon
was a stickler for no eating before the game, and after this
game had started, I walked out to the bullpen with two
hot dogs, sat down beside Mel, and started eating them.
Mel hollered, "What did the man say?" I said, "He said
no eating before a game." He said, "Yeah, right, so?"
I said, "I'm not eating before the game. The game has
started." Mel said, "Jesus Christ, if you can't eat before
the game, you can't eat during the game." I said, "Well,
all right," and I threw the hot dogs down. Mel went in
and told Virdon anyhow.

The best one I pulled on Mel occurred in Anaheim
one day. The gates had just opened, and I was in a crazy
mood, so I zipped down my fly and took my nuts out. I
was standing in the outfield in my uniform with my balls
hanging out, shagging flies, having a good old time, and
I must have been doing this for about five minutes until
Cecil Upshaw noticed me. He cracked up. He was laughing so hard, he was drawing a lot of attention, so I
stopped. I put my nuts back inside. The next day when
I came to the ball park, Virdon called me into his office.
He said, "I have a favor to ask of you." I said, "What's
that, Bill?" He said, "Please don't shag balls in the outfield with your nuts hanging out anymore."

On August 2, 1975, Bill Virdon was fired and Billy
Martin was named manager. Billy had managed the Minnesota Twins, won the Division title and was fired, managed Detroit, won the Division title and was fired, and
managed Texas, finished a surprising second, and was
fired. The Yankees hired him only weeks after the Rangers
let him go. Billy's problem is his temper. Plus he always
wants to be the boss, which offends the guys who own
the team. They figure that for the money they paid, they

have the right to be boss. Unfortunately for Billy, he can't fire them. They can fire him, and often do. The players, on the other hand, dig him. Billy, see, is different from most managers. He fights with the ballplayers, drinks with them, and he gets closer to them than most managers. Billy is really easy to play for because he treats his players like men, whereas many managers treat you like kindergarteners. Billy doesn't have a curfew check, and if I want to stay out till a bar closes, all I have to do is ask him, and he'll say yeah. He still remembers what it was like to be a player. Other assholes, as soon as they switch from player to manager or coach, they immediately forget they were ever a player. Billy hasn't changed his style from player to manager, except now he has a title. When Billy took over the Yankees, everybody on the team really loved him. We were excited about having Billy as a manager, because he'd make a move, pinch-hit or steal or bunt, and he'd walk up and down the dugout and explain why he did what he did. The guys liked that. We finished the year pretty good, and we were really looking forward to spring training to start the season with him running the club. He was doing all the things Virdon hadn't been doing, and we felt that with him we had a good shot at winning the pennant.

Sure enough, in '76, we did win the pennant, just as owner George Steinbrenner had promised when he took over the Yankees in 1973. At that time he promised to build the Yankee Dynasty back up to what it used to be. That made the players feel good because we had confidence that he would do that. We knew George would go to any length to build a winner. The man is ruthless. Ask Mike Burke. When George bought the team from CBS, Burke was supposed to be a partner. Burke had run the Yankees for CBS for ten years and loved it so much he decided to buy the team. Burke needed money and got in touch with Gabe Paul, who fixed him up with George. After Mike and George bought the team, George forced Burke out, set himself up as bossman, and made Gabe the general manager.

When George took over the club, he really didn't know much about baseball. I remember there was a runner on third base and two outs, and we were losing 3 to 2, and

Roy White hit a slow ground ball, and the fielder had to scuffle to throw Roy out at first. Horace Clarke was on third, and he actually crossed the plate before Roy was thrown out at first for the third out. Well, George was sitting in his box behind the Yankee dugout, and he was clapping and yelling, "All right, all right. We tied it up." Someone asked him what he was talking about. He said, "We scored before they got the man out at first, so it's tied." Even little kids know that when you get the man at first the run doesn't count regardless of when it crosses the plate. He just didn't know the game. And he would try to get involved when he didn't know anything. When one of our guys would strike out or pop out in a crucial situation, George would say, "Get rid of the son of a bitch." If George had had his way, he would have gotten rid of all of us.

We also found out early how impersonal George can be. We played our home opener against Boston. Before the game the teams were lined up on the foul lines for the national anthem. Boston was neat and clean. They had their hair cut and they looked good, and they kicked our ass. George was sitting in his box behind the dugout and apparently he felt that some of our players were wearing their hair too long. George wrote a note to Ralph Houk and ordered him to read it at a meeting before the game. The letter said, "I want numbers 19, 47, and 28 to cut their hair." He didn't even bother to find out who they were. I was number 28.

The funniest thing George ever did happened in Texas. George used to be an assistant football coach. He likes discipline, or, rather, the appearance of it. There's a lot of that bullshit in football. It's like being in the Army. Army men shouldn't fool around, and all that crap. Well, this one afternoon in Texas, Gene Michaels was playing shortstop, and Gene is scared of any little thing that moves. Gene is afraid of an ant. On this day somebody took half a wiener and stuffed it into one of the fingers of his glove. Gene ran out to short to take some ground balls before the inning started. He put his fingers in the glove, felt the wiener, and jumped a mile, throwing his glove 50 feet in the air. Well, George went crazy. He was sitting beside the dugout, and he ordered the batboy to find out what had happened. When they got the wiener out of the glove, George ordered them to give it to him. He kept it, and after the game he went to Ralph and said, "Someone put this wiener in Gene Michaels's glove. I want you to find out who did it and give that man a reprimand." Ralph couldn't believe it. Neither could we. We called it The Great Wiener Caper.

In 1974 George was prohibited from running the club for more than a year by baseball commissioner Bowie Kuhn. We didn't think anything about it, but we did know that even though George wouldn't be there physically, he'd still be involved as much as ever. Instead of his calling the manager and meeting with the players, George all the time would contact Lee MacPhail or Gabe, whoever was the general manager at the time. But the thing is, the way George is, it must have killed him not to be able to be there. He's always been successful in business— he built up his father's shipping business to one of the most successful in the country—and the prime reason he is successful is that he doesn't depend on others to make the decisions. George does it. He tells his employees what to do and expects them to follow his orders explicitly. If they vary one bit from what he tells them, there's hell to pay. That's why whenever George sees the team going bad, he feels, "Goddamn, I'd better do something," and he steps in. Son of a bitch, you can laugh at him, but it seems that every time he does step in, we start winning again.

During the time he was forbidden to run the Yankees, he wasn't allowed near the clubhouse. One time Boston really kicked our ass, and this was the time when George would usually come busting into the clubhouse to chew us out. Bill Virdon was the manager, and he called a meeting, and I saw that he was standing there holding a tape recorder. "That's awfully strange," I thought. Virdon said, "Gather round here and listen." Virdon turned the tape recorder on, and it was George. George said, "I'll be a son of a bitch if I'm going to sit up here and sign these paychecks and watch us get our asses kicked by a bunch of rummies. Now Goddamn it, like they say down on the docks, 'You have to have balls.'" And he was going on and on. We thought it was really funny. For weeks we were grabbing our nuts and saying, "You have to have balls." Still, when you really think about it, you have to admire his competitiveness. The guy hates to lose. In 1974 we were in first place for a couple of weeks in September, but we faded and we ended up losing the pennant by two games to Baltimore. We lost to the Milwaukee Brewers the second-to-last game, and that eliminated us, and that night George held a party for us. Before it was over, he got up to speak. He said, "Tomorrow is one of the biggest games of the year. You go out and show 'em that you can win tomorrow, and that way you'll get your minds off losing the pennant. Go out there tomorrow and kick their asses." That's how competitive George is. Everyone kinda said, "Jesus Christ, the season's over and he wants us to kick their ass tomorrow." It made a big impression on us. We went out and beat the Brewers the next day 2 to 1.

Just so you don't get the idea that George isn't good to his players, it's important to note that George does a lot of things for us other owners don't do. Last year and the year before, he gave every player $300 to spend during the All-Star break. When we get into Cleveland, there's a restaurant-bar called the Theatrical, and we can eat and drink there and sign the tab. George believes in giving you these little rewards, and I really appreciate that. Where I disagree with him totally is that he tries to run his baseball team like he does his other businesses. You just can't do that. You can't treat baseball players like accountants or like a herd of cattle. George can get away with treating an accountant or a secretary like a pack rat, because he can find a million accountants or secretaries to replace them. In his businesses, he's always firing his employees, and those he doesn't fire end up quitting 'cause he can be such a bastard. You can't do that with baseball players. You can't tell one of your pitchers, "Well, screw it, I don't like you, you're not going to pitch the rest of the year." Unless he can find someone to replace him, George is going to have to put up with him. George isn't going to be able to treat the players like they're lower than life, like he does most of his employees, because if he tries it, the player will tell him to go stick it.

Monday, December 12   Demarest, New Jersey

I was listening to the radio when it was announced that the Yankees have bought pitcher Andy Messersmith from the Atlanta Braves. According to the report, George paid the Braves $100,000 for the right to sign him. My question is: What's George paying Andy?

Messersmith had been the first free agent signed after the courts ruled against a club's being able to own a player indefinitely. After winning 20 games, and then 19, Andy was unhappy with the contract offer made by the Dodgers, so he sued baseball and the reserve clause and won. The courts ruled that he was a free agent who could sign up with any team, and after listening to a dozen offers, Messersmith was signed by the Atlanta Braves to a three-year, million-dollar contract. As it turned out, it was a bad deal for the Braves, because in '76 he missed half the year with an injury after winning 11 games, and this year, after winning 6 games, he broke his elbow and again missed the second half of the season. Andy's 16 wins cost the Braves' owner $40,000 a win.

Now George has bought Andy, and he has no idea whether he'll ever be able to pitch again, let alone win, and if my guess is correct, George has picked up his contract, meaning that he's paying Andy $333,333 for this year to find out.

Goddamn George. First he gets Gossage, then a couple of days ago he signs another pitcher who had a bad year last year, Rawly Eastwick, to a five-year, $1,100,000 contract, and now he pays someone who's disabled $333,333 for one year to find out if he can pitch. Until now, I was perfectly happy with the $135,000-a-year I'm making, but after this, how am I supposed to feel? I just won the Cy Young Award, and here George is paying a guy with a broken arm $200,000 a year more than I'm getting. The man is giving my pride a shellacking. If I find out for sure that Andy's getting $333,333 this year, George is going to have to answer to me.

Tuesday, February 21, 1978   Demarest, New Jersey

Spring training opens in Fort Lauderdale for our pitchers
and catchers today, but as usual I've decided not to go for
another couple of weeks. No big deal. I don't need six
weeks to get ready, and everybody, including Billy, knows
it. When the bell rings, I'll be ready. I really don't know
why spring training is six weeks. Abner Doubleday or
John McGraw or Connie Mack or somebody once decided
it had to be six weeks long, and since then it's always been
six weeks. That's the way baseball is. No one ever questions why things are the way they are. No one ever thinks,
"Maybe spring training should only be five weeks, or two
weeks." No, John McGraw said it should be six weeks,
so it's six weeks. But McGraw's been dead for fifty years.

They like the pitchers to go down to Florida and throw
real easy, and only gradually to start throwing harder. I
like to go down there late, throw as hard as I can the
first day, and get the adhesions broken. My arm is sore
for a few days, but after that I'm ready to throw in a
game. I then spend the next two weeks throwing fastballs
to give my arm strength to throw my slider. I don't need
six weeks of spring training. The last month would be
a boring waste of my time. I'd get tired standing around
all day just to throw batting practice for twenty minutes
every other day.

Wednesday, February 22   Demarest, New Jersey

Cedric Tallis, George's left-hand man, called me from
Florida this morning. He said, "Jeez, Sparky, you gotta
get down here." He sounded very upset. He said, "There's
holy hell down here. Where the hell are you? How come
you're not down here?" I was hearing this, but for the life
of me I couldn't figure out what the big deal was. I told
him, "I hadn't planned on coming down this soon."

We hung up, and about an hour later Al Rosen, George's
right-hand man, called saying that George was having a

tantrum. I couldn't imagine why, but I told Rosen that if it meant that much to George, I'd be down Saturday after I got my affairs settled up here. He said fine.

A reporter called and read me a press release George had distributed. It said, "If Sparky Lyle isn't mature enough to understand that he has a contractual and moral obligation to the New York Yankees, we certainly are not going to waste one minute of our time attempting to find out where he is." I mean, where the hell did he think I was? Cedric reached me. Rosen reached me. Even a Goddamn newspaper reporter knew where I was.

I think I can guess why George is being so insistent. All the years before this one, I didn't sign my contract until a few weeks into spring training, so I had no obligation to be there. He couldn't make me come. Last year I dickered with him all spring and finally signed a three-year contract for just over $400,000. I was happy over it, he was happy over it, and I think that when I didn't show up yesterday, he got mad because he felt I was taking advantage of him. George has a big ego. That's the way he thinks sometimes. If he's gonna get his balls in such an uproar over this, I'll come down. It's not that big a deal.

Saturday, February 25   Fort Lauderdale

Mary and I flew down to spring training this morning, and after the jet landed, we were walking through the terminal when I saw Cedric Tallis waiting to meet me. Right behind him was a hundred-piece high school band that started playing *Pomp and Circumstance*, which is what they used to play at Yankee Stadium when I came in to pitch. There were baton twirlers, and a few of the band members were holding up a sign that read, "WELCOME TO FORT LAUDERDALE SPARKY—FINALLY."

Sunday, February 26   Fort Lauderdale

George came up to me in the clubhouse, winked, and
said, "I'm one up on you." I said, "Yep, you sure are."

Tuesday, February 28   Fort Lauderdale

Gossage was pitching batting practice, and after throwing
a couple of pitches to Piniella, Goose sailed a burner
right by Lou's head. Lou dropped his bat and walked
away. He yelled over to George, who was watching us
practice, "Hey, George, how 'bout signing some outfielders, huh?"

After doing some snooping around front office types,
I have been able to confirm what I had suspected all along
—that George is paying Messersmith $333,333 to pitch
this year. It's about time I had a meeting with George.

I never ever cared about the money George paid the
free agents. When George paid Catfish Hunter $2,850,000
for six years in 1974, I thought it was great. When he
gave Reggie $2.9 million, Gullett his $2 million, Gossage
his $2.7, and even Rawly's $1.1, I wasn't bothered because
a lot of teams were bidding for their services, and in order to get them George had to pay them that much.
Messersmith, though, he was not a free agent when
George got him. Messersmith, he's a totally different story.

Reggie Jackson arrived in camp today, and I was amused
to see that he hasn't stopped talking his bull. A group of
reporters were asking him about his three home runs
against the Dodgers in the last game of the Series, and
Reggie began talking about what a lesson it was for everybody, the rich and the poor, blacks and whites, and he
said what was most important was that he, his closest
friends, and the Yankees had made it together as a team.
As he was saying this, I was thinking, "Who are these
closest friends he's talking about? They're certainly not

his teammates." 'Cause when he walked into the club-house, the only player I noticed going over to say hello was Cat. Then Reggie started talking about why he's looking so fit. He said he's down to his playing weight because he cut out meat and junk food from his diet. This was right after telling reporters about the great taste of the chocolate and stuff that's in the new candy bar that was named after him. Reggie's really a piece of work. He'll say anything, and be real quotable every time, whether what he says makes any sense or not.

I remember last spring when Reggie came to camp for the first time. Kenny Holtzman, who played with Reggie at Oakland, told us, "You definitely won't believe this guy." Holtzie predicted the crap Reggie would be coming out with. He'd say, "You wait, pretty soon Reggie will be saying how he's the leader and how he's the key to the team," and sure enough, that's exactly what happened. When Reggie joined the club, everybody was just waiting to see whether what Holtzie was saying was true. It didn't take long to find out that this guy was coming from somewhere I've never been. The first time I saw him sitting around with all the Goddamn writers in the lobby of our hotel, I said, "Jesus Christ, what's with this guy? He must want to get his name in the papers real bad." I would never sit around and take writers out to dinner in order to talk to them. It's not that I don't like them. It's just—what the hell would I want to do that for? He was holding a lot of press conferences, and I couldn't figure out why in the world he was doing that.

The last straw, so to speak, what hurt Reggie more than anything else, was when he ripped Thurman Munson in an article in the June issue of *Sport* magazine. Thurman's our captain, and he's been an All-Star catcher for years, and whether they like Thurman or not, everybody has a lot of respect for him. They respect the son of a bitch as much as anybody, and when that article came out where Reggie said he'd be the straw to stir the Yankee drink and that Thurman could only stir it bad, that got Reggie off on the wrong foot, and I don't think some of the guys have forgiven him for that to this day. Why did he have to do it? We were asking each other that, and everyone kept saying, "I don't know. I don't know."

We were wondering if maybe something had happened between them, but no, no one had heard anything like that. It was just, "Hey, Reggie's just trying to come in and take over." But this club was too close to let him get away with badmouthing Thurman and saying his crap. If he had kept his mouth shut, he could have done everything he had wanted to do. If you play in New York, just do the job you're supposed to do, and keep your mouth shut, you'll be recognized. Everyone knows Willie Randolph, Roy White, and Bucky Dent, and they never open their mouths. But that's not Reggie's style. Reggie doesn't want just to be recognized. He wants to be idolized. If Reggie had kept quiet, he would have gotten his candy bar named after him, *and* he would have been popular. But when he tried to nail Thurman, that was going too far. Reggie had no reason to dump on Thurman, especially Thurman. Everybody else on this club understands Thurman. No one else knocks him or says bad stuff about him. And all of a sudden, here's this new guy who doesn't even know him but who knows how sensitive Thurman is, so what's he do? Bang, he tries to nail him right off the bat.

Then, to top it off, after everyone was so pissed because of the article, Reggie got up and hit a home run, and as everyone stood in the dugout ready to shake his hand, instead he made a beeline for the other corner of the dugout, and he refused to shake hands with his teammates. That's like a little kid to me. I don't give a damn that he was mad at us. You don't do that. Alex Johnson was different. Alex felt, "It's my job to hit a home run. You don't have to shake my hand for doing my job." But Reggie, all of a sudden he doesn't want to do it. It was as if he was telling everyone, "Screw Munson, and screw you guys too if you don't like me."

And yet Reggie turns around and has the balls to say, "Why is everyone always on my case? Why does crap always happen to me?" After everyone got so ticked off at him for all the terrible things he said, he was genuinely surprised. That's the kind of guy he is. He can tell a writer that you're the biggest moron and the worst ballplayer who ever lived, and the writer will come over and tell you this, and the next day Reggie will come over and smile at you and say, "Hey, how're you doing, buddy?" as if to say, "I wasn't serious about the stuff I said. I was just doing my thing for the writers." Well, he's not entitled to get away with bull like that. And the thing is, not many guys rip Reggie as hard as he should be ripped because they don't want to be like he is. They don't want to do what he does. Instead of confronting him and telling him, "You asshole," and putting an end to that crap, they figure, "Screw it. I don't want to be like him."

Monday, March 6   Fort Lauderdale

I got myself worked up so much that I finally went in to talk to George. I told him, "You bought Messersmith's contract from Atlanta for $333,333. The man has just had an arm operation, you don't know whether he can throw, and if he can throw, you don't know whether he can make our pitching staff, it's the final year of his contract, and next year he'll be a free agent again." I said, "I'll be a son of a bitch if after performing like I have for you since you've taken over this ball club and after you give him double the money I'm making, I don't get what he's making." In baseball, owners and general managers are always telling players that how valuable you are to the ball club is determined by how you perform and how many years you're with the club. But then a new guy is signed, and none of that crap matters.

I also told him I was deeply concerned about what's going to happen to me in the Yankee bullpen once Billy starts going with Gossage full time. I knew it was ridiculous for me to ever try to explain why Goose's presence means my burial. I said, "I'm not going to get in enough pitching to be effective." He said, "Come on, you know damn well you're going to be in there plenty." It wasn't worth the time trying to explain why I wouldn't because he would have told me I was crazy. I can't tell him he's wrong. How can I prove it? But I know damn well that this season is going to be a disaster for me unless he trades me the hell out of here. I said, "George, I want you to trade me," and I told him I would OK a trade if I could negotiate with the club before the trade was completed.

He said, "If you stay with the Yankees, you have a chance to go into the Hall of Fame. Did you think of that? But if you go someplace else, your chances will disappear." The Hall of Fame had never occurred to me. Later, when I thought about it, I admitted that that would be the greatest honor ever bestowed upon relief pitching. It would be a milestone.

But I hate to think that the difference between my getting elected and not is where I play. Does George think that just because I don't play for the Yankees, I wouldn't pitch as well?

After George told me I had a chance at the Hall of Fame if I stayed on the Yankees, he said, "You get in shape and get ready to pitch, and we'll talk about this." As for my getting traded, George said he isn't sending me anywhere.

Tuesday, March 7   Fort Lauderdale

There's been talk that George is going to fly the Yankees to Cuba to play against a Cuban All-Star team. Tell you what: if that's true, this Yankee isn't going. No way. I don't care how much I get fined, I'm not going. If I have to, I'll go into hiding until the team leaves. I understand Fidel Castro is going to play in the game, and it would be just my luck that I'd be pitching and I'd accidentally brush him back, or the ball would get away from me and I'd bean him, and that would be it for me. I'd never get out of the Goddamn place. My control is not that good in the spring. I only have three, four years left in the majors. I just can't take the chance of having to pitch to Castro.

Pitcher Mike Torrez, who won 16 games for us last year, became a free agent, and signed for a couple of million with Boston. In the papers today Torrez claimed that Thurman let down behind the plate whenever he got into a batting slump. When Thurman saw that, it hurt his feelings. He was quite upset. He went to Cat and asked, "If I had been horseshit, you would have told me to my face, wouldn't you?" Cat told him to disregard what Torrez had said.

How can Torrez make a statement like that after all Thurman has done? I'll tell you what: Munson and I have played together six years, and I never saw him let down when I was on the mound. The guy plays hurt, never complains, and he's great at catching my sliders in the dirt. To me, Munson's the best catcher there is.

This year Thurman is continuing his boycott of the press. When a reporter comes near, he growls at him or pretends he isn't there. Thurm is convinced, and I agree with him, that life would be a lot easier around here without the reporters printing their crap in the papers. Thurman stopped talking to the press last August after they made such a stink about his beard. George has a dress code that prohibits beards, and to show he was pissed off at George, Thurm grew a beard. And the press made a big deal of it.

Thurm was mad at George for several reasons. George had promised him that he would be the highest-paid Yankee as long as he was on the team. Then Reggie became available, George signed Reggie to that huge contract, and Thurman was no longer highest paid. Then as the season went along, Thurm felt that George was blaming him for not getting along with Reggie, despite that terrible article Reggie had written about him. And, finally, Thurm was angry with the circus atmosphere that Reggie brought to the Yankees. Eighty percent of the crap that went on between Billy and George was because of Reggie. Thurman couldn't take it anymore, and he asked to be traded to Cleveland to be near his home in Canton.

Thurm is keeping quiet for another reason. Last year a reporter got him to criticize George in the papers with the promise that the quotes would be anonymous. Thurm ripped George for butting in on how Billy was running the team, not letting him DH Reggie, and for causing such dissension on the team. Somehow, though, George found out it was Thurman who had made the comments, and reamed him out about them.

Oh yes. Thurman cut off his beard just as soon as the

press made a big deal about it in the papers. Right after he cut it, he told the writers, "Don't even bother coming over to my locker."

The thing that got me about the beard was, how in the hell was he able to catch with a son of a bitch like that? I'm telling you, to be back there with a sweaty mask rubbing against your beard the whole game, that's got to be terrible.

George learned that Thurman is going to continue his silence in the press. George's comment: "I think Thurman is being 'overprotective.' "

Thursday, March 9   Fort Lauderdale

Reliable sources have informed me that Brad Corbett, who owns the Texas Rangers, said he would pitch me the way I want to pitch and pay me a million and a half dollars for three years if he could get me in a trade. I'm now making $400,000 for three years, which isn't bad, but it isn't a million and a half either. Shit. If I went to Texas, we'd win our division, because relief pitching is all the Rangers need. They have this kid Barker who's young and throws real hard, but he's inexperienced. He'll be good, but Corbett wants to win now, and we could win if I was there. We'd have an even chance of beating the Yankees in the play-offs, too. It's nice to know that someone believes in you and is willing to pay you what you're worth. It's so near and yet so far.

I read in the papers that the Yankees were talking to Texas about trading me. The article said that Texas proposed trading Paul Lindblad and Claudell Washington for me and Chris Chambliss. George, of course, turned that deal down. He would have had to be crazy to make that one.

George doesn't seem to give a damn about me, so why should I give a damn about him? When I saw Rosen today, I told him that I'm not in shape to pitch in the exhibition games. I'll be ready to pitch, but I won't pitch until George is ready to talk about my contract. Other years, I wouldn't pitch in the exhibition games because I was unsigned, and I'd be damned if I'd take a chance hurting my arm while I was unsigned. As usual, it would be screw the ballplayer. What if I had hurt my arm while I was unsigned? Hell, I'd be in deep trouble. I'd be gone. They'd say, "Tough luck. You don't have a contract. See ya." I feel the same way this year, even though I do have a contract. They want me to go on the hill, telling me, "Hey, if you pitch we'll get this thing settled," but there's no guarantee of that. So I figure there ain't no way I'm going to pitch until we settle this thing. If I go out there and get batted around or get hurt, I'm defeating my purpose. So I just keep telling them I'm not in shape to pitch.

Friday, March 10   Fort Lauderdale

This thing with Steinbrenner is starting to get ridiculous. I was walking to the clubhouse, and George walked past me, and he didn't even say hello. In fact, he sneered when he saw me. I just can't stand that. My business dealings have absolutely nothing to do with my personal feelings toward him. This is strictly business. What gives him the right to sneer at me? What have I done to him? I went in to see Billy, and I told him, "You call Rosen, and you tell him that if I don't get to talk to him, I'm not showing up when we get back to New York."

Tuesday, March 14   Fort Lauderdale

Rosen evidently got Billy's message, because I received word that Rosen wanted to see me. I went to Rosen's office, which is in a trailer sitting in the parking lot just outside the ball park. He was at his desk, and after I sat down opposite him, he told me that he had tried to trade me to Texas but that Texas had turned down the trade offer. I asked him if he was talking about the Claudell-Washington-and-Paul-Lindblad for me-and-Chambliss trade. He said yes. Did he expect me to believe that Texas had turned down that trade? Bullshit. Rosen had turned down the trade. Yankee fans would have hung him by the balls if he hadn't. It was just a variation on another ploy management uses when you ask to be traded. They tell the player, "We put you on waivers, and you know what? Nobody claimed you." It happens every time you start bitching about wanting to be traded. The general manager will say, "We *can't* trade you. Nobody wants you." That's when they don't know what else to say.

Rosen finally said, "We're not going to trade the Cy Young Award winner. There is just no way." What he's saying there is "We don't want you pitching for another team, winning fifteen games, maybe coming back and beating us and making us look bad." I told Rosen, "The Cy Young Award is the most important thing that ever happened to me, but you can take that award and stick it, 'cause that was last year and it doesn't mean a thing to me this year. It's over with. The day I received it, it was over with. Don't worry about embarrassing me. I don't care if you trade me for a jockstrap. You're not going to embarrass me, Mr. Cy Young Award winner. I take it year by year, game by game. You're only as good as tomorrow, so let's not even talk about the Cy Young Award. It's irrelevant at this point."

Again I gave Rosen all the reasons why if they were refusing to trade me they at least had the obligation to give me more money. I told him about my feelings about Messersmith and Cliff Johnson, who is making $100,000 a year as a pinch-hitter and part-time player. I said to Rosen, "Another thing. I've been hurt, but I've never missed a game with the Yankees because of arm trouble or anything like that. Twice I've broken my toe on the morning of a game, cut the shoe out, put shoe polish over my sock, and pitched. Several guys who are accident-prone are getting a lot of money. If you get a half a season out of any of them, you're lucky."

I thought I was eloquent and convincing, but Rosen didn't want to hear it. He kept emphasizing that I had a binding contract, that I had been happy with the money when I signed it, and where in hell did I get off asking for more? I agreed with him. I said, "You're right. By legal rights, I shouldn't even be sitting here arguing, but yet the way I look at it, based on what others are getting, I deserve a lot more than what I signed for, and as a result I do have a right to be here arguing with you."

Rosen refused to discuss it. He said, "Get in shape,

start throwing, and then we'll talk." That didn't make any sense to me because that meant that once I got in shape, I had to negotiate all over again.

Before George hired Rosen this year to be, in effect, the general manager, his last contact with baseball was as a player for the Cleveland Indians in 1956. I said to him, "You say you're a baseball man, but you don't understand what is happening today. You've been gone too long."

That made him mad. He shouted, "Who the hell do you think you are?" I got mad and shouted back, "What the hell difference does it make! This is what I believe." I told Rosen, "I'm going home." He screamed, "Well, then why don't you go home." I said, "All right, I will." He shouted, "Good, go ahead. Just go the hell home." I was standing there in my uniform, and when he said that, I ripped the buttons off my shirt and said I was going home. I huffed out of his office, slammed the door of the trailer behind me, and started across the parking lot to the clubhouse in order to get dressed. I wasn't even showering. I was ready to go because I had told Mary earlier, "This is what it's coming to. And when I say I quit, I'm going to go home."

I didn't know it, but the whole time I was in Rosen's office yelling, Steinbrenner was sitting in the next room on the couch. When I stormed out of Rosen's office, Rosen came after me yelling, "Sparky, please come back here. Please come back here, Sparky." I left him standing there hollering. I got to the clubhouse, and started getting dressed when Billy came over. Rosen had come over and was in Billy's office when Billy called me into his office. Billy said, "Listen, Sparky, we'll get things worked out. I promise you. Don't leave. Get in shape, get ready, and it'll be worked out." I have great respect for Billy, so I said, "OK. If you ask me, I'll stay." And I will stay. But I'm not pitching an inning in one of these exhibition games until George works something out with me.

It's ironic. George wanted to get rid of me last year. I had been 7 and 8 with 23 saves in '76, but most of those saves I got in the first half of the season. Plus I was arguing contract again. They couldn't get me to sign. But the big reason they wanted to get rid of me then was that at the end of the year I would come under the ten and five rule. I'd have ten years in the major leagues and five with one club, and when that happens, a player cannot be traded without his permission. Once I passed that point the Yankees were screwed because they couldn't trade me unless I let them. Last year, then, was their last chance to trade me without their having to get my permission. They were figuring that Ron Guidry could pull through and take my place as the left-handed short reliever, but, fortunately for me, Gid was absolutely horrible in spring training last year. He was doing so poorly at one point that Billy said to him, "If there's anybody you can get out, tell me, and I'll let you pitch to him." Billy knew that the kid had great stuff and that it would just be a matter of time before he'd start winning, but it was frustrating to see Gid go out there and walk guys and not get anyone out. The Yankees were forced to keep me. The thing is, very few pitchers have good springs, and those who do are always the control pitchers, not the power pitchers like Gid. I never pitch well in spring training either. My ERA has got to be 10.00 down in Florida. I don't give a damn about the exhibition games. I'm having fun playing. I don't throw sliders until just about the final week. I'm just pumping fastballs in, making my arm strong, and they're knocking the shit out of them. It doesn't mean anything to me. The game doesn't matter, and even if I'm in the game in a key situation, I laugh out there. If I ever had to make a ball club based on my spring training record, I'd never do it. I remember the Red Sox almost sent me down one year because I wasn't pitching well in Florida. They told me that if I didn't do well this one day, it was the end. Boy, I got my ass kicked, but they ended up taking me and this pitcher Garry Roggenburk to the big leagues. As soon as the season started, I was pitching good, and Roggenburk was sent down. They had been worried because I hadn't been throwing any breaking balls. They thought my arm was hurting. I told 'em it wasn't. I hadn't been doing anything different than I ever did.

Because Gid was getting banged around last spring, George gave up on him and decided to trade him to Chicago as part of a deal for Bucky Dent. Gabe Paul, who was George's right-hand man last year, knew that it was only a matter of time before Gid started rolling, and he talked George out of it. It's a good thing they kept him, and kept me too, for that matter. I ended up signing a three-year contract for $135,000 a year, and you know what kind of a year I had. Gid got into the starting rotation when Cat and Gullett got hurt, and he ended up the year 16 and 7.

What worries me this year is that Gabe is no longer around. He's now a part owner of Cleveland, leaving George and Rosen to wheel and deal for the Yankees, which is a frightening thought. I wonder whether Rosen would have been able to talk George out of trading Guidry. I doubt it. Gabe may have been a cheap bastard, but one thing he knew was talent.

Thursday, March 16   Fort Lauderdale

All spring Andy Messersmith had been pitching real well, super for a guy who had just had his elbow operated on. His fastball was moving, he had good control, and it was looking like George's gamble might have paid off, until today. We were playing the White Sox in an exhibition game, and in the fourth inning, Ralph Garr hit a grounder to Cliff, who was playing first. Andy ran to cover the bag, and when Cliff threw behind him, Andy fell trying to reach back for the ball. He fell hard on his shoulder, and now doctors think it might be separated. He may miss the rest of the season. It's the second serious injury we've had in the last few days. A few days ago our shortstop, Bucky Dent, fouled a ball right down onto his shin. Bucky dropped like he'd been shot. He's in terrible pain and won't be able to play again for a couple of weeks.

Friday, March 17   Fort Lauderdale

We lost our fourth spring training game out of our last five, which doesn't mean squat, of course, but George is starting to get nervous. He has such a football mentality that the guy ought to buy the Green Bay Packers. Rah

rah rah. Sis boom bah. Winning isn't everything, it's the only thing. That's such crap. The exhibition games are for getting in shape. George was telling reporters, "Billy better start buckling down, or we won't repeat. We'll have trouble winning the East. Some guys better start thinking about defending the championship." We don't pay any attention to that nonsense. It's nice to win the exhibition games, but I'll tell you, I've been with clubs that kicked everybody's ass down here, and then as soon as the season would start, we'd lose our first six or seven games. Spring training doesn't prove anything, no matter what George or anybody else says.

Sunday, March 19   Fort Lauderdale

Billy came to me and said, "Sparky, if you'll pitch against Boston tonight, George promises that he'll get this money thing straightened out." I said, "OK, I'll do it for you. I'll pitch." In my mind, I was thinking, "Screw it. I'll pitch once, pitch an inning, and get it over with." I came into the game in the ninth with the score tied 4 to 4, and retired all three batters I faced. I pitched mostly fastballs, but I pitched good. Now it's up to George.

Monday, March 20   Fort Lauderdale

I've been reading stories in the papers that George is trying to trade Graig Nettles for Dave Winfield of San Diego. Graig is thirty-four and Winfield is young and a great outfielder, but trading Nettles would be a terrible mistake. He's the best third baseman in baseball and will be for the next five years.

I'd say that without him at third base, my years on the Yankees would not have been half as productive as they were. He's probably the number one factor in my success here. You ought to see some of the balls hit down to him when I'm pitching. He dives, makes unbelievable plays, half in defense of his life, half just in defense. I kid his wife, Ginger. I told her, "Let's take out a life insurance policy on Graig and make you and me the beneficiaries, because one of these days when I'm pitching, he's gonna get killed."

George really amazes me sometimes. They don't know when they've got something really special right in their own backyard.

Every ballplayer has to have an outlet to relax him, and Lou Piniella's is handicapping the horses. It gives him great satisfaction when he picks a horse and is right. Lou really takes his track handicapping seriously. He's quite good at it, but lately he's been on a losing streak. He's been getting his ass kicked every day, it seems. Lou's been saying to Roy or Holtzie or Mickey Rivers, "Hey, I have a hunch on such-and-such a horse, and I'm betting it," and the horse would come in dead-ass last or wouldn't place or would get nailed in a photo finish. Yesterday Lou was moaning to Catfish. He was saying, "I'm losing so often I can't feed my horses anymore."

Today Lou was sitting in his locker in the clubhouse, and Cat walked in and dumped a big bale of hay in front of Lou's locker. "Now you can feed your horses," Cat said. Lou just sat there, and real slow and sarcastic he said, "Ha . . . ha . . . ha. Ha . . . ha . . . ha."

Wednesday, March 22   Fort Lauderdale

Rosen asked me to come see him today in his office, and when I got there he told me that if I would agree not to change my present contract, he'd give me $250,000 for the extra year George had added back in November, plus a $35,000 bonus. I said, "What the hell is that? That's nothing. Nothing. What good is one year at $250,000 three years from now? I could be dead by 1981." I told him to stick it.

That's absolutely ridiculous. If they want to give me $200,000 a year through 1981, then I'm happy. That would make me feel like I'm part of something.

Saturday, March 25   Fort Lauderdale

This afternoon Rosen came up to me and asked me to
pitch against the Reds tonight. I said no. Later Art Fowler
said to me, "They're on Billy's ass. Just pitch one inning."
They were saying Billy had no control over me, and I
didn't like that. I said, "OK, I'll pitch." I pitched an inning, threw about eight pitches, and I was out of the
inning without giving up a hit. They then called down
to the dugout and asked me to pitch another inning. I
told Fowler, "No. I'm pitching one inning, and that's it."
They had wanted me to pitch, and I pitched. I headed
for the clubhouse, and Fowler came running after me. I
told Art the same thing. I said, "Art, I'm not pitching
another inning in spring training. I pitched my one inning, and that's it." He said, "You only threw eight
pitches." I said, "I don't give a good Goddamn if I only
threw three pitches. One inning."

Easter Sunday, March 26   Fort Lauderdale

We scored six runs in the bottom of the ninth to beat the
Mets 9–6. Paul Blair hit a three-run home run to win
it. Steinbrenner still hasn't let up in his criticism of how
the team is playing. After the game he said, "Billy Martin
and Al Rosen tell me we're on schedule, but personally
I don't think we are. The manager better start pulling his
team together." It would be helpful if George would go
back to Cleveland and help wash his boats.

Billy's laxness has nothing to do with our real problem:
the physical problems of our starting pitchers. Gid, who
has had bronchitis all winter, is weak. He pitched a couple
of innings a few days ago and gave up five runs. We've
lost Messersmith. Don Gullett's arm has been sore, and
he's pitched only a few innings, and Holtzie hasn't been
very effective. Billy had been saying nice things about
Kenny until a couple of weeks ago when he gave up seven
hits in a row and eight runs against Atlanta. George would
like to trade Kenny, but he has a no-trade clause in his

contract, and he'll allow them to trade him only to Milwaukee or Chicago. Today in the papers Rosen said that if he traded Kenny to the Cubs, he'd want Bobby Murcer in return. Why not ask for Dave Kingman, too, Al? It looks like Billy isn't figuring Holtzman in his starting rotation again this year. Holtzie's in a bind. He hasn't pitched enough to be sharp, so Billy doesn't have enough confidence in him to pitch him in spots. I guarantee you that once the season starts he'll start a few games, but that's not enough work. If he goes through this year the way he went through last year, sitting on his ass, he's not going to be able to pitch anymore.

Billy says it's not that he doesn't like Kenny. What I gather is it's between Billy and Steinbrenner and Holtzman. Last year, Gabe had planned to trade him to Texas for Johnny Ellis and Ken Henderson. The trade really sounded good for us, and George was all enthused about it. Brad Corbett, the Texas owner, was saying that he'd let Holtzman renegotiate his contract, and I guess George figured Holtzie would jump at the chance. For George, it was the opportunity to get rid of Holtzman's $165,000-a-year contract.

Holtzman had been sitting in Steinbrenner's office, and when George told him about the trade, he looked George straight in the eye and said one word: "Veto." George must have gotten mad, really mad, because he said to Kenny, "I guess I'll just sit in my box, and you can sit in the bullpen, and I'll wave to you every day." And that's what happened.

If Billy doesn't use Holtzman, that leaves us Ed Figueroa and Dick Tidrow, who are solid, Ken Clay and Jim Beattie, who are rookies, and Catfish, who is questionable. Five years in a row Cat won 20 games in a season, he's won four Championship Series games and four World Series games, but more than that he's a class guy who we all admire. Until last year, he was the guy you sent out there when you needed a key win. Cat looked great in spring training last year, but he was hit on the foot by a line drive opening day, got a sore arm, was hit with a urinary disorder, and finished the year with a 5 and 5 record and an ERA over five. Now the doctors just found out he has diabetes, and he's really worried about it. He has to give himself an insulin shot every day, and the doctors say he should be able to control it, but still, diabetes can kill you, and I'd be worried too, if I got it.

Monday, March 27　Fort Lauderdale

George named Rosen president of the Yankees to fill Gabe Paul's shoes. At the press conference, George said he isn't going to interfere as much as he did last year. He announced, "I am leaving the running of the ball club in the hands of Al and Billy Martin. They will continue to be responsible for the performance of the team. It will be in their hands." Billy and Al, "The Good-Hands People." George may have seriously believed what he was saying. Just wait for the first series when Boston kicks our ass. We'll see then whose hands it's in.

Tuesday, March 28　Fort Lauderdale

Rosen came up to me in the clubhouse and said, "Goddamn it, Sparky, if you had just pitched that other inning the other night, we would have had this thing settled." According to Rosen, George felt, "If he only wants to pitch one inning, doesn't want to pitch the other inning, then the hell with him." Rosen said George was going to give me another $50,000 for each year of my contract.

I said, "Why didn't you tell me that? All you said was 'We want you to pitch another inning.' You didn't say, 'Pitch another inning and we'll talk to you after the game.' "

Christ, Rosen could have said that George would have given me another $100,000 for each year. He could have said, "If you had pitched the other inning, George was going to give you a million dollars." But the fact is, nobody gave me anything. The thing is, I feel that I'm just as much in the right as they feel they're in the right. They're looking at it one way. I'm looking at it another way. The problem for me, of course, is that George is in the driver's seat. There isn't a hell of a lot I can do, either to get my money or to keep myself from getting buried. It won't matter how good I pitch. By July, when Goose has his act together, I'm going to be the long man or the mop-up man, and I'm telling the world right now, I won't do that for anybody. Not for Billy, not for anybody. George should just trade me the hell away from here. It's really the only workable solution. But George, he won't trade me. George won't trade away his Cy Young Award winner. In other words, no matter what I do this year, I'm going to be screwed.

Thursday, March 30   Fort Lauderdale

Gid worked five scoreless innings against the White Sox today. He was a little wild, but it looks like he's regained his strength. The Gid has so much natural ability, it's frightening to think how overpowering he'll be when he finally gets it all together. If he reels off 20 wins this year, it won't be a surprise to me. Gid is kinda quiet. I don't see him very often. He doesn't go out to bars and drink that much, and that leaves me out. He's a good kid, keeps to himself, doesn't say much. He has an air of cockiness about him, which comes with success. It took Gid six years in the minor leagues before he stuck with the Yankees. Gid told me once that he always knew he could pitch in the majors and felt that the Yankees should have brought him up sooner. He's a little resentful they took a couple of years in the majors away from him.

  I've been kind of depressed over the box George has put me in. Now that I know he has no intention of trading me, I go over in my mind how Billy can possibly use both me and Goose, and it always comes out the same: bad. I keep coming back to his 100-mile-an-hour heater versus my 80-mile-an-hour slider. Plus, I have to have enough work for everything to go right for me. Goose doesn't. Even if he's a little off, 92 miles an hour still isn't bad. If I end up getting buried and my statistics show a drastic drop-off in productivity, baseball people are going to wonder whether I'm washed up. At age thirty-four, you can have been a great short relief pitcher for ten years in a row, but if you have one off year, they start saying, "He's done. He's burned out." And then they'll look at my $135,000 salary and wonder whether it's worth taking a chance on a "burned-out" aging relief pitcher who's making a ton of money. I've always known that one time or another late in my career a high salary would be a detriment, 'cause if you're a relief pitcher and they no longer think you can do it, you're gone. If you're a nonpitcher, they can always make a designated hitter out of you. If you're a starting pitcher, they can make you a long man or a spot starter. But when you're a short relief man and you lose your stuff, there's nowhere to go. You're just gone. That's why before the free agent bonuses, I never wanted to make $100,000 a year. I didn't want to price myself out of the market when I got older. When Tug McGraw was saying how he wanted $100,000, I stayed conservative. I said to myself, "He's going to have to be good for a long time for that money. If he has a couple of bad years or he hurts his arm, he's gone." I didn't want that to happen to me.

Tuesday, April 4   Fort Lauderdale

Some of the New York writers and a few of the guys were remarking that I haven't been my usual crazed self. I have a reputation for playing practical jokes, but since I've gotten down here my mind is preoccupied with this contract thing, and I haven't been in the right mood to fool around.

I pulled a good one on our trainer, Gene Monahan, during spring training last year. It was April first. I went in to pitch in one of the exhibition games, and just before I went out to the mound, I told Tidrow, "Make sure Monahan is watching me." It was something I had decided to do on the spur of the moment. I threw a warm-up pitch, and after I followed through I grabbed my pitching arm. I was bent over, grimacing, acting like I was in real pain. Monahan comes out to the mound immediately, and he's saying, "What's wrong?" I'm groaning and moaning, and I say, "I think I blew my elbow out." I'm going on and on, "Fuck, does it hurt!" and he's being real concerned

and he's saying, "Christ, let's go in," and real gently he
takes me by the other arm and starts to lead me to the
dugout. I take a couple of steps and I yell, "April Fool."
Ooh, he was mad. He says, "Why, you son of a bitch,"
and he picks up the resin bag and fires it down. Nettles,
who's standing there with us, said to Gene, "You could
hurt your arm throwing like that." That was it. Away he
went.

Another time a few years ago I went to see a doctor
friend of mine in Fort Lauderdale. I thought it would be
terrific if he could fit me with a full body cast, but that
would have taken almost a half a day to put on, so instead he put a cast on my pitching arm and another cast
on one of my legs. Mary drove me to the ball park,
where I went onto the field with these casts, walking on
crutches.

When I got onto the field, I was watching Bill Virdon.
He looked over, and he did a double take, as if to say,
"Oh Jesus, what is this?" I had him for a second. I could
see it. Virdon told the press, "Nah, he didn't fool me.
Once I saw it was Lyle, I knew he wasn't hurt."

The funny part of that prank was at the doctor's office.
I had gotten the casts on and I was walking out with my
crutches, and it's hard to walk on those things, so when
we got outside, I asked Mary to go and get the car and
pick me up. There was a crowd of people standing out
there watching me, and in front of all these people, she
says, "Nah, you can walk to the car." *She* knew I didn't
need the crutches, but the people didn't, and they're looking at her like, "What a nasty woman she must be. Here
she's going to make this poor, crippled guy walk all the
way to the car. He's hurting, and she's telling him, 'Screw
you, buddy, I'm not picking you up.'"

Until the press ruined it for me, the thing I enjoyed
more than anything was sitting on cakes. I used to do
it all the time. It started when I was playing with Boston.
Kenny Harrelson had a birthday party, and he had a
lemon meringue pie, and he hit me in the face with it.
I told Kenny, "I'm going to get you back for this."

Later someone sent him a great big cake that was Kelly
green and shaped like Fenway Park. It was beautiful. Har-

relson just loved it, and he didn't want anything to happen to it. So before batting practice ended, I went into the clubhouse, took off all my clothes, and waited for him. When he came in, I yelled, "Hey Kenny," and I did a half-gainer and sat right on top of the damned cake. Really squashed it good.

From that day on, every time someone had a birthday, the guys would start yelling that so-and-so has a birthday cake. For a little fun, I'd take my clothes off and go and sit on it.

When I was traded to the Yankees, a few of the guys knew I had been doing this. I was in New York about two weeks, and sure enough, someone got a cake, and Thurman, who knew about me, said, "Hey, Sparky, a cake." I took my clothes off and went and sat on the cake, and the other players absolutely couldn't believe it. They were saying, "Boy, that takes balls," and I couldn't understand what the big deal was. The big deal was that it turned out to be manager Ralph Houk's cake! I just about died. I figured, "Syracuse, here we come." But, no. Houk sort of growled, but he took it the right way. And as time went by, I sat on more and more cakes. Our pitching coach, Jim Turner, a really nice man, loved cake. I told him that the only way he was going to get a piece of the Yankee cakes was to cut a piece out before I got there to sit on them. I had warned him fair and square. Well, from that day on, you should have seen Turner. As soon as a cake would come in, the players would start hollering for me, and Turner would run and get a knife and try to get some of the guys to hold me back while he got to the cake. Poor Jim, he never beat me to the cake. Not once.

Then the media took that fun away from me when they started writing about it. There was a full-page story in the *Los Angeles Times* about me sitting on cakes. After that article, I said to myself, enough. I figured that some idiot would put a needle in the cake.

I remember one writer came up to me very seriously and he asked, "Why do you do that?" I said, "Did you ever sit on a cake bare-assed?" He said no. I said, "Number one, I strive for leaving a perfect ass print on the cake after I sit on it. If the icing goes right up in that little point where your ass cracks, then you've done it right. And it takes practice to do that." I'm going on and on, and this guy is writing all this down. I couldn't believe it.

One time, Ron Swoboda got me real good while he was playing with the Yankees. It was my birthday, and I had a couple of cakes in my locker, and apparently Ron went in there, pulled his pants down, bent over, and took a shit on one of those cakes. I'm sitting in front of my locker, and I'm sniffing and smelling this, and I'm saying to myself, "Goddamn, it smells awfully funny." I looked down and I saw this beautiful cake, and on top of it was a big, brand-new shiny brown log. Swoboda looked up at me and he started laughing like he was going to die.

Friday, April 7   Tuscaloosa, Alabama

We were playing the University of Alabama today, and Catfish pitched to 21 batters and retired 21 batters. I came in in the eighth and ruined his perfect game. In the ninth I walked a guy. Everyone was giving me the razz: "Perfect game, and you have to come in and screw it up. Cy Young Award winner, my ass."

Tomorrow is for real. It's about time.

Saturday, April 8   Arlington, Texas

Opening day. In seven innings Guidry allowed the heavy-hitting Rangers a run. That's all we got, so it was tied when Billy brought Goose in to relieve him. In the bottom of the ninth, Goose faced Richie Zisk. He threw two heaters by Zisk, then threw a slider that got up too high, and Zisk deposited it in the left-field seats to end the game. Only 161 games to go. We'd better win tomorrow or George'll get on his plane and give us one of his pep talks if we don't. George will only be happy when he has a team that is ten games in front in May and then slowly pulls away.

Sunday, April 9   Arlington

George can cancel his flight. Figgie pitched a three-hitter,
Reggie got four hits, we won, and everything's under control.

Monday, April 10   Arlington

Zisk hit another home run, this time off Tidrow, and we
lost to Dock Ellis, 5 to 1. I mopped up, didn't have squat,
but still only allowed them two hits in two and two-thirds.

Dock won 17 games for us in '76 and played an important part in our winning that first pennant. He had had
a reputation for being a troublemaker when he was with
the Pirates, but when he came here, he was quiet. He
never wore hair curlers on the bench like he did with
the Pirates. We had fun with Dock. Even though he
pitched well, he ended up getting in a fight with George,
and he was traded away the next year.

Sometimes it seemed that Dock went out of his way to
antagonize George. Dock was a free spirit, and I think
George represented a stifling of that spirit to Dock. The
things he said in the press were unbelievable. We weren't
doing too hot in spring training last year—as usual—and
as usual George was hollering at us, and Dock told a reporter, "The more we lose, the more Steinbrenner will fly
in. And the more he flies, the better the chance there will
be a plane crash."

The final straw came around early April. George walked
into the clubhouse and noticed that Dock was wearing an
earring. To Steinbrenner, Mr. Macho, this must have
looked weird, and Steinbrenner told him he wasn't exactly
happy one of his ballplayers was wearing an earring. Dock
told him that if he didn't like it, he'd wear the earring
when he pitched. "The only reason I don't do it is 'cause
I don't want to rock your little boat," Dock said. George
became angry. "If you do, you wouldn't rock the boat a
second time," he replied. Ellis screamed at him, "OK,
mother, get ready to trade me. This is war."

George traded him a few days later. George wanted to get pitcher Mike Torrez from Oakland. Oakland owner Charley Finley couldn't sign Torrez, who would have become a free agent if he couldn't trade him. George also wanted to trade Mickey Rivers, who was in George's doghouse. George figured a trade of Ellis and Rivers for Torrez and Bill North, Oakland's center fielder, would rid him of two headaches at once. Gabe Paul, though, didn't give a damn what aggravation Mickey was causing. He knew that few players in the majors can do what Mickey Rivers does. He knew that Mickey was the key to our offense, and that on defense, even though he throws funny and doesn't always get a good jump on the ball, he's still the best center fielder around, if you don't count Paul Blair, and we already have him. Gabe talked George out of trading Mickey. Finley, who had a lot more experience than George, offered Torrez for Ellis, Mickey Kluttz, a rookie infielder, and Guidry. Again George was willing. Again Gabe talked George out of it. They ended up trading Torrez and Ellis even up.

Tuesday, April 11   Milwaukee

Cat pitched, allowed six hits and six runs in two innings, and took the loss. Cat insists that his arm doesn't hurt, but you have to wonder.

Wednesday, April 12   Milwaukee

Goose is so fast that batters have to be ready on every pitch for his fastball. If he throws you a slider, he's doing you a favor because he doesn't throw it nearly as hard as his burner. Against Larry Hisle today, Goose fired two fastballs right by him. It was awesome to watch. Then he went to his slider, didn't get it away enough, and Hisle lost it in the seats. That's two times in two appearances that Goose has done that, Hisle today and Zisk in Texas. Holtzie started and looked good. In five innings the only run he allowed was a home run by Sal Bando.

* * *

I found out that George damn near fired vice-president Cedric Tallis after I made an issue of Cliff Johnson's signing for $100,000. Cedric had been the one who signed him. To me, that's horseshit because Steinbrenner's just looking for a way to say, "Don't blame me. I didn't do it, he did."

The reporters were asking me whether I had solved my differences with George. I told them no, that I was madder than ever and said that I would quit the team if my contract differences weren't resolved. I said, "Tell them to go ahead and give me away. Tell them to trade me back for Danny Cater."

Thursday, April 13   New York

We won our home opener in the first inning when Reggie came up and hit one of his line shots into the right-field seats for a three-run home run. I hadn't known it, but each of the 40,000 fans who showed up were given free Reggie Bars, the candy bar Reggie finally convinced somebody to name after him. A Reggie Bar looks like a flying saucer. It's shaped like a B-cup with a bright orange wrapper and a picture of Reggie swinging a bat on it. Ever since George signed Reggie, Reggie's been bragging that he's so great someone will name a candy bar after him, and somebody finally broke down and did it. After Reggie hit the home run, he was trotting around the bases, and I saw two of these orange Reggie Bars come flying out of the stands and land near the plate. It took the rest of the fans about ten seconds to realize the beauty of that act, and from the bleachers, from the mezzanine, from the upper deck, from the box seats came thousands of these Reggie Bars flying onto the field. It was a hailstorm of Reggie Bars. They covered the outfield and the home plate area like a lawn overgrown with dandelions. The umps had to call time while the ground crew went out to pick up the candy bars, and they would still be out there except that a dozen or so kids jumped out of the stands and gathered Reggie Bars piled high in their arms. At twenty-five cents each, they did pretty well for themselves.

A few of the candy bars being thrown from the bleachers fell into the bullpen. Holtzman retrieved one, unwrapped it, and took a bite out of it. He said it tasted like cowflop.

After the game Chicago manager Bob Lemon was talking about what happened. "It must be a great tasting candy bar if they throw it instead of eat it. They should advertise it as the candy bar made to throw."

Friday, April 14   New York

We had an off day today, so George scheduled a charity luncheon for the Yankee players this afternoon and made attendance mandatory. I didn't go. I really hate those things, and I didn't think it was fair to make the guys go on our only off day for two weeks. It was more important to everyone to get the families settled and get everything at home straightened out. It's bush, if you ask me. George can go ahead and fine me. I don't care.

When I do something like this, I have a damned good reason for it. That's one thing I want everyone to understand about me: when I do something like this, I'm not doing it merely to be defiant, to say, "Screw it, I won't do it." That's not the reason. Last year the Yankees had to fly to Syracuse in the middle of the pennant race to play a game against our farm club. A couple of the players decided not to go. This player was one of them. That was my way of protesting our having to play a meaningless game against a bunch of minor leaguers in the middle of a tough season. George had been complaining about how the club was playing so badly. Why in hell didn't he give Syracuse $5,000 or whatever they were going to make, and let the players go home and enjoy a day off? We've been playing, scuffling, and getting ridiculed for not winning, and it's bad enough because we know how good we should be. And now we gotta go and play Syracuse so the people up there can get their jollies. I said, "We need a day off and I'm not going." And I didn't. I got fined $500. They took it out of my check.

Saturday, April 15   New York

Thurman, Graig, Mickey, were also fined $500 apiece for
not going to the luncheon. Munson and Nettles were so
angry, they refused to play against the White Sox today.
They didn't see what the big deal was, and it was their
way of retaliating. Thurman has a cyst behind his left leg
that's been bothering him, especially when he squats and
runs. Thurm said his cyst was acting up. Puff said he had
the flu. Nettles told the press, "I've played when I'm sick,
but they think so little of me now, why should I play when
I don't feel good?" Nettles said he had taken his preg-
nant wife to the doctor. He didn't ask Rosen if he could
skip the luncheon. Maybe if Rosen had known, he wouldn't
have fined him, but Rosen never asked him why he didn't
go.

They couldn't tell the writers what they had done because they had to protect Billy. If George found out they
didn't play because of the fine, George would have come
down real hard on Billy. He'd be saying, "Don't you have
any control over these guys?"

Nettles was funny. In the clubhouse after the game he
told the reporters, "If they want someone to play third
base, I'm ready. If they want an entertainer, they can hire
Georgie Jessel." When I came over to talk to him, he said,
"You better not talk to me any longer. You're liable to
catch the flu."

Mickey also was angry about the fine, and he told reporters that George had also fined him during spring training for being a few minutes late for a couple of practices.
"There's always something hanging over this team, and it's
the front office. They wonder why we can't win with all
this stuff," Mickey said.

Mickey's right, of course. I wish they would leave
Mickey alone. Don't fine him. Don't threaten him. Don't
bug him. Don't mess with him. Just leave the guy alone,
and he'll play great ball.

Mickey reminds me of another guy we used to have,
Alex Johnson. Alex had tremendous ability. In fact, one
year Alex led the league in hitting, finishing about .330,

but he was like Mickey. He didn't like to be hassled. He was into his own thing. In baseball you run into guys from different walks of life, and Alex was a guy who didn't get all enthused about things. He didn't give the manager any of the false hustle managers always seem to love. He didn't like to talk it up on the bench. If they would have left him alone and quit getting on his ass, he would have played good ball.

The thing was there were times he would do something so spectacular you couldn't believe it, and everyone would say, "Why can't he do that all the time?" Being so good in a way hurt him. When he played at less than his peak, the manager would get on his case. The same thing sometimes happens to Mickey.

I didn't get a chance not to go into the game today. Figgie pitched a complete game and won 3 to 2. Mickey scored one of the runs. He drove in the other two.

Sunday, April 16   New York

Holtzman is in George's doghouse because George wants to get rid of him to make room on the roster for Tacoma pitcher Jim Beattie. Kenny, though, still won't let George trade him anyplace but Milwaukee or Chicago. After what Kenny did today, George is probably ready to lynch him. Holtzie called Marvin Miller, the president of the Players Association, and told Marvin about the fines. Marvin told Holtzie that the Yankees had no right to fine us. He said that under our contracts we are obligated to attend promotional events. This luncheon, though, was for charity, it wasn't a promotion, and the Yankees are not allowed to fine us for not going to a charity. We've filed a grievance to challenge the fines. That sounds kind of bad, not going to a charity affair, but my family comes first. This thing will now go before an arbiter and probably won't be settled until Christmas.

Holtzman, who's the Yankee player representative, can be a real pain in the ass for an owner. Charley Finley once called him "the most miserable man in baseball." That's quite a statement, coming from Finley. Not only is Holtzman our player rep, he's also on the board of the Players

Association, so he knows just about everything that's going on. He's a very good representative. He knows the rules backward and forward. If you need any information, you don't need to look it up. Just ask him. Before, teams were always getting rid of their player representatives. These days it's not so easy. If Holtzie hadn't had a no-cut contract, the Yankees would have gotten rid of him a long time ago.

Rosen's about at the end of his rope, and when he finds out about the arbitration, he's going to go crazy. Always it's Rosen's ass. Rosen's the one who's supposed to be taking care of the day-to-day problems on the Yankees, and you have to understand that George feels that when something goes wrong, it wouldn't have if he'd taken care of it himself. Rosen has gone through a heap. Every little thing that comes up, everyone goes to Rosen, screaming and hollering.

Like tonight, the wives' room wasn't open for some unknown reason, and I had to go raise hell about it, and he's the guy I had to go to. If the Goddamn popcorn machine doesn't work, he's going to hear about it. You can go nuts. I'm always up in his office asking him, "Where's my money?" Holtzman's telling him, "Trade me, but only Milwaukee or Chicago." Mickey Rivers is always up there asking for more money. Whatever it is, Rosen gets the call.

Tidrow pitched a neat four-hit shutout for six and two-thirds innings to beat the White Sox. I relieved, kept them from scoring, and got my first save.

Graig got a telegram from Georgie Jessel. It said, "Thanks for getting my name in the paper."

Monday, April 17 New York

When Catfish Hunter came to the Yankees in 1975, he was the best pitcher in baseball. Starting in 1970, his record over the five-year period was 18-14, 21-11, 21-7, 21-5, and 25-12. In his first year with the Yankees he was 23-14, then 17-15. Watching Cat, I felt he would be able to pitch as long as he wanted to. He was such a great competitor, had good stuff, and had such great control. Even without speed, I felt his ability to put the ball exactly where he wanted to would enable him to keep winning. When he's right, nobody can set up hitters like he can. But last year doctors thought he had a hernia. He couldn't get his hips working like they should, and he began pitching unnaturally. His arm started bothering him, and he finished the year 9 and 9. They never did figure out what caused it, but he hasn't been the same since.

Against the Orioles today, Cat got rocked again. This time it was six hits and five runs in four and a third, as we lost 6–1. Goose came in to replace him and immediately gave up a home run to Doug DeCinces, their third baseman. That's three home runs in three games for Goose. Rick Dempsey was the next guy up, and Goose threw a burner right by Dempsey's nose, sending him sprawling. Early Weaver, the Oriole manager, came flying out of the dugout demanding that the ump give Goose a warning, which the ump wouldn't do. Weaver turned to Munson, who was standing there waiting for Weaver to leave, and he said to Thurman, "I'm going to get you," which Billy apparently heard because immediately Billy came flying out of our dugout. Billy began swearing at Weaver, and Weaver made a move to go after Billy. If Frank Robinson hadn't held him back, we might have seen an exciting fight. Billy had to be satisfied with giving Weaver the finger. Billy screamed that if one of our hitters went down, he was going to come over to the Oriole dugout and punch the living shit out of him.

Everyone really dislikes Weaver because he's always trying to intimidate you and intimidate the umpires. When you're on the mound, you can hear him hollering at you all the time, trying to get you to screw up. He yells, "Get that shit of yours over," or "What are you doing out there, jerking off?" The same old baseball stuff. Boy, he's a bastard. That's one reason he wins.

Because I've publicly asked to be traded, a Toronto poster company wrote me to say they're no longer interested in putting out a poster of me in a Yankee uniform.

They said they were afraid to put it out because if I got traded, they'd be stuck with a lot of posters. If they knew George, they wouldn't be afraid to put it out.

Tuesday, April 18   New York

We go on the road tomorrow for a couple of days, so before today's game I went up to see Steinbrenner to tell him I'm quitting. I won the Cy Young Award last year; I'm the only lefthander in the bullpen, and I'll be damned if I'm going to play for what he's paying me. I went in and I said, "Why do I have to pitch to prove what I'm worth after what I've done already? You want more and more, but you won't compensate me for all I've done."

And he agreed with me. He said that I have a legitimate gripe. But George is in a corner because Gossage, who he paid two something million for, is 0 and 2, and if Steinbrenner renegotiates with me now, it'll look to the public like he's dealing from weakness.

He said, "If you wait and let everything quiet down, I'll take care of you, and you'll be happy. On the other hand," he said, "if you're going to quit, I'm going to have to let you do that." Then he said, "But you're not financially stable enough to do that, are you?"

What could I say? I told him I wasn't. So he said, "Wait till things die down. I'm not sure how long it will be. It may be a week, it may be a month. We'll have to see." He showed me the door, and as I was leaving, he said, "Don't call me again. I'll get in touch with you."

This contract thing has my head so messed up that I don't even want to go to the ball park. I told Steinbrenner, "Ordinarily I'm more relaxed at the ball park than anywhere, including my house." It's not that way anymore. Usually I go to the park at two o'clock for an eight o'clock game because I enjoy going there. Now I wait until the last minute.

The reporters have been asking me why I'm down because I've really been quiet, which is unusual. I can honestly say that until now I've never been depressed in the major leagues.

* * *

I relieved Gid in the seventh with the bases loaded, and I walked some Oriole rookie I never heard of to tie the score. I didn't have a thing today. Thurman kept advising me of that fact. I kept telling him, "I know. I know."

I got the win in the ninth when Reggie homered into the right-field stands off Tippy Martinez. Reggie later came over and said, "We picked up right where we left off last year." It was funny, but last year when I came in to pitch, even if Reggie had been 0 for something, he'd get up and get the game-winning hit. We were talking about that. He said, "When you pitch, I hit." I said, "You just keep doing that."

Reggie was talking to reporters after the game. That's something you can count on. Reggie once said that the only people he can relate to are the writers. That's because they're the only ones who benefit from hearing his crap. Today after the game, he told them, "When I get up in a pressure situation, I swell up with confidence and relaxness. It's like everyone is saying, 'Reggie's up. Everything's going to be OK.'"

Only Reggie would say something like that. I never would, and none of the other guys on our club would either. Not one. There are steadier guys than he is who would never say a thing like that.

Cat has Reggie pegged perfectly. He was making jokes about the Reggie Bars. Cat said, "Don't ever put a Reggie Bar in your pocket or you'll get mustard all over your pants." Cat also said, "When you unwrap a Reggie Bar, it tells you how good it is."

Cat was telling me that when someone asked Reggie if he was going to that charity luncheon Friday, Reggie said, "Of course, I'm coming. Everybody's coming to see me. What the hell would it be if Reggie Jackson wasn't there?"

Don Gullett's arm is really hurting him. He was placed on the disabled list today. Jim Beattie was called up to take his spot on the roster.

Wednesday, April 19   Toronto

During spring training we were laughing at Tidrow because he would always walk from his hotel to the ball park to keep his legs in shape. This afternoon we were in our hotel, and Dick says, "Where's the ball park?" Nettles looks out the window and points to the tower of the Canadian National Railway building, which looked to be about a mile away. Graig said, "The ball park is just past the needle there, that Canadian National tower." Tidrow thanked him, and since it was still a few hours before game time, he decided to walk to the park. I can just picture Tidrow walking up to that tower, and in the distance there are the lights of the ball park, and they're very, very small because the ball park must have been a good five miles from that tower.

As a result, Tidrow barely got to the park on time. We took a cab and got there a good hour before he did. When Tidrow got to the clubhouse, he was sweating like a pig. Dick went up to Graig and said, "If I'd a seen your cab, I would have flagged it down, hauled your ass out of there, and taken the cab myself." He threatened that he was going to give Nettles a whirly and make him throw up. Tidrow is 6 feet 4, about 225. He's deceptive. You don't think the man's that big, but he is. When Nettles messes with him too much, Tidrow picks him up, puts him on his shoulders, and spins him around until he's about to throw up.

With the score 3 to 3 and a man on first in the bottom of the ninth, Goose fielded a bunt and threw low to second for an error. When the next guy bunted, he fielded the ball and fired a bullet three feet over Chambliss's head to lose the ball game.

Goose is overthrowing. He's trying too hard. The pressure is on him to perform, and he's letting it get the best of him. Also, he's upset by the stuff that's going on with me. He knows how his presence is affecting me. I told Goose, "You've got to protect yourself. You can't let what's happening to me affect your pitching." He'll come out of it. It may take a little while longer, but with his speed and ability, he's going to be something when he finally gets it together.

Thursday, April 20 Toronto

Our game with the Blue Jays was rained out, so we took the bus to the airport for our flight back to New York, and when we got to the airport, traveling secretary Gerry Murphy stood in the front of the bus and announced that each player had to carry his own bags through customs. Normally we don't see our bags from the time we leave the ball park until we get to where we're going, but in Canada, before they allow you on the plane, you have to go through customs with your bags so they can search them.

Everyone got out of the bus, and Mickey Rivers went up to Murphy and told him, "I'm not carrying my bags. Get someone to do it." Murphy again told Mickey that he had to take his own bags, and he said that he wouldn't get a boarding pass until he did. Mickey got mad and ordered Murphy to take care of the bags. Again Murphy refused, and Mickey went nuts. He grabbed Murphy, pushed him down to the floor, and started choking him. Finally, the airport police came over and broke it up. It took a lot of fast explaining to get out of that one.

Friday, April 21 New York

We were sitting around the clubhouse before the game this evening when Billy called a meeting. He stood in the middle of the room, and he really aired everyone out. He told us he was tired of all that bullshit about money. He said, "When I was playing, no one was making the money you guys are making, but whatever we were playing for, we enjoyed playing." He said that if we didn't start playing better and start winning, he was going to fine us and have a curfew check and generally make our lives miserable as hell. He said he was going to start fining guys for not being out for infield practice. The starters don't ordinarily have to take infield if they don't want to, but we've been lax, we're playing badly, and Billy wants more discipline. If you look at us, you think, "These players don't want to win," because our attitude doesn't look very good. If we get our asses kicked, we'll still laugh and carry on and play our tape recorders on the bus, and it's tough for Billy to take. He feels that after you lose, you should be able to hear a pin drop, even if it's the tiddlywinks championship you just lost.

We're in fourth place, three and a half games behind Detroit. We've been playing .500 ball against teams that aren't nearly as good as we are, and I guess Billy's trying to get something going so we'll play better. He was trying to get us pissed off at him so we'd go out and play harder and do better. Billy didn't chew anyone out individually. He never does that. He said, "If you have anything to get off your chest, do it now. If you don't like me, it's tough. If you don't agree with what I'm doing, if you don't want to play, I'll make it miserable for you." As he was talking, he was getting madder and madder until his voice cracked and he had to stop. When his voice cracks, you can tell he's really angry.

By now, Billy had fire in his eyes. He shouted, "I'll fight one of you, I'll fight all of you." No one made a sound.

Tidrow's locker is alongside mine, and I was looking over at him, and from the other side, Guidry was also looking at him, and without moving a muscle, Dick was whispering under his breath, "Uh uh, uh uh."

Whenever Thurman and Cliff are both playing in the game, and we have to warm up two pitchers, we use an extra infielder to do the catching. If only one pitcher is warming up, Fran Healy usually takes care of it, unless he's passing time in the clubhouse watching TV, as he often does. It was late in the game tonight, we were losing 8–2, and Art called the bullpen for Kenny Clay to warm up. Healy was in watching TV, so infielder Mickey Kluttz had to warm up Clay. When you know you're going in, you throw as hard as you would in the game. Clay throws real hard, and he has a very good sinker ball, and he threw a pitch to Kluttz that was right down the heart of the plate and dipped real quick. Kluttz caught the ball with his thumb pointing down, and the ball caught his thumb and

ripped the webbing of his hand. It was the same hand
Mickey broke last year.

After he got hit, he caught two more pitches, and I told
him, "Get in the dugout and see the trainer." I made him
go in. He didn't want anyone to know he was hurt. Mickey
had just come up to the big leagues, and he suffered
through being on the disabled list and going back to the
minors after the break last year, and he didn't want to
go on the disabled list again. Finally, though, he went in.
The trainer examined the hand and told him his thumb
was broken.

Saturday, April 22   New York

Steinbrenner wants us to drop the grievance case on the
$500 fines. Billy came up to me today and said that Rosen
told him they're ready to talk to me about money. He said
only one thing is standing in the way though. The grievance. I told Billy I wasn't going to back down.

With Kluttz hurt, George Zeber, another infielder, was
sent out to the bullpen to catch, and he's going to get
smoked too. I don't know what they're going to do. They
better hire someone with experience to come out here and
catch.

Lucked out for another win today. After Tidrow allowed
only two runs in nine innings, he went out of the game
without getting the win because we weren't able to do
much with Mike Caldwell. I went in in the tenth and as
this kid Molitar was coming to the plate, Graig Nettles
came over from third to tell me that he often bunts. The
first pitch I threw him was a slider that didn't break, and
the kid hit the hell out of it, put it about 15 rows deep
into the left-field seats. I turned around and stared at
Nettles. "Yeah, he bunts," I yelled at him. Graig walked
over and said, "You have to throw him more than one
pitch for him to bunt."

In the bottom of the tenth Willie Randolph tied it with
a sacrifice fly, and in the twelfth, after I held the Brewers,
Roy White blooped a single to drive in Fred Stanley with

the winning run. Earlier, Roy, who the Yankees talk about trading every year, reached over the left-field wall to rob Charley Moore of a home run.

Billy still isn't too pleased with the way things have been going. After the game, a reporter asked him whether his pep talk had worked. "I guess so," he said. "We only left eighteen men on base."

Sunday, April 23   New York

Cat had retired 15 batters in a row and looked real sharp when Cecil Cooper singled in the seventh. With two outs Oglivie doubled Cooper to third, and with Sal Bando up and Gorman Thomas on deck, pitching coach Art Fowler came out to talk with Cat. Fowler says to Cat, "Don't give Bando anything good to hit." Great advice. Cat says, "I'm not planning to," but by now Cat's rhythm is so messed up because of Fowler's interruption that Cat throws a fastball a little too far over the plate, and Bando doubles to left for two runs and the game.

Monday, April 24   Baltimore

Sailing along with an 8 to 0 lead in the fifth, Gid swallowed a glob of tobacco juice when Rich Dauer hit a ball back at him through the middle. Gid told me he was just getting ready to spit when he threw the pitch. Usually, as you deliver the ball, you spit, but this time it was hit so quickly, and he had to jump for it. When he did, he swallowed all the juice he had been about to spit. He was bending over behind the mound, trying to get himself going again, but eventually it was too much for him. He pitched another inning, went into the clubhouse, and threw up. Goose finished up.

Gid said he was chewing Levi Garrett, which isn't as juicy as Red Man, what he usually chews. If he'd been chewing Red Man, he probably would have vomited right on the mound.

Of all the pitchers who chew tobacco, very few of them chew on the mound. Catfish chews almost every day, but he doesn't chew when he pitches. On the other hand, I rarely chew away from the ball park. In fact, I can't remember ever pitching without a chaw of tobacco in my mouth. I enjoy having it there, like some people enjoy chewing bubble gum. Levi Garrett is my favorite. I've gotten notoriety from pitching with chewing tobacco because, as the game goes along, in between innings I'd stuff more and more into my mouth, and sometimes the chaw would get so big, I'd actually have trouble getting it out after the game. It gets so big it looks like my cheek is going to burst.

I only chew a little bit in the wintertime because I'm in the house all the time, and I'm a sloppy chewer.

I started chewing tobacco when I was a teen-ager working for my father fixing roofs in Reynoldsville. One day I was putting on shingles, and I kept running up and down the ladder for water 'cause it was so damn hot. Dad was complaining that my going up and down was costing him an hour a day and suggested I chew. He handed me some Levi Garrett, showed me how to chew it, and I was up on the roof, putting the shingles on and chewing, and I finished, climbed down the ladder, and said, "Let's go." He climbed up to inspect, and he said, "Come back up here." The roof had white shingles, and they were covered with brown spots where I had spit. He made me scrub clean every spot. I've been chewing ever since.

Tuesday, April 25   Baltimore

In the outfield before the game I overheard pitching coach Art Fowler telling Figgie that he should do his running. "I'm not running," Figgie yelled at him.

Later Fowler came over to me and said, "The son of a bitch won't run because he's pissed off that he's not pitching today." Jim Beattie just arrived from Tacoma, and Billy shoved him into the starting rotation in place of Figgie for tonight's game. Figgie got up in the air about it.

Figgie likes to pitch every fourth day, and because tomorrow is an off day and the next day is the Mayor's Trophy game against the Mets, which he's not pitching in, that means it'll be seven days between starts for him. Figgie's pitching pretty well, and when a pitcher is going

well, he doesn't want to vary his routine. I can't blame him
for being angry. Nevertheless, a pitcher has to run, has to
keep his legs strong. Believe it or not, your legs get weak
if you don't run for even three or four days. They start
to get heavy. When my legs feel heavy, I don't pitch well.

I haven't thrown the ball well my last two outings, but
I've been lucky. Lucky is better, but still . . . tonight, Goddamn, that was scary. Beattie held the Orioles to a run
when I came in in the seventh with a couple of runners on
base. He had pitched beautifully for his first major league
start, throwing a live fastball and a major league curve
and change-up. I really think he'll stick up here. I got the
final out in the seventh, and when I came back to the dugout, the kid was so grateful, he came over and shook my
hand. I never saw that before in the middle of the game.
    I had nothing. Absolutely nothing, but the Orioles didn't
hit the ball hard—not until the ninth. In the top of the
ninth Jim Spencer, who was our DH, hit his hundredth
major league home run, giving us a 4 to 1 lead. I went
back out there to finish the game, my fingers were nice
and warm and sticky with resin, and I was raring to go,
feeling great, but Goddamn, they didn't hit anything
shorter than 400 feet. Even the outs were towering fly
balls. They scored two runs, making it 4 to 3, and they
had runners on first and third with two outs and Rich
Dauer coming up. Thurman called time. He came out to
the mound and he said, "I want to ask you something."
    "Ask," I said.
    "Are you trying?"
    He was serious. I said, "Of course I'm trying." Then
Billy came out of the dugout. He walked to the mound and
asked me how I felt. I told him. "I feel fine, but I don't
have squat. Nothing's breaking."
    I don't think he expected me to say, "I don't have squat."
He said, "What do you want me to do?" I said, "You're
the manager." I should help him decide what to do? So he
said, "OK, go get 'em." Quite frankly, I was surprised he
left me in. Either he's crazy or he has a hell of a lot of
confidence in me.
    Dauer stepped in. I figured that he's a line-drive hitter,

so I more or less just threw the ball up to him hoping he would hit a liner at somebody. It was a high meatball, and he swung and hit a nice high liner to Mickey Rivers in center field. We won 4 to 3.

In the dugout Spencer came over and rolled his eyes and made a loud sigh. I told him, "I had to make it a game. What good is hitting your hundredth home run unless it's a game winner?"

After the game, I was sitting in a bar with Nettles and Tidrow when Art Fowler came over and said, "If women didn't have pussies, there'd be a bounty out on the sons of bitches."

Fowler's a big guy, with real skinny legs, a red face, and tiny little feet. Everybody calls Fowler ten to two, because that's the way his feet point.

Fowler came up to Cincinnati to pitch relief in '54. He was thirty-one, and he had spent many years in the minors. When he finished pitching, he became a coach at Denver when Billy was managing there. This was 1970, and that year a lot of the pitchers got hurt, so Art activated himself at age forty-eight and won 9 games and saved 15 more. He would have been the league's Most Valuable Player, but he asked the league to give it to one of the kids instead. Fowler's been with Billy ever since then, at Minnesota, Detroit, and Texas. When Billy came here in '75, Gabe Paul refused to let Billy bring Art. Once when Fowler was pitching at Cincinnati, Gabe was the general manager, and he once called Gabe a son of a bitch to his face. Also, Art doesn't mind having a drink or two, and Gabe didn't feel Art would be a good influence on Billy. Christ, with that thinking, maybe we should have hired Billy Graham as our pitching coach. Finally last August, after one of George and Billy's bury-the-hatchet meetings, they finally agreed to let Art join Billy.

Thursday, April 27   New York

We beat the Mets in extra innings in the Mayor's Trophy game tonight. Catfish, who's had a painful pitching arm, started and really threw well. We ended up having to go into extra innings, and nobody wanted to play extra innings because we were leaving after the game to go on the road. In fact, nobody wanted to play the game at all.

In the dugout, Nettles said to me, "If I get a ball hit to me, I'm going to let it beat against my chest, and I'm going to throw it into the stands." I listened to this, and I really didn't think he would. One thing about Graig, if he makes a bad throw, it's always in the dirt. So we're in extra innings, and the ball was hit to Graig, and he bobbles it just like he said he would, and he threw it straight into the stands, a good ten feet over Chambliss's head. The batter ended up on second. And you know, those sons of bitches still couldn't score! This kid, Brian Doyle, who we brought up from Tacoma because Kluttz broke his hand, was playing second base, and the game would have been over, thanks to Graig, except Doyle made a tremendous play on a ground ball to get the final out and save the run. Everyone was pissed off at the kid. They were mumbling, "Goddamn it, what are you trying to do out there?" The kid didn't know what was going on. Here he made a great play, and everyone was mad at him. We ended up winning the game anyway.

After the game Fran Healy came up to Graig and asked him whether he had really tried to throw the ball away. Puff said, "Hell, yes, I did. I wanted to get the hell out of there." Healy said, "I can expect that from some players on this club, but not from you. I thought you always wanted to win."

In a game like that, who the hell cares? We would rather have not even played the damn thing. We were talking in the bullpen during the game. I said, "Christ, when you're pitching against the Mets, you don't know whether you're pitching well or not, they're so Goddamn bad." I'll tell you, if I had been pitching against them and it was extra innings, I'd have thrown the ball right down the cock. After playing ten games in eleven days and traveling all around, we don't need this aggravation, especially to have to play extra innings. I would have made it batting practice just so we could get the hell out of here. Who cares about beating the Mets?

I take that last sentence back. George does. He has this thing about beating the Mets. It's one of his biggest things. He always wants to beat them, just as the Mets always want to beat us. George gets all uppity before we play them, making a big point of it. He'll say, "I want you to beat these guys bad. We're both in New York, and we don't want to lose to them. Pride's involved. We gotta beat them."

For two years, 1974 and 1975, we had to play our home games in Shea Stadium while Yankee Stadium was being remodeled. I think that's one of the big reasons George hates the Mets so much. They wouldn't give the Yankees a percentage of the concessions or the parking, and they cut down the number of guys from our ground crew who were allowed to work there. They said their guys had to do it. Really, they kind of screwed the Yankees.

Personally, I thought Shea was a horrible ball park. The bullpen was terrible. It was a Plexiglas wall, and as the sun was going down, it hit right in the Plexiglas, and it was so scratched the bullpen pitchers couldn't see the field. Also, it was hotter'n a son of a bitch in there. Plus there were planes flying overhead every three minutes. You couldn't even hear yourself think.

My most memorable day at Shea occurred on Italian-American Day, or something like that. They had two big cannons sitting in the outfield with the barrels pointed toward the outfield wall, and they fired those babies ten times. Well, this one cannon was too close to the fence, and they were firing the son of a bitch and shooting and shooting, and by the fourth shot the cannon had blown a hole in the fence! We're in the bullpen, and we're saying, "Well, look at that. Those guys are for real!" The cannon went off again, and boom, the fence caught on fire, and it was burning. You could see the flames, but the guys shooting the cannon didn't pay any attention. They were supposed to fire ten shots, and they were going to fire those shots even if the entire stadium was falling down around them. They just kept firing that thing like nothing was happening.

Friday, April 28   Minneapolis–St. Paul

Just before the game today, Fran Healy and Ed Figueroa
almost got into a fight. Figgie was the starter, and Fran
was warming him up in the bullpen. Figgie threw a curve
ball in the dirt that bounced up and hit Healy in the
shin. A pitcher, I don't care who it is, who hits a catcher
warming up can't help but laugh. I'll laugh out loud. "Did
I get you good?" I'll yell, but catchers don't get pissed
off at me. Figgie sort of smiled and turned his back on
Fran, and boy, did that piss Healy off. In a matter of
three seconds, I was standing between these two bastards,
and Goddamn it, Fran had his arm cocked. I'm trying to
break it up, saying, "Now, Fran, leave him alone. Be nice,"
stuff like that 'cause I don't want to get my ass kicked
either. Finally, Fran cooled off and he said, "Ah, it was
just a misunderstanding." But Fran would not walk back
and get the ball they were using that had bounced past
him. Now, remember, Figgie was warming up to get ready
to pitch a ball game, and he doesn't have a ball to warm
up with. Figgie walked off the mound and said, "I ain't
throwing to that no good son of a beech anymore."

Ellie Howard, who runs the bullpen, was frantic. He's
calling on the phone to the dugout, "Get a catcher, get
a catcher," but no one would come out. It was three
minutes to game time, and Figgie's saying, "I no throw
to that son of a beech."

Billy played tonight's game under protest. In Minnesota
the visiting bullpen is in right-center field. Both bullpens
used to be beyond the outfield fence, but the Twins'
pitchers now warm up near their dugout. We warm up
in a padded cell. When the Twins put up a cyclone fence
around the outfield, they put the bolts in facing the wrong
way, with big, long bolts facing the field. Outfielders were
going back against the fence, and one of their players had
his side ripped open. Other players have also gotten hurt,
so the Minnesota players filed a grievance, and Lee Mac-
Phail, the American League president, came out and in-
spected the fence, and the Twins were ordered to put pad-

ding along it. They did that. They put the padding *all the way* around the outfield, including where the bullpens are, and now we can't see out from the bullpen. It's like we're in a room with no windows. So me and Rawly and Goose said to ourselves, "Hell, we're going to sit in the bleachers," which we did, but the umpires made us move. So Billy protested the game.

Figgie won the game, allowing five hits and one run. He went all the way. Imagine how he would have done if he had been able to warm up properly.

Saturday, April 29   Minneapolis–St. Paul

Billy was going to protest today's game against the Twins because one of their pitchers didn't have the same color shoes as everyone else. Billy was screaming that the guy was out of uniform, which is against regulations. Everyone on Minnesota wears red shoes. This one guy had black shoes. Billy was just busting their balls because he knows their manager, Gene Mauch, gets the red ass.

Mauch's a good manager, but he doesn't know how to handle pitchers. He's always screwing up his pitchers. When he was manager of the Phillies in 1964, he blew a ten-game lead at the end of the season because he had fouled up the staff so badly. When Mauch goes out to talk to a pitcher, he really chews the guy's ass out. He's a manager who just doesn't like pitchers. Some managers are like that. They feel a pitcher is somebody who's just there. This type of manager feels he could take any infielder or outfielder, tell him in spring training, "I'm going to make you a pitcher," and the guy'd end up winning 20 games. He doesn't feel that a pitcher has a talent like the rest of the players. That seems awfully funny coming from a major league manager.

Mickey Rivers didn't play tonight because of his knee. On this day it apparently acted up over a card game. It seems that besides baseball, there are only two things Mickey likes: going to the track and playing cards. Nothing else.

We have a rule, no card playing in the clubhouse be-

fore the game unless it's raining, and yesterday Mickey
and Holtzman and a couple of others were playing cards,
and they played right through infield practice, which really
pissed Billy off. Today before the game, Mickey asked our
clubhouse boy for a deck of cards, and the clubhouse boy
told him no. Mickey said, "What do you mean, no?" He
was really mad. The clubhouse boy said, "Billy told me
no more card playing at all." So Mickey said, "Screw it.
I ain't playing." And it was at that point that his leg
started hurting him real bad.

After the game, which Tidrow lost 3 to 1, Thurman
almost got into a fight with a fan because the guy wanted
a Goddamn autograph. It's tough to understand a ballplayer's position about autographs unless you have to go
through it. A funny thing, autographs. On the road I
get out of bed at one, two in the afternoon, and I leave
my room and get in the elevator to go down and get
something to eat, and as soon as the car reaches the
lobby and opens, they're there. They hang out in the lob-
bies, at the ball parks, everywhere. You're constantly involved with this, and after a while it gets very tiresome.
They even come to your table when you're eating. People
don't think. They're not involved at the other end of it.
They wouldn't want people coming to their house, ringing
the doorbell, and saying, "Can I have your autograph?"
Sooner or later, they'd say, "Hey, buzz off." And that's
the point Thurman reached. It's gotten to where they
don't say, "May I have your autograph?" They say,
"Gimme your autograph," and when someone says that
to me, I don't even look at them. I ignore them. Those
people don't deserve autographs. I think to myself, "If
you're gonna be that way with me, then screw ya." And
they call you asshole or something like that, and after
going through that enough you get further and further
away from wanting to sign autographs for anybody.

Thurman is a nice guy, but I think New York has
taken its toll on him. New York is a hard city. You hear
people say, "If you can make it in New York, you can
make it anywhere," which is true. But on the other hand,
to make it in New York, you have to become a little bit
harder than when you play in Minnesota or Cleveland or

another city. Thurman can't even wipe his ass without someone knowing about it. He has been through so much media exposure, I think he feels he has to protect his privacy very carefully. Not wanting to be bothered is the only attitude he feels he can have to maintain any privacy. He's very intelligent, and has a fine business head. He's as successful in business as he is in baseball. He's taking flying lessons, getting ready for the changeover when his career comes to an end. He's ready to quit. He's heard too many people yell, "Horseshit throw," or "Ya can't hit for beans, ya bum," or "You're too old," and he's getting tired of it. He's extremely sensitive about criticism, and he's had it, especially with the New York fans.

Sunday, April 30   Minneapolis–St. Paul

Rawly Eastwick is a great explorer in the bullpen. He should have been a treasure hunter. Or a garbage man. In the bullpen he'll hunt around and find little doodads, and no matter what it is, he'll give it to me. For no reason. Last week, he found a little piece of copper wire, and he sculpted it into a tiny pair of glasses. He gave it to me, and I pinched it and put it on my nose. I'm going to save all the things Rawly gives me during the year, and at the end of the season I'm going to give them back to him, and he's going to make a sculpture. I told him, "Make the sculpture according to what kind of year you have. If it's horseshit, we'll make it horseshit." But I don't expect it to be horseshit because he's a very good pitcher.

Yesterday he found a golf spike on the field. I don't know how it got on the field. We hadn't been out there five minutes. He walked over, smiled, and handed it to me.

Today Rawly found the back of a tie tack. He gave that to me along with a little metal thing that looked like a wrench. I said, "All right. I'll find you something." I walked over to the bullpen the Twins used before they put up the padding. It's down aways, and there was this old guy guarding it, but he wasn't watching. The telephone was still on the wall, and I figured I'd give it one

good try—yank it once as hard as I could—and I ripped
it right off the wall. I hid it under my warm-up jacket
and walked back to our bullpen. I came over to Rawly
and said, "I found something you didn't find, and it's
been here the whole time, and you didn't see it." He
says, "What?" And from behind my back I pull out the
telephone receiver. I said, "Here, this is for you." Rawly
went, "Ooooooooooooooooooooh." He liked that.

Later I found him a big hook, one of the hooks used
to hold up the padding. As with everything I give him,
he examined it closely. I don't give a damn if it's a piece
of wire, he'll hold it up to his eye, turn it around, look
at it from every angle, and try to learn everything about
it before he puts it away.

He's an unusual guy. The bullpen pitchers get pastrami
sandwiches in the bullpen when we play at home, but
Rawly doesn't eat red meat. He's into health food. The
other day I had Frankie Albano, who drives the relief
pitchers in the cart from the bullpen to the mound, get
Rawly a salad along with our pastrami sandwiches. Rawly's sitting there, and we're eating our pastrami, and I
said to him. "This is for you," and handed him the salad.
He said, "Right on, this stuff is goooood," and he got
everyone to try some. Then he ate the whole cup of salad.

Everyone on the club thinks Rawly is weird because he
buys *Rolling Stone* magazine. Everybody else reads the
Sporting News. Ballplayers aren't the greatest readers, me
included. One day during spring training, Rawly left his
magazine upside down on a bench. Yogi, who for all his
money wouldn't spend a penny if he had to take a crap,
picked it up as soon as Eastwick left. Yogi thought he
had a free copy of the *Sporting News*. He started walking
away, and pretty soon he looked at it, did a double take,
and looked at it again. He scrunched up his nose like
he'd just smelled rotting cheese. Finally, he threw it back
on the bench and said, "This ain't no *Sporting News*."
Eastwick, who had watched the whole thing, just smiled.

They think he's spacey because he keeps to himself a
lot. When he does say something, everyone goes, "Woooo-
ooooooooooooooeeeeeeeeeeeeeeeeey," like space music, because if you didn't know him, you'd think he was a space
cadet, that he had no damned idea of what anybody is

talking about. He just walks around the bullpen and listens and smiles. Before, if the guys were ripping someone, Rawly wouldn't say anything. But now, every once in a while, he'll join in. Today Holtzman said, "Did you notice that Rawly dropped a few 'fucks'? In another three or four weeks, he'll be just as sick as the rest of us. He's getting closer all the time."

Rawly is getting used to us, and he likes it here. At first, I don't think he really cared whether he was a Yankee or not. Now he's really having fun. Rawly isn't a derelict like the rest of us.

Willie Randolph jammed his hand yesterday, so today Billy played the Doyle kid at second base. Doyle is a good player, but the only reason he's here is that Mickey Kluttz broke his thumb. As far as I'm concerned, whoever Billy wants to play is fine, but what he fails to remember, here's a guy, Fred Stanley, who was our starting shortstop in '76 when we won the pennant; he did an outstanding job, and then George got Bucky Dent—and Fred lost his job right away, which depressed the hell out of him, and here he is, keeping himself ready, and now Kluttz gets hurt, and all of a sudden after one good play in the Mayor's Trophy game, Billy thinks, "I'll give the kid a chance to play," and Stanley's out.

Fred is very down, and I can't blame him. See, Billy wasn't thinking about that. If a manager had ever done that to Billy Martin when he was playing, there would be hell to pay. If Doyle was going to take Fred's job, then I could see it, but he isn't, because he can't play short and third like Fred can. Say Nettles or Bucky gets hurt, now Stanley has to play. So why play Doyle? Why not let Fred play when there's a chance to put him in? Managers always figure you should be able to go out there and do it. That's not the way it is.

On our flight from Minneapolis to New York, Goose was sitting in his seat talking, not paying attention to anything else, and I stuck the head of a match into his earth shoes and lit it. The damn thing went out. I did it again, and again the damn thing went out. Goose kept talking, and Fred Stanley came over to me and said, "Let me try that," and he lit it up. I tell you, as Goose was tap-dancing in the aisles we thought he was Mr. Bojangles for a minute. It burned his whole shoe up, made it black.

We used to have a pitcher by the name of Mike Wallace. Mike used to be so tired during the day because he was always partying at night. He didn't do anything different from anyone else. He just didn't have any stamina. So I used to light up his cleats every day just to keep him awake. That didn't help much either. He didn't last here very long.

Monday, May 1   New York

We hired a kid who got released from "A" ball to catch the pitchers warming up in the bullpen. They hired him just to warm us up, and I guess he's going to go on the road with us too. All I know about him is his name is Dominick. Today he walked up to me and said, "Hi. I'm Dominick." I didn't know who he was. I said, "You want me to kiss your ring?"

Since Kluttz broke his thumb, Cliff Johnson has been refusing to come out to the bullpen to catch. He flat-ass refuses, and the times he does come out there, he won't catch unless two pitchers are warming up, which pisses Fran Healy off because since we got Cliff not only does Healy not get to play anymore, all he does is warm up pitchers. Even before that, Healy wouldn't warm up pitchers unless he absolutely had to. Healy would warm up the starting pitcher, go to the clubhouse to change his shirt, and he'd be in there screwing around for three innings. He'd always come back at the bottom of the third. If we had to get two pitchers up early in the game, Healy wouldn't be around, so we'd have to use whoever else happened to be out there. Ellie Howard sometimes has to do it, but he shouldn't because he has a bad knee. When he crouches for a long period of time, he has to have it drained. Last year it was Cloyd Boyer, the pitching coach. Cloyd is fifty-seven years old. He shouldn't have had to catch guys. This went on and on, and finally Cloyd and Healy almost had a fight. Cloyd told him he was a lazy son of a bitch, which he is.

Tonight they made Cliff go out to the bullpen. Out there were Cliff and Fran and Dominick. The phones were ringing in the bullpen for guys to warm up, and Fran wouldn't move off the bench, and neither would Cliff. Dominick, who was catching everybody, was getting his blessed hand knocked off out there. Ellie told Fran and Cliff, "Goddamn it, you guys are out here to catch. You're gonna have to take turns. That's the way it's gonna be." Fran just stood there with his hands on his hips staring at Ellie. Ellie was pleading with Fran, saying, "Goddamn it, you can't let this kid warm everybody up." Fran didn't move an inch. Ellie looked over at Cliff, and Cliff was sitting on the bench with his hat over his eyes dropping sunflower seeds into his mouth. Fran said, "When that big son of a bitch gets up to catch, I'll catch." Aw hell. Cliff is 6 feet 6 and Healy is 6 feet 5. Who's going to stop them if they get into it? Then I thought, "I hope nobody breaks it up. A big fight could end our problem right here. The loser catches."

This stuff has been going on all year in the bullpen. You'd never guess this was the big leagues, the Yankees, the World Champions. You'd expect something like this in Little League. Ellie tells them to do something, and neither one of them will listen. When Ellie complains to Billy, he's got enough other things to worry about; he doesn't want any part of it. Billy will tell Ellie, "You tell them to catch or I'll fine their asses." So Ellie tells them that, and they say, "Big deal. Fine me." Billy will tell them, "Don't worry. We'll work things out." Then he'll tell Ellie, "Goddamn it. Make them catch." Billy, by not backing up Ellie, makes his job harder, and I think Ellie's getting fed up with the whole thing.

Billy has been trying to alternate Goose and me as best he can, and he's doing a good job of it. The problem is that I'm still not able to get real sharp. I'm still pitching poorly. I've got two wins and a few saves, but I've been lousy. Red Foley of the *News* asked me, "How can you be pitching poorly if you haven't lost a game?" I said, "Compared to what I'm capable of doing, I'm not pitching well." I'm getting guys out because they're missing pitches they should be hitting.

Goose got his first win yesterday, but he's been having his troubles too. He doesn't like the situation any more than I do, but there's nothing we can do about it. We're still good friends. We were before. Last winter, right after the Yankees got him, I had him over the house and told him exactly how I felt and what I was going to do. I told them they'd have to promise to pitch me a lot or trade me. I said, "Anything you read in the papers where a writer has it sounding like I'm knocking you, don't believe it. This has nothing to do with you personally. It's strictly from a business point of view. You need a lot of work. So do I. I'm trying to establish myself, to get more work and more money, or to get out of here."

Gossage is a fun-loving guy, always happy. I've never seen him in a bad mood. Goose told me a story that when he was pitching with Chicago, he hit Thurman. He hit him right on the elbow, and as hard as he throws, it must have been God-awfully painful. I remember when it happened. I thought Thurman's elbow was broken. But Thurman didn't even rub the son of a bitch. He just walked down to first base. Goose told me that after the game Munson sent him a note. It read, "I took your best shot right on the elbow, you big donkey, and I'm still playing." He signed it, "The White Gorilla."

Goose was sitting in his locker sandpapering his earth shoes to get the black off from us lighting them up. Nettles came over and said, "I thought you were supposed to shine your shoes. I didn't know you sandpapered them! That must be why mine never turn out too well."

Rawly got his first win today in relief of Beattie. He pitched three and a third innings of scoreless ball and looked very sharp. I finished up and saved it for him.

Tuesday, May 2   New York

In the bullpen today Dominick said to me, "I guess I'm going to be warming you up a lot." I said, "Don't be expecting too much. I'm no flamethrower. I just get loose nice and easy and go into the game." The first time he warmed me up, I was throwing nice and easy, and I started throwing sliders. Now every once in a while my slider will break left instead of right. I threw Dominick the ball, and it started to break out and suddenly it broke back in and hit the kid right in the chest. Boom. He groaned at me, "It's backing up." I said, "I know. I forgot to tell you. That's one of my pitches too." Now this poor kid doesn't know what to do. Before, he was comfortable because he thought he knew how the slider was going to come in. Once it broke the wrong way it screwed him up, 'cause now he's missing the ones that break in *and* the ones that break out.

I relieved Cat after he threw seven beautiful innings. He allowed only five hits, including two long home runs by Porter and McRae, and won his first game since last August. Lou won it with a two-run home run. I gave 'em nothing on nothing in two innings for save number four. They were hitting the ball like I was throwing it—terrible.

The only reason Billy is letting me pitch more than I thought I was going to pitch is that right now I'm throwing more strikes than Goose, which I've always been able to do. Goose'll find it soon, and then we'll see where I end up. It's like a 100-mile-an-hour sword hanging over my head.

After the game Mickey Rivers was standing in the clubhouse wearing a chest protector strapped to his back. Mickey said it's supposed to protect him as he runs into the wall chasing the missiles hit off Cat. As Mickey pranced around the room, Cat sat in his locker smiling.

Then Cat and Piniella started ripping each other. Piniella was complaining of wall burns from running into walls going after Cat's home-run balls. He told Cat, "The next time you pitch I'm going to buy a seat in the bleachers. I have a better chance of catching the ball." Cat said, "Oh yeah, well, anyone who loses his job to Jim Wohlford has no place criticizing anybody." Wohlford took Lou's job at Kansas City after the Royals traded him here. "Imagine," Cat said, "losing your job to Jim Wohlford." As Cat kept giving it to Lou, Mickey Rivers, the scorekeeper, was hollering, "Farmer Catfish one hundred and ten, Cuban Piniella twenty-two." Finally when everything got real quiet, Lou said, "Why don't you give yourself a shot and settle down for a while."

Wednesday, May 3   New York

When Dominick was warming me up yesterday he was throwing the ball back with a real high arc. I mean, real high. It almost brought rain. After you throw a pitch, you have to wait forever until the ball gets back to you. I told him, "Throw the ball back with something on it, understand?" So before the game today, Dominick started warming Figgie up, and Dominick smoked the ball back to him, whooooooooooomp. He almost broke Figgie's hand. Figgie's going, "Hey, Goddamn you, son of a beech, what you trying to do? What the hell is going on?" Dominick came over later and was obviously confused, and he asked me, "Am I throwing it back too hard?" I told him, "That's a little too hard." It was tough to keep a straight face. First Healy and now Dominick. Figgie must be wondering whether the catchers are conspiring against him. Despite all that, Figgie still won his fourth game.

Our hitters are starting to hit a little bit—we scored six runs tonight—even though they're still not setting the league on fire. We're winning right now because even though Nettles, Munson, and Randolph, guys who usually hit, aren't, our other hitters are. We're winning ball games with a different guy every night. I don't think it'll be too long before we're really playing well. Our pitching has been excellent, and it looks like Guidry is going to be something special this year.

There's going to be a lot of crap, though. Boy, I can see it coming. Tonight I was about to take a shower after the game, and Cliff came in and cut in front of me and took my shower. I pushed him out of there, which is no easy task. I said, "Get the hell out of here, you big donkey." He said, "Awwwwwww, that's all right. The Count can push me around. He's my buddy. But there's one guy who ain't gonna be able to do that." Nettles mentioned a player. Cliff said, "It ain't him."

I said, "I know who it is. Could it be your co-catcher
in the bullpen?" Cliff smiled. "It could be him," he said.

I can understand how Healy feels because here's a guy
who went from being the starting catcher at Kansas City
to being the backup catcher to Munson here. That right
there was a big blow because Fran wants to play, he
wants to catch, yet Thurman is so much better than he
is. When Healy came over here, I heard him say, "I can
take it. I can take warming up pitchers all day because
I know I'm not going to take that man's job away." When
we got Cliff from Houston, Cliff told them that he didn't
want to be a catcher. He had bone chips in his ankles,
and it was killing him to squat down. Over the winter,
they operated on his ankle and got it fixed, and now
Cliff is catching and Healy isn't, and that's just too much
for Healy to take. Thurman catches 150 games a year,
and the few Thurman isn't catching, Cliff is catching,
keeping Healy stuck in the bullpen. In a way you can't
blame Fran for retaliating the only way he can, by saying, "Screw it, I'm not warming up those pitchers." It's
the only job he has right now. But frankly, I think Fran's
burying himself. If we can hire a kid like Dominick, we
can just as easily bring up one of the young catchers
from the minors and say to Fran, "Take your sixty grand
and see ya."

In the ninth tonight, Goose was awesome. He struck
out two out of three batters to get his first save. We
were up by a run, and Kansas City sent Pete LaCock up
to hit against him. Goose was throwing 100 miles an
hour, and the first pitch he threw to LaCock was up in
his eyes. LaCock swung at it as if he had an axe in his
hands and he was trying to split a piece of wood. Then
he threw the next one right by him, and the third strike
was on the black, on the outside part of the plate at 100
miles an hour. Just being on the black normally is enough.
LaCock just carried his bat back to the dugout. I knew
just what the poor son of a bitch was thinking: "Goddamn, he throws a hundred miles an hour and he's paint-
ing the black. I don't care if I ever face him again."

Thursday, May 4   New York

This has not been an easy job for Mickey Morabito, who is in charge of public relations for the Yankees. It was bad enough during spring training because Mickey had to be in his room every night at eleven so he'd be available when George wanted to talk to him. Now Mickey's ass is on the line because a reporter asked Tony Kubek about George, and Kubek said that George is a tyrant who rules by fear and that George has an expensive toy and won't let anyone else enjoy it. Which is all true. Even so, George got so mad at Kubek when he found out what he said that he gave the word that no Yankee player is allowed to be interviewed by Kubek for the Game of the Week show. George called in Morabito and told him that if just one player talks to Kubek, Morabito's fired. When Mickey told me this, with a straight face I said, "Jeez, Mick, I'd really hate to see you lose your job, but if Kubek asks me for an interview, I really can't say no."

George has the attitude that if you don't like it, you can leave and find another job, and many of his employees do. It's not surprising his front office staff turns over twice a year. After Mike Burke left, a year later George had a whole new staff. Lee MacPhail, Tal Smith, Pat Gillick, Elliott Wahle, Clyde Kluttz, they all left. Bob Fishel, who had been the PR man for years and years, quit. His successor, Marty Appel, who started with the Yankees cutting newspaper clippings while he was in high school, a guy who loved the Yankees more than anything, finally quit. Christ, I heard that George fired one secretary because she didn't bring him a tuna fish sandwich fast enough!

Friday, May 5   New York

We won our fifth straight game tonight, as Gid won his third in a row. Again Goose was tough in relief. Thurm

had three hits and drove in two runs to break a Texas
seven-game winning streak.

Among the letters Ellie got in the mail today was an
application to join the Society for the Preservation of
Whales. Ellie says that he keeps getting this whale literature and thinks Fritz Peterson is the guy who's sending it
to him. Fritz was here from 1966 through 1973, and
while Fritz was a Yankee he always called Ellie Boilerston
Tuna Howard. Ellie was always wearing this big rubber
belt around his waist to slim down his stomach, and he
called that a tuna belt. The boiler was his big belly, so
Fritz named him Boilerston Tuna Howard. Ellie used to
get pissed all the time when Fritz called him that, so
Fritz used to send him literature on tunas and whales and
weight-reducing pamphlets.

As soon as the whale stuff came, Ellie immediately
said, "That son of a bitch Peterson, I know it's coming
from him." But he didn't really. That's what made Peterson the greatest practical joker I ever saw. You could
never catch Fritz doing anything. He'd repeatedly call
someone a name until the name stuck, and then he'd
start sending you literature relating to the name he gave
you. He'd also send Ellie a lot of porno stuff, stag pictures, and I mean oodles and oodles of the stuff, and boy,
would Ellie get the red ass.

Four guys, Peterson, Mike Kekich, Steve Kline, and
Mel Stottlemyre, were constantly doing things to each
other. When Stan Bahnsen was here, they pulled a lot
of stuff on him. Once they sent Stan's clothes to Hawaii.
We got home from a road trip, they took his clothes, put
them in a box, stamped it, and mailed it to Honolulu.
Kekich once bought a waterbed in Milwaukee, and he
kept going on and on about what a terrific waterbed he
bought, and the next day the waterbed was hanging from
the flagpole in front of the scoreboard at County Stadium.
It was about 80 feet in the air, this big rubber thing
flapping in the breeze.

Fritz must have signed Stottlemyre up for every damned
encyclopedia there was in the world. Stott got home from
a road trip, and waiting for him at his home were boxes

and boxes of books worth thousands of dollars. Stott was furious. He said, "I'm not accepting any of this. I didn't order it. I don't want it." And he sent the books back. But more books just kept coming and coming.

I remember when I first came to the Yankees, around 1972, Thurman had ordered a gun holster from a magazine. Thurman likes pistols and guns, and he wanted to buy a holster for his .357 magnum. It cost $40. He filled out the order blank, ordered a holster for a .357 with a four-inch barrel, put his waist size as 36, and said it was for a right-handed person.

Fritz intercepted the letter to the company, which was in California, and Fritz took the order blank and erased what Thurman wrote. Fritz ordered a holster for a tiny .38 snub-nose, put down a size 20 waist, said it was for a left-handed person, and mailed it out. It took six weeks for the package to come, and Thurman was all excited, and he ripped off the wrapper, opened the box, and inside was a holster about three inches long, it had a 20-inch waist, and it was for a left-hander. Thurman was so pissed. He was moaning, "I waited so long for it, and son of a bitch, I have to send it back." He was singing the blues. He put it back in the box and returned it. Fritz intercepted it again. The box never left the clubhouse. Fritz kept it in his locker for a couple of weeks, wrapped it up as if it were coming back from the company, and put it back in Thurman's locker. Again Thurman went nuts. Three times Fritz did the same thing, and three times Thurman opened the box, and every time he got the same tiny holster, and he couldn't figure out why.

Meanwhile, Fritz was writing letters to the president of the holster company, signing Thurman's name and saying how much Thurman loved the holster and that if he wanted any tickets for a Yankee game when we got to California to call Thurm at such and such a number. That was Fritz. He was beautiful.

I remember one day Steve Kline got some flowers from a girl friend. It was his birthday, and this girl had sent him a flowerpot with flowers in it. Steve thought it was nice because he had never gotten flowers from a girl before. He was saying, "Man, this is really nice." And he kept asking everyone, "Wasn't that nice?" And everyone was saying yeah. Steve said, "It's so pretty. I'm going to keep it and watch it grow." He was like a little kid. As soon as Steve went out onto the field, Fritz poured about a half a bottle of alcohol into the flowerpot. By the time Steve got back to the clubhouse, the flowers were bent over, wilted, and turning black.

Steve wasn't nearly as clever as Fritz was. My first year here I used to have my clothes washed at the ball park. The clubhouse man would wash them and put them back in my suitcase. I went into the clubhouse one day, and when I opened the door, I saw Kline putting a greasy window fan into my suitcase with my clean clothes. He was rubbing the grease from the fan all over the clothes. I shut the door before he could see me. I never said a word. He had bought a pair of high-heeled fancy shoes. He really loved those shoes. Wore them all the time. A couple of days later, during the game, I took his shoes and put a couple of eight-inch spikes through them. The old "nail-the-shoes-to-the-floor" trick. When the game ended, we had a bus to catch to the airport, and he hadn't realized what I had done until it was time to get on the bus. It was really funny watching him scramble to get the spikes out so he could catch the bus. That was enough satisfaction for me.

Saturday, May 6   New York

Singlehandedly I ended our winning streak. It was 2 to 2 in the sixth, and with men on first and third and one out, Billy brought me in to relieve Tidrow. The first batter, Sundberg, batted one back to me. I looked to see if I could get Harrah running home, saw I couldn't, and when I couldn't, I turned to throw Sundberg out at first, but it was too late to do that too. The next guy, Campaneris, flied out, which should have been the third out, and Bump Wills doubled home two runs and we ended up losing 9 to 5. Kenny Clay pitched the last three innings, allowing Richie Zisk, who is slower than everyone in the league except maybe Rusty Staub, to steal two bases on him.

We're still three behind the Tigers, one in back of Boston.

Sunday, May 7   New York

Pete Sheehy, the clubhouse guy, has been here since Yankee Stadium was built in the twenties. That old son of a bitch knows more about what's going on than anyone around, including George. I happened to see Pete before the game, and he was holding a few metal nameplates, the ones that go on top of the lockers. I saw them and said, "Hey, Pete, what do you have there?" He said, "Oh, nothing." He laid the nameplates face down, and I went over and looked at them, and the first nameplate I picked up was Jerry Narron's, our big young catcher at Tacoma. I held up the nameplate and said, "What the hell does this mean?" Pete didn't know what to say. He hesitated a few seconds and said, "I watch and anticipate if we might take someone new. I try to guess who it's going to be. I figured I'd get the nameplate made just in case."

We call Pete "Gabby" for Gabby Hayes. I said, "Gabby, you son of a bitch, let me know when they're taking my nameplate down."

Pete is seventy and stooped, and if you didn't know him you'd think he is very serious all the time. He likes to play around sometimes, though. When most guys put their uniform on, they pull their pants to about thigh level while they pull their shirttails down. Pete will shuffle around the clubhouse, and he'll see a guy getting dressed with his pants down, and he'll lay a baseball in the seat of his pants. Then he'll shuffle over to a corner, sit down, and light up a cigarette. The guy will yank his pants up hard, and it feels like the ball has gone right up your ass.

Billy sent me into the game in the sixth inning, and I pitched a couple of innings and took myself out. I'm depressed enough as it is that George won't talk to me, but I'm getting vibes that Billy is trying to slip me into the long relief spot. I feel like quitting.

Billy had to put Goose in, which I felt bad about, and Goose had to pitch four innings before Chris Chambliss homered to win it. Goose now has two wins and two saves in his last four games.

Chambliss is a hell of a hitter. He's improved a lot since Gabe Paul got him from Cleveland in '74. You might make him look silly the pitch before, but if he gets his pitch, he's not going to pop up or ground out. He's gonna lose it. He isn't the type of hitter who swings from his ass all the time to try to hit the ball out of the park. He takes his time and swings at good pitches. He's the only guy who rarely gets in a slump, and as a result the last couple of years he's driving in 90 or more runs a year.

Chris is one of the nicest guys on the club, never says a bad word about anybody, never gets mad, and never makes excuses for himself if he makes an error. The umps love him too. When Chris gets called out on strike, he never says anything, never throws his helmet. Some guys will argue just for the sake of arguing but not Chris. If an ump calls a guy safe at first and you see Chris arguing, you can be sure the guy was out. Chris is a very nice guy, he's an intelligent person, and he's considerate of others, which isn't a quality you find in a lot of ballplayers.

For as long as he lives, he'll be remembered for the home run he hit off Mark Littell of Kansas City in 1976 to get us into the World Series. What's funny is that Chris doesn't like to talk about the home run. I always thought it was funny he never got any offers for any real big-money commercials afterward. If he didn't deserve it, who did?

Like I said, Gabe Paul brought Chris to the Yankees. Chris is Gabe's man. When Gabe was at Cleveland, he signed Chris out of college, and in one of his first deals after he and George took over the Yankees, he traded to get Chris back: Peterson, Kline, Freddie Beane, and Tom Buskey to Cleveland for Chambliss, Tidrow, and Cecil Upshaw. We were really pissed off when he made that trade because we were losing good guys. We were doing pretty good at the time, and it didn't seem to us that the guys Gabe were trading were doing a bad job. Upshaw used to be good, but he'd hurt his finger. We thought Tidrow was a pretty good pitcher, but we didn't know how much better a pitcher he was than the guys we were giving up. Chambliss we figured would be a pretty good ballplayer, but we couldn't figure out why

Cleveland would want to get rid of him. As it turned out, they shouldn't have.

Since George got Jim Spencer in a deal with Chicago over the winter, I suppose it's possible now that Gabe's gone that George wants to trade Chris. George feels that Chris doesn't hit enough home runs for a lefty batter in Yankee Stadium. If George does trade Chris, it would be a big mistake.

Roy White, another player George has never been particularly fond of, is going through a really tough period. At the beginning of the season, they were talking about trading him, as they always do, and they didn't. Then they told him, "Don't worry, we're going to get you in eighty games." (That's half the games.) But now Roy is down because Billy's been playing Cliff instead, and I don't think Roy's ever sat out so many games in a row. Tonight Roy finally played. Billy had him bunt and he popped out to the catcher. Roy's normally as quiet a guy as Chris, but this time he came back to the dugout and he started yelling, "Play somebody else. Get me out of here. I can't play like this. I can't go up to the plate every week or ten days and do the job." He was screaming so loud you could have heard him in the press box.

Monday, May 8   New York

The game against Minnesota was rained out, so a few of the guys were sitting around the clubhouse playing cards. Rivers and Holtzman and a few others were playing poker. A few of the other guys were playing pluck, a game like bridge, where you have to win a certain number of tricks. Just about everybody on this club plays it. Most ballplayers gamble, whether it's cards or horses, because it's a fun way to kill a lot of time, and one thing we have on the road, it's a lot of time. Mickey loves to gamble more than most. He loves to follow the horses. Billy thought Mickey was using the clubhouse phone too much for that purpose, so he had it taken out. Mickey said he doesn't care. All it means is he'll have to send somebody out to call in his bets. But that's Billy's way of

punishing him. Granted when you're not playing well—
and we're not, and Mickey's not—you grab for anything
you can get. So Billy figures, "Well, Goddamn, if he's
worried more about the horse in the second race than
about the ball game, I'll take that away from him." With
someone else, that might have worked, but Mickey's attitude is, "Screw it, if they're going to punish me, I don't
care if I play or not."

Now Mickey sends a guy out to find out the race re-
sults. The guy comes back and tells Holtzie in the bullpen, and when Mickey comes out to play the outfield at
the start of the inning, Holtzie calls out the winners to
him. If Mickey's horse wins, he gets all excited.

Billy called Rosen for me, and Rosen got in touch with
Steinbrenner about renegotiating my contract. Rosen called
me back and repeated what George had said before: that
George was going to do it on his own time. In other
words, tough. Rosen said, "I'm not going to tell you anything different. That's what George said, so if I told you
anything different, I'd be lying to you. George said you'd
get your money in due time, not before."

I figure, what the hell, I'm not going to get anywhere
taking myself out of games, so I won't do that again.
I'll just go ahead and pitch and wait for George.

Sheehy's nameplates didn't lie. Healy got his release
today.

Tuesday, May 9   New York

Yesterday's game was rained out, and if we had stayed
in rotation, it would have been Figueroa's turn to pitch,
but Billy decided to go with Cat tonight, and when Figgie found out he wasn't starting, he was hot. Lemme tell
you what kind of guy Cat is—when he found out Figgie
was angry, he went to Art Fowler and told him, "Let
Figgie pitch. I'll throw batting practice."

Oakland owner Charley Finley gave Catfish his name.
Finley's the one who gave a lot of those guys their nick-
names, like Blue Moon Odom. Cat told me Finley wanted

one guy to change his name, and the guy said, "You kidding me? I ain't changing my name." That's the way Finley is. He likes things to be colorful. Catfish Hunter is a lot more colorful than Jim Hunter or Jimmy Hunter or Big Jim Hunter. Cat tells stories about the damn mule Finley had out there. Finley took it everywhere they went, even into the hotels. The mule had gotten so old his hair had fallen out, so Finley had a tail made for the damn mule.

One day when we were playing the A's, I was going to pull the mule's fake tail off. I got pissed because they would walk it around the outfield, and it would always take a dump right in front of our bullpen. It was like Finley had trained it. Once I even stepped in it, and you have no idea how tough it is to get it off your spikes. Finally, I decided to rip its tail off. But I chickened out. I was afraid I would never play again, that I wouldn't be quick enough and that the mule would nail me with his hooves before I could get out of the way. Eventually it died.

Cat was on the mound taking his warm-up pitches to start the game when the phone rang. It was Art asking Holtzman to get up and start throwing. I said to myself, "Uh oh, there's definitely something wrong with Cat." When they called Holtzie to warm up, they told him to pretend there were runners on base and to work on holding them. Rawly stood behind him, acting like he was the second baseman, and the rest of us were sitting in the pen cheering Kenny on, saying, "C'mon, we have to get the double play," and stuff like that. We were clapping for him, and he was tipping his hat to the fans in the bleachers, and they were cheering. He did this for four innings, and Kenny said, "I know what's going to happen. I'll warm up for five innings, and then you and Goose'll get up, and that'll be it for me." And that's just about how it happened. In the sixth I was warming up to go in.

It's ten years and a day since Cat pitched a perfect game for the A's. Today he pitched a one-hitter for six innings. I came in and pitched from the seventh and got my fifth save. Cat hates to be taken out, I don't care if he gives up ten home runs, he hates to come out, but after the game, he didn't seem pissed at all. He was just glad he won. He said to reporters, "It's great to show everyone that you can win again, rather than get your ass kicked every night." Later I saw his arm packed in ice. Also, his shoulder's stiff and hurting. I hope it's nothing serious.

Art Fowler's been really down lately. Billy's been getting on his ass. Art keeps saying that Billy wants to win so badly that you can't tell him anything. Art and Ellie have talked to Billy about getting guys up in the bullpen earlier and giving them more time to get ready, but Art says Billy just forgets about it. All he keeps saying is "I pitched for twenty-eight years. Goddamn. I know a little bit." Usually Art is jovial, and you can hear him all over the clubhouse, and he makes guys laugh wherever he goes, but recently he hasn't been very cheerful. Art said today that he's never been through anything like this in his life. Apparently, George is blaming Art 'cause the pitching hasn't been so fabulous, and Billy has been on Art.

I was sitting in the bullpen, and Art was just sort of staring into space as Catfish was warming up. I came over to him and said, "What do you think, Art?" Just saying hello really. He said, "About what?" Usually if you say to Art, "What do you think?" he'll come back at you with something funny, but when he said "About what?" it took me by surprise. I said, "Errrrrrrrrrrr. Catfish. What do you think about Catfish?" He said, "I wasn't even thinking about baseball. I was thinking about something else." Then he muttered, "You can't tell that man a damn thing, he wants to win so bad."

Friday, May 12   Kansas City

The Yankees officially announced that Healy had asked for his retirement. He said that an old neck injury was the reason he was quitting. What I think is, they plain released him. After he got his release, he didn't fly with us to Kansas City, but when I got to the ball park today, there he was, only he was wearing a suit and tie and he was carrying a tape recorder. The Yankees, it turned out, made him one of their radio announcers.

I was never close to Healy. He and Reggie are good friends. They sit together at dinner and talk business. We call him "The Professor." If you ask him a question, he always answers with another question. I can't talk to the man. When he was a player, he was kind of aloof. He felt he was an adult, and he wanted to act adult, which was fine with us so long as he wasn't ruining our time.

In the clubhouse before the game, Healy came up to me and said, "Hey, Spark, what do you guys do in the bullpen during the game?" and he shoved his microphone in my face. I said, "Jesus Christ, Fran, you've been out there with us for three years, and now you want to know what the hell we do out there?"

Catfish yelled over, "Gee, Healy's dressing better now, wears a suit and tie." Piniella said, "Yeah, he had to quit baseball to become a star."

A girl came up to me today and said she was doing an article on Thurman. She wanted to know why Thurman is mean. I told her I didn't think it was fair to him or to me or to anyone else to ask a question like that. Everyone's tired of this bullshit, tired of getting ridiculed, tired of hearing this stuff and of talking to writers and answering the same questions over and over about other people. I told her, "Just leave the guy alone." If you had to worry about driving in runs, throwing guys out, catching balls in the dirt, and making plays at home where some big son of a bitch, running just as fast as he can, is trying to knock the ball out of your hand and kill you at the same time, and also worry about somebody calling you a big prick, you're not going to walk around smiling all the time either. Then a writer comes up and asks you an asinine question after you go 0 for 4, when if you had gotten just one hit, it would have meant the ball game, and then you ask why he's mean? I said, "Thurman just wants to be left alone. He knows how good he is. Quit writing about why he's so mean. Just accept the fact he has an off day like everybody else, except that he has more of them." I told her,

"Maybe the guy doesn't like to talk to strangers. Did you ever think of that?"

Poor Figgie. If the poor bastard only wins 19 games again this year, tonight'll be the game he'll point to and say, "That was the one that got away."

Figgie was winning 3 to 2 in the bottom of the ninth when he walked Porter. Billy brought Goose in to end it, and that's what he did. Amos Otis hit a line drive to right-centerfield. Paul Blair, in for Mickey on defense, ran way over into right field to catch it, and just as the ball hit his glove, Reggie, who is built like a bulldozer, smashed into Blair, knocking the ball out of his glove and sending them both sprawling. As they lay on the ground, Porter and Otis scored, and Goose had his fourth loss, one he didn't deserve.

The inning before, the phone rang in the bullpen. I answered it, and Art was on the other end. "Get Gossage up," he shouted, and he hung up. Well, Goose was taking a crap in the head, and you have to understand that when Billy wants a pitcher up, he expects him to be throwing before Art hangs the phone up. Goose, doing what he was doing, wasn't out there, and sure enough, the phone rang again. "Goddamn," yelled Fowler, "where is he?" I said, "Art, the man is taking a dump, that's what he's doing. He's taking a dump," and I hung up the phone. Then Goose comes running out of the head, and he's pulling up his pants as he's running out to warm up. After the game, Art went up to Goose and told him to dump on his own time.

Saturday, May 13   Kansas City

The Gid won his fourth game, allowing two runs in eight innings. Goose pitched the ninth and saved it. The Red Sox are now in first, but we're only two games out and no one's worried except George, who can't understand why we're not undefeated.

Gid hasn't been throwing well—as consistently as he was last year—but he's winning. He gives up only one or two runs a game. Gid's going to his slider more, which is causing him to tire a little. He's been spending a lot of time in the trainer's room because his back is tight. He wears heat packs for it, and almost every day he gets treatment.

During the game Mickey Rivers didn't run out a grounder and in the field didn't look like he was trying very hard. Billy was extremely upset. He was yelling, "I want a guy out there who tries. Mickey says his leg hurts, so until he tells me he can play, he'll sit on the bench."

Benching Mickey isn't going to turn him around. If you say, "Well, screw you, buddy, if you don't want to hustle you can sit on the bench," that doesn't matter to Mickey. By benching him, you're trying to embarrass him in front of the other players to make him change. With Mickey, though, that's not going to work. There is nothing that can make Mickey change. But the thing is you don't have to do anything with him. He'll play good again. Just leave the damned guy alone. Leave him alone, and he'll snap out of it. Every once in a while, as fast as he can run, whether he's hurting or not, he'll hit a one-hopper right at the shortstop and loaf down the line because he knows he's going to be thrown out, which I can understand, but the crowd boos 'cause they're used to seeing him fly down that line. Maybe one time in a thousand if he had run all out, the shortstop would have thrown the ball away, but yet the manager feels, hey, this guy's not hustling, and he fines him or benches him, and this only makes Mickey feel resentful. If the game is on the line, Mickey's going to run. Let him play. Just leave the guy alone. All these rules and regulations and punishments are a bunch of crap.

Piniella went to Mickey and told him it didn't look like he was giving a hundred percent. Mickey told him, "When I go out there, I play the best I can. I don't give a damn what you think." Lou said, "I'm just telling you how it looks from where I'm at." Mickey said, "I don't care how it looks. I'm telling you I'm playing the best I can. My leg hurts."

Who's to say whether it does or doesn't. Mickey doesn't like to give the extra effort when he's hurt. Other guys do, and they end up getting hurt worse. I gather it was the same when he was with California, that they felt he didn't

always play up to par, and out there he said the same
thing: "When I'm healthy, I play fine." And the thing is,
at California, here, wherever he plays, Mickey's going to
be the nucleus of that club. He's what makes the club go.

I believe that man can do anything he wants to do on
the field when he's healthy, and after hearing him talk to
Lou, if I was the manager I'd leave him alone. I'd let him
come and tell me when he wants to play.

Sunday, May 14   Kansas City

I relieved Tidrow in the fifth inning and again got my
ever-loving ass kicked. Tidrow allowed five runs, and in two
and a third innings I allowed four runs, but with everyone in our starting lineup getting at least one hit. When I
went to the showers, the score was tied 9 to 9. In the
eighth Piniella hit a two-run double to tie it up.

With the score still tied and a runner on, Otis hit a ball
into centerfield that Mickey Rivers sort of jogged after. As
the runner rounded third and headed home, Mickey didn't
even try to throw him out. He just flipped it in halfheart-
edly, and we lost the game 10 to 9, and everybody was
really pissed off about that. I was in the clubhouse when
the game ended, and when coach Dick Howser came
through the door, he was saying, "What the hell is going
on? I never saw anything like this in my life." I didn't
even know who was involved, and I didn't want to ask. I
figured it was Reggie, but it wasn't. It was Mickey. For the
second day in a row he had played horseshit, like he didn't
care, even though Billy hadn't benched him like he said
he would. In the clubhouse Billy kept pacing, saying things
like, "Yeah, you guys sit in the back of the bus and play
your tape recorders and laugh, ha, ha, ha, ha, you bunch
of low-grade bastards." He was boiling.

During the game Billy and Cliff had gotten into a shouting match. Cliff was catching, and he was getting on
umpire Bill Wunkel's ass real bad. Billy was screaming at
him from the dugout to shut his mouth, and Cliff got
pissed and started yelling something back. Cliff has become
paranoid. He thinks everyone is against him. Whenever a
coach asks him to do something, he says, "Why me?" Why

are you picking on me?" Billy was just telling him, "Just sit back there and catch, because you're making the umpire mad and he's taking pitches away." When Cliff got back to the dugout, Billy said, "I'll take care of the umpires, and you take care of the catching."

I didn't mind coming into the game in the fifth inning tonight. Billy had told me he might have to use me early. I said, "OK." He said, "Maybe as early as the fifth." I said, "All right. Once in a while is all right." But I'm not going to let him make a habit of it. I'll flat out tell him no.

I haven't thrown the ball well the last three times out. I haven't had enough work and my arm has been too strong for my slider to be sharp. I was pitching OK for a little while, but then this was my first chance to pitch in five days, and I can't pitch that way. If I could pitch three or four days in a row, take a day off, then pitch three or four more days, I'd have my act together where I'd be all right at least until the All-Star break in July. But since I haven't been getting any better, Billy now has to keep Goose sharp. He can't worry about me anymore.

We took the bus to the airport, and after having some drinks at the bar, we got on the plane for the trip to Chicago. In the back of the plane Mickey, Holtzman, Chambliss, and Lou were playing pluck.

Billy was feeling his oats. He was still madder'n hell, and when he saw them playing cards, he walked back to where they were playing and started chewing out Piniella's ass for playing cards with Mickey. Billy shouted, "You're always going on about how this should be done and that should be done, and then you turn around and sit and play cards with the guy who is screwing up." Lou said, "Hell, Billy, I didn't do anything. I didn't lose the game." Billy stood there for a few seconds, shook his head, and went back to his seat.

Everyone was pissed off at what Billy said to Lou. If he had something to say to Mickey, say it to Mickey. But Billy said it to Lou with Mickey sitting beside him, hoping, I guess, that Mickey would say something. When Mickey didn't, Billy walked away disgusted.

Nobody said a word. You could see guys going, "What

the hell is going on?" And then the traveling secretary, Jerry Murphy, walked to the back of the plane and told everyone that they couldn't play their tape recorders without headphones. Billy doesn't like to hear the music after we lose.

This was a commercial flight, with a couple of hundred other passengers. Billy and the coaches were sitting up front in first class. Thurman was sitting in the front of the coach section with the other players, and he kept pulling the earphone plug out of his machine, letting the music blare for a few seconds, then he'd plug it back in. I don't know if he was teasing Billy or just having fun or if he was pissed off because we weren't allowed to play our music out loud.

The plane landed, and Thurman got up, ready to get off, and in front of all the passengers Billy started yelling at him that he should be a better influence. Thurman and Billy were bickering back and forth, and Thurman said, "The only reason you're saying this stuff now is that there are nine guys between us." Thurman really didn't mean it in such a way that he wanted to fight, he was just telling Billy more or less that hey, you've had too much to drink, keep quiet. But when Thurman said that, Billy went crazy. He tried to get to Thurman, and the coaches had to grab Billy and hold him back. All the while, Thurman was watching as Billy struggled to get free, laughing and shaking his head, which made Billy even more livid.

We got off the plane, and I figured, "Aw Jesus, I'm not going to get on the bus and get involved in any more crap. I'll take a cab." I figured that someone was going to punch someone else's lights out on that bus. But Billy and the coaches took a cab, so I went on the bus with the rest of the players.

I never saw anything like that flare-up, and really it never should have happened. It was uncalled for. If Billy had something to say to Mickey, he should have said it. Why he didn't, I don't know, unless Billy can't touch him. Maybe he's waiting for George to do something.

Tonight I was in a bar with Art Fowler, and he was upset with Mickey too. He said to me, "Goddamn, the ballplayers ought to do something about this and take a hand in it." I said, "No way. That's the worst thing that could happen. It's the manager who's got to take care of this, or the front office. You can't have ballplayers starting stuff like that. It'll make us all hate each other." I refused to talk to him anymore. I don't want to hear weak stuff like that. The real problem is that Billy wants to reprimand guys, only he doesn't want to do it himself. He's scared they'll hold a grudge against him and won't play for him. That's always going on in this club. The coaching staff may be an arm of the manager, but when you're having trouble with a player, that's for the manager to handle. A coach shouldn't do it. Billy likes to use coaches a lot in situations like that. The coach delivers the reprimand, and if the player gets mad, Billy can get himself out of the situation by saying, "I really didn't say it that way."

We're only two out, and we could really play ball if everyone would just leave us alone.

Monday, May 15   Chicago

After what happened yesterday, Thurman didn't even feel like playing today. Thurman plays when his legs are hurting him so badly he can hardly bend down, yet he runs everything out and keeps playing. After Billy chewed his ass out, Thurman was saying, "Screw it. I'm not going to do it anymore if that's all the man thinks of me about what I've done." Thurman said, "Hey, if the man doesn't think enough of me to give me a little respect, when I don't feel like playing from now on, I'm not going to. Just because he's in the sauce doesn't mean I have to listen to him yell at me."

Billy apologized to Thurman, but Thurm won't forget what happened for a long while.

Billy said he would keep Rivers on the bench for the rest of the road trip—two games against Chicago, two in Cleveland, and three in Toronto. Howser told Mickey that Billy wanted to speak to him in his suite. Mickey wouldn't go. "If he wants me to come to his suite, he can come and tell me himself. I'm not going just because some damn coach asks me," Mickey said.

Mickey is contemptuous of the whole incident. Mickey said, "You can't get the respect of people by shouting at them like that. I can overlook it, though, because anything can come out when a man is drinking."

Billy said that Holtzman will be gone within the week because he's such a bad influence on Mickey. I don't know where Billy got that idea, unless it's because they're always playing cards together. Christ, you get two guys who are friends, what are they going to do? If they sat around and sucked lollipops, no one would say a word. They say Holtzman is a bad influence on Mickey. Last year, Rivers hit three hundred something, led us to a pennant, and now Billy is saying that Holtzman is a bad influence? I don't think Holtzie should get traded because of this. We need his arm. Gullett is on the disabled list, Tidrow's got a bad thumb, Cat's arm is sore, and we need him.

I relieved Jim Beattie in the sixth and again saved his win. I pitched three and two-thirds innings, allowed two hits, no runs, with no stuff. The batters must be swinging at last year's slider. It hasn't been around this year, that's for sure, and it won't until I get more work.

Tuesday, May 16   Chicago

Cat was scheduled to pitch today, but after walking into the clubhouse, he said his arm was bad and he can't throw. It looks like he'll join Gullett on the disabled list. Cat's shoulder is so stiff he couldn't even reach home plate. Holtzie pitched in his place, gave up three runs in five and a third, and won his first game since last May.

Billy is very sick. He almost passed out in the middle of the game, and when the doctor came to look at him, he ordered Billy to check into a hospital immediately. Billy wouldn't go. Billy's pale and looks terrible. Everyone's been telling him to take it easy, but he takes losing so hard, and with this other stuff popping up, it's killing him. Crushing him. We're only one game out of first, but it would be the same way if we were ten games in front. Billy's deathly afraid he's losing control of the ball club, and I think that if he continues the way he has been, he just might. If he's going to try to turn the guys who are for him against the other guys, he's going to fail.

After the plane incident, everything has quieted down to where there is no talking on the bus at all. Billy's usually the first one off the bus, making sure everyone has a tie on before we get on the plane. Before we got on the plane for Cleveland, Billy was the last one off, and he was the last one off the plane. He didn't say a word to us.

I read in the papers that Chicago traded Bobby Bonds to Texas. Gabe got him in a trade with San Francisco for Bobby Murcer in 1975. A year later Gabe traded him to California for Figgie and Mickey Rivers. Bobby is going to get traded forever because for all his power, he can't hit in the fourth spot. He strikes out too much, so the manager always ends up leading him off 'cause you gotta get him out of the way as quick as you can. Let him do his damage if he's going to do any, and that's it. When we had him here in New York, we were expecting great things of him, but the next thing we knew, he was leading off. I mean the guy hit 30 home runs and he was leading off! And you can't bat him sixth or seventh, not for what you're paying him. You might as well not even have him. That's why he keeps going from team to team because everybody who gets him figures here we've got a powerful guy with all kinds of talent who can run like hell, steal 30 bases, but then he starts striking out, and son of a bitch, all of a sudden they realize they have to lead him off. That's what happened at San Francisco, with us, with the Angels, with the White Sox, and I guarantee you, next year he won't be wearing a Texas uniform. If he leads off, he doesn't have a chance to drive in that many runs, and that's why Texas got him.

Wednesday, May 17   Cleveland

George is filled with great ideas, and one of those great ideas has cost me a ball game tonight. Our scouts chart our opponents, and a computer tells them where their hitters have been hitting the ball. Bill Kane, one of George's assistants, sits in the press box with the charts and calls down to Yogi on a walkie-talkie and tells Yogi where to position our fielders. In the bottom of the tenth, Paul Dade got up, and Yogi moved Lou, who was in right, way over toward center. I was pitching, and on the next pitch Dade hit the ball right where Lou had been standing before Yogi moved him. Lou couldn't get it, and Dade got a triple. I then hung a slider to Rick Manning, who smashed the hell out of it to win the game for the Indians.

After the game was over Lou came over to Yogi's locker and told him, "The next time you move me over, I quit."

Last year when I pitched, Reggie would often get the winning hit. Today, when he had a chance to win it for me, he struck out. I said, "What the hell's going on? I'm pitching, aren't I? You should have hit the ball out of the park." He just laughed. Last year, you couldn't have said that to him. For the first time, he's enjoying himself in New York, doing what he wants, and he's having fun playing ball. This year he's trying to be more of a team player, and I think there are several reasons for this. One, I think he realizes that we're not going to take his crap. He doesn't want to play on this team and have nobody like him, which is what happened last year. Also, he's finally realized that there are a great bunch of guys on this club. Third, he wants the people of New York to say, "Jesus, what a transition this guy has made." I think he wants to be able to park his Rolls-Royce on the streets of New York and not get a parking ticket.

If he goes along like he's going now, he just might do it.

Thursday, May 18   Cleveland

Roy White pulled a leg muscle running out a hit in the sixth, so Billy put Mickey in his place, the first time Mickey's played in a week. In the seventh the score was tied, and Mickey hit the ball in the gap to drive in the go-ahead run, and as he rounded second and headed for third, he looked back and saw they were getting the ball back in, and he just turned it on, vroooooooooom, and he slid in no contest. The next batter scored him, and when he came back to the dugout, he didn't say a word. He didn't even smile. Gid won his fifth. Goose got the save.

Billy's still real sick He isn't looking good, and he's down. I think the combination of all this stuff plus the fact that the Red Sox never lose is doing it to him. Billy's close to the edge, and everybody's very uneasy, wondering if we lose a game we shouldn't lose, the crap won't break out again.

Saturday, May 20 Toronto

Billy got in the sauce last night, even though the doctors have told Billy to lay off. He has ulcers or something, and he's getting sicker. This morning I walked into the trainer's room and Billy was lying on the trainer's table, and if he hadn't had a little color in his face, I would have thought he was dead. He's been subjecting himself to some punishment. I think the bullshit from the front office is getting to him and taking its toll.

Ellie told me he's gonna quit at the end of the year. Ellie has to answer the phone in the bullpen, and the constant ringing drives him crazy. Like today Art called down, and he asked Ellie, "How long before Sparky can be ready?" So Ellie asked me. I hadn't started warming up! I told Ellie, "Tell them to get me up, and we'll see." Ellie got back on the phone, hung up, and said, "They don't want you up." A minute later the phone rang again, and Ellie said, "Sparky, get ready. Hurry. Hurry. Hurry." Ellie said, "I swear, this is my last year. I can't take any more of this."

I can understand what's going through Billy's mind. The front office has him where he's always second-guessing himself because he knows he can't afford to make a wrong decision. Billy'll be thinking, "Maybe I should take a pitcher out now. But, wait, the guy in the bullpen isn't ready. I'll let the pitcher face one more batter. Hmmmmm, the guy in the game is throwing a little better. Maybe I won't take him out." That phone will ring ten times an inning, and then, whether the guy in the bullpen is ready or not, Ellie'll get a call, "He's in the game."

I told Ellie, "Why can't you just tell them, 'We know what we're doing down here. We've been at this long enough. Just tell us who you want, and we'll take care of the rest. He'll be ready to go in.'"

We got beat 10 to 8 by Toronto, and it's beyond me why this happens because we should never, ever lose to Toronto. I guess they have nothing to lose, and they're relaxed against us, and we're overconfident. It's like what Reggie was saying yesterday: "We're coming to play Toronto, and I got seven motherfucking taters, and I'm going to leave Toronto with at least eleven."

Piniella said, "Who you kidding? The only eleven that you'll get is 0 for eleven."

I remember Guidry last year. He was about to face the Blue Jays, and he said, "I'm going for a strikeout record today." He got his ass kicked. Toronto is a mediocre club, and they only have a couple of guys who can drive in runs if the other guys happen to get on. Against us, they have guys on first and second, and we figure, ain't no way they're gonna score, and boom, a guy gets a base hit and there goes the ball game.

Billy made Holtzman go into the game tonight, and you should have seen him. Holtzie was hurt and he couldn't throw. I had gone in before him, felt fine, and got my ass kicked. Would you believe five runs in two-thirds of an inning? Holtzie came in to relieve me, and he was just about lobbing the ball in, and these guys were popping up, grounding out. It was almost funny. Kenny Clay gave up no hits, walked one, and lost it when the one guy he walked turned out to be the winning run.

Sunday, May 21   Toronto

We beat the Blue Jays twice today. Figgie won the first 2 to 1, and we were winning the second game 9 to 1 behind Kenny Clay when they called down to the bullpen in the seventh and asked whether I wanted to pitch. I said, "No. Not if I don't have to." I hate to pitch if we're way ahead or way behind. They got Holtzman up, and he could barely throw because he was still stiff from pitching yesterday. Eastwick is stiff from pitching two days ago and couldn't throw either.

Holtzman went in there in the eighth, and again he just lobbed the ball up there with nothing on it, and son of a bitch, he got three outs like it was nothing. I ended up pitching the ninth anyway.

One thing bothers me about Billy. He doesn't think about pitching that much. Pitchers are there, and he respects you, but you're still just there. You're there to do what he wants at any time, and that's not always possible.

Lou was talking about this guy Garvin who pitched the second game for Toronto and got shelled. Lou was hitting right behind Reggie in the batting order, and Lou was saying that he was watching Garvin throw fastballs right by Reggie, and Lou was thinking, "Damn, this guy throws hard." He said, "I get up there, and I'm waiting to see this blazing fastball, and the guy didn't have squat. I'm pulling the ball down the third base line. 'Course," Lou says, "when you're hitting behind Reggie, all you're doing is leading off the inning every time."

Cliff hit a home run to win the first game. Afterward he said, "If I played every day, I could do that all the time."

Rawly's getting married tomorrow. Tonight, before I left the park, I went over and shook his hand. He was kind of nervous about it, and I told him to get a good night's sleep. I told him, "Don't worry. Things'll work out. She can only take half your salary."

We were in JFK waiting for our luggage after returning from Toronto. Cliff Johnson, the big donkey, is always walking around trying to lie on top of you, just screwing around, but tonight I wasn't in the mood to be squashed. He had had a little bit too much to drink, and he was being obnoxious. He started coming in my direction, and I saw that he was intending to shove me out of his way like a freight train coming through. When he came near, I shoved him right on his ass onto the luggage conveyor belt. He didn't know what hit him. Cliff just lay there laughing, spinning round with the unclaimed luggage.

Cliff may get drunk every once in a while, but he was nothing compared to Sudden Sam McDowell when he played with the Yankees in 1973 and 1974. When Sam was with us, he had a terrible drinking problem. He was big, about 6 feet 6, and he threw real hard. Five times he led the league in strikeouts. He had as much talent as anybody I've ever seen, and he was past his prime when he was with us. But Sam, for some reason, could not control his drinking then, and it cost him badly. I understand that since Sam has gotten out of baseball, he's been able to control his problem, which makes me feel real good because being with Sam was one of the highlights of my career. He was one of the most fascinating guys I've ever known.

We used to call him Teen Angel because he always slicked his hair back. Sam was notorious for getting in the sauce, getting real rowdy, picking a fight, and getting beat up. This one day we were on a plane heading for a road trip, and Sam's hair was blow-dried, and he had it combed and styled. Everyone was buzzing: "Teen Angel got his hair done."

We were taking bets because we knew something must have happened. When Sam fell asleep, Pat Dobson went back to where Sam was sleeping, lifted back his hair, and there were two big knots on his forehead where somebody had knocked the crap out of him. He had his hair blown dry to cover the knots because Bill Virdon had told him, "No more drinking. One more time and you're gone."

I remember one night Sam had had a few, and he tripped while walking down the sidewalk and sprained his ankle.

This was '73, when Ralph Houk was managing. The next day Sam was supposed to pitch, and his ankle was hurting him so badly he could hardly walk. He went to Ralph and said, "You know what happened? I went shopping yesterday, and I went up the store escalator, and I hurt my ankle." And Sam made up the name of one of Minneapolis's department stores and made up all this stuff.

Houk said, "Yeah. Yeah." Sam said, "Really, Skip. It hurt real bad." Ralph didn't say anything, but he had known what had happened. But to show you how Sam would work things through, the next day he went back to Ralph and said, "I just want to tell you everything's OK. I was going to sue those guys in the store, but I went and talked to them today, and I told them I was all right and not to worry that I was going to sue them for that escalator hurting my ankle."

That night we went to the airport, and there was an escalator. Ralph waited for Sam and made him walk up the stairs. Ralph told him, "I wouldn't want you to hurt your ankle again."

Sam used to say, "I have complete control of all my pitches." Graig would say, "Yeah, you can walk any batter on any pitch." Later we started calling him Topper. It didn't matter what you said, Sam had always done something a little bit better. One day someone said that Warren Spahn held the season record for walks. Sam said, "No he doesn't. One year I walked three hundred and fifty batters." It was about 20 over the first number. After that we started making things up to see what he would say, and always he had done whatever it was, only better. Always.

But he was a joy. For all the trouble he caused, he was really a very nice guy. It was one of those things. A lot of people have drinking problems, except Sam happened to be a baseball player, and that made it sound much worse. It was too bad because he could have been so much better than he was. He only won 20 games once, when he was with the Giants.

I remember after he left us, we were flying from Detroit to Cleveland, and there was a copy of *Cleveland Magazine* on the plane, and damned if there wasn't an article on Sam. In the article they were talking about all the things Sam might have achieved. And they asked him about his drinking. Sam said, "I finally licked my drinking problem. I had a pill sewn into the lining of my stomach, and if I have one drop of alcohol, it makes me violently ill." I read that, and I said, "Aw Jeez, I just can't believe this. He never changes."

Sudden Sam. He was a joy and a treat. I wish the guy all the best. He deserves it.

Tuesday, May 23   New York

Ellie's been threatening to quit, but he's done that every
year since he's been a coach here. They want him to go
into the front office, but he doesn't want to do that. They
wanted him to do that last year too. Maybe they're going
to put him in charge of the walkie-talkies. That's what
Yogi does all game long.

Since I've been a Yankee, I've been trying to figure out
what Yogi's job is. I still don't know. He hits fungoes to
the outfielders before the game. Sometimes he even hits
grounders to the infielders. To me he doesn't do anything.

Yogi's supposed to have said a lot of funny things, but
I don't know how anyone hears all the things he says because he doesn't talk. Yogi's also the most frugal guy I've
ever seen, but last year I fixed him good. All last year he
kept using my toothpaste. He'd walk over to my locker
and take it. I guess he wasn't about to buy any. I said to
myself, "Son of a bitch, I'm going to fix him." So I took
White Heat, the burning hot stuff you put on your arm to
take the tightness out of your muscles, and I injected some
of this stuff with a syringe into my tube of Ultrabrite.

I'm sitting there in my locker in the clubhouse, and
Yogi comes walking over with his toothbrush. He squeezes
out some of the toothpaste, goes into the john, and brushes
his teeth. I'm in the shower, and everybody knows what's
going on, and as Yogi comes walking into the shower
room, he's blowing on his hands. "My gums. Whoooooooo.
My gums are on fire," Yogi says. And they were. They
were smoking. The next day he cut all my shoelaces. I
pulled my laces tight, and they came off in my hands. This
year, I've been using Yogi's toothpaste.

During the game a bunch of kids sitting by the bullpen
were chanting for Dominick. Every time he got up to
warm up a pitcher, they started clapping for him. He's
having as much fun as anyone on this ball club. And
every day he gets his hand blown away. It's like: "Excuse
me, Dominick, I'm a reporter and I'd like to ask you what
you do for a living."

"Why, of course, I'd be glad to tell you. My job is to get my hand blown away."

Gid won his sixteenth win in his last 17 decisions over the last two years. The son of a bitch may never lose again. Today he beat the Indians 10 to 1 and struck out 11. He's now 6 and 0.

Wednesday, May 24   New York

A reporter was asking Ellie if he was interested in taking the job as Oakland manager now that Bobby Winkles has resigned. I overheard him and yelled, "Ellie, please take me with you."
Ellie said, "As a pitcher or a coach?"
I said, "Either."

Cat tried again to throw, but he still can't. His shoulder is hurting him something fierce.

I just bought a new 1000 c.c. Honda motorcycle, and I can't wait to ride into the stadium. George and Rosen will have a heart attack. Mary bought it for me. On the first nice day I'm going to drive the son of a bitch in there. Steinbrenner will go bananas, the phone will ring, and he'll say, "You get up here right now." It's in my contract: no motorcycles. I have a guaranteed contract, which means that if I get hurt, I still get paid. But there's a paragraph about a foot long of things I can't do. Want to know what I can't do? It would be easier to list the things I can do. I can drive a car, play tiddlywinks, and screw. Anything other than that, I can't do. If I get hurt doing anything else, they don't have to pay me. The way things are going, it doesn't matter to me anyway.

Thursday, May 25   New York

I got a fan letter. It says, "Dear Sparky, I've been a Yankee fan since I was ten years old, and that's when the Yankees were real Yankees. After reading about you bitching because you're unhappy with your contract, here you are making $500,000 for three years, and you're unhappy. Try this out. I'm making $10,000 a year. Why don't you shut your mouth, you big bastard?"

A couple of years ago I got a letter that said, "You promised me a ball during batting practice, and after it was over, you didn't give me one." What this guy did was send a copy of it to the Yankee front office. The front office wanted to know what the hell was going on. I said, "OK, I'll sign the ball for him." I took the ball and wrote, "To whatever his name was. Kiss my ass. Sparky Lyle." I packaged it and sent it to him. Well? He got his baseball.

The fans I hate the most are the ones who bring their cute little kids to the park and yell at you, "How 'bout giving the kid a ball?" You feel like saying, "How 'bout sucking on this?" but you end up giving him the ball anyway.

The fans don't ordinarily give me much trouble. There's the normal crap you have to listen to every night: "Your mother wears Army boots," that kind of stuff. That's standard procedure and has nothing to do with the uniform you have on your back or your number. Then if you give a ball away to a little kid while you're in the outfield shagging flies during batting practice, from then on every time you pick up a ball, they start hollering. If you don't give the next one away, it's "You suck." Me, I'm not smart enough not to give any away. I got to give the one away in order to hear, "You asshole." Perhaps that makes my whole night.

George fined me once for giving a fan the finger. Cost me $500. This was in 1973, George's first year, and I had been pitching real great. I'd saved I don't know how many games in a row, and this one night against Oakland, I gave up five straight hits, the ones that dribble though the infield, and we ended up losing the game. I walked off the mound, and the fans were booing the hell out of me 'cause they were acknowledging that "Goddamn, Sparky Lyle just doesn't do that." I didn't mind the boos, but there was this one guy sitting right behind our dugout wearing a T-shirt with mustard all over him, one of these assholes who if there were 70,000 people there, you still could hear his voice. He was hollering, "You bum, Lyle. You suck."

When I saw him, I couldn't control myself. I put my glove underneath my arm, and I gave him the double bird. Both middle fingers, and I held them way up and was looking right at him as I walked the entire way from the first base foul line to the dugout.

Ralph Houk, who was the manager, didn't see me do this because he was waiting for the new pitcher to come in, so when George, who was sitting behind the dugout and saw the whole thing, told Ralph what I had done, Ralph said, "Oh no, Sparky wouldn't do a thing like that. He was probably giving the fans the peace sign." George wanted to fine me a thousand dollars, $500 a finger. Ralph said he couldn't do that, that the most he could fine me for something like that was $500.

Ralph called me into his office and asked me if I had given the fans the finger. I said, "Yeah, I did that," and I told him why. He said, "Jesus, I told George that you didn't do that." I said, "I don't know what to tell you. Just fine me and don't worry about it." So he did.

The funny thing was that my mother and father were there that day. My mother almost had the big one when she saw me do that. I could just hear her saying, "Oh, Albert, look at him." She'll never forget seeing her son flipping the bird in front of 40,000 people.

On the road, every park is different. You get used to seeing the faces and hearing the voices of the people who come to agitate you, and you know exactly where they sit. I just let them agitate the hell out of me, and then I wait until I can get in one good zinger, where everybody goes, "Oh, ho, ho," embarrassing the hell out of him. That's enough to shut the guy up for the rest of the game. I remember one line delivered by Ron Swoboda when he was with us. We were in Boston, and the gates had just opened, nobody was there, and this one guy started getting on me. He was saying, "You bum. You stink. You're no good." Not bad words. Swoboda turned around and yelled to him, "How can you get on an athlete? You don't even sweat when you jack off!" Rocky stopped the guy right in his tracks.

* * *

Boston's tough. There's a lady, if you can call her that, who absolutely despises me. Why, I don't know. But every time we go up to Boston, she makes it a point to be there early to wait for me to come on the field. The minute I walk out there, she's yelling, "There you are, Lyle. You're horseshiiiiiiiiiiiit. Horse Shiiiiiiiiiiiiit. HORSESHIT. I don't know how you lasted this long. You were horseshit when you were here, and you're horseshit now."

This spring the Red Sox came down to Lauderdale, and she made the trip just so she could yell, "You're horseshiiiiiiiiiiit, Lyle. Horseshit." When she said that, I said to her, "You made my whole spring." I said, "I thought I was never going to see you again." She said, "Oh, you'll see me. I'll be in Boston. I'll be there." So I have that to look forward to.

They get wrapped up in it. I don't mind that this woman dislikes me. I'd just like to know why.

Tidrow pitched a complete game win over the Indians tonight. We got 15 hits, scored 9 runs, and though we're 19-6 lately, we're still a game back of the Red Sox.

Tidrow has been pitching very well this year. He's one of the nicer guys on the club, and he's a great competitor. Also, he knows how to pitch. He's the type of guy who if he needs a new pitch to win on a particular night, will come up with it while he's warming up for the game. If something isn't working, he'll struggle till he finds something that does work and get you out with that.

We call him "Dirt," a nickname that stuck from when he first came over to the Yankees from Cleveland. When he joined us, before the games we would play a game called flip. It's usually played behind home plate near the screen while the other team is taking batting practice. The pitchers—this year it's me, Tidrow, Kenny Clay, Gid, Figgie, and Catfish—get in a line, and you bat the ball with your glove over to one of the other guys, until someone isn't able to bat it cleanly. The idea is to advance to the front of the line, and if you miss, you go to the end of the line. Whoever loses that day has to serve the rest of the guys Cokes or whatever in the clubhouse after the game.

While the rest of us played the game nice and easy,

Tidrow would be diving after balls, getting his uniform
filthy. We started calling him "Mr. Dirt" after the guy in
the Mobil commercials, and it stuck with him.

Friday, May 26   New York

I don't know what the hell's wrong with Cat. He's been
placed on the disabled list, and he went home to North
Carolina. Messersmith and Gullett were both throwing on
the sidelines yesterday, and if they can come back, it'll be
a big help.

I relieved Beattie in the seventh, losing 2 to zip with
men on first and second, threw one pitch, and this kid
Bosetti grounded into a double play to end the inning. It's
the easiest way to get out of an inning, but the thing is,
the pitch was terrible. If anything was satisfying about it,
it was that. I threw a slider, and it broke the other way
a little bit. It moved just enough for him to top the ball.
That's what the secret to pitching is, to get the ball to move
just a little. During the game, I kept looking over at Chris
at first base, and I'd signal with my fingers two and five,
which I told him was my ratio—two good pitches and five
bad ones. I have to get the five out of the way and get the
two good ones in there somewhere.

After I got the double play, Chris came over and said,
"That wasn't one of the two good ones." I said, "I know,
but it was good enough." That's what I've been doing all
year, getting guys out on sliders going the other way.

In the bottom of the seventh Jim Spencer got up and hit
a home run with the bases loaded to win the game for me.
For Spencer it was very uplifting. He wants to do so well
here. He's the type of guy who wants to win the first base
job, even though there's no way he's going to. Yankee
Stadium is built for him. All he has to do is get his bat on
the ball, and it's out of here. But with Chris at first, about
the best job he's going to be able to get is left-handed DH.
It's going to be tough for him, but he's just going to have
to accept that. He's a great defensive first baseman, but
he's just not going to get the chance to play, and he's

really not the consistent hitter that Chris is. Spencer's a left-handed hitter with power on a team that doesn't need another left-handed hitter with power. We have Reggie, Nettles, Chris, and Rivers. What do we need another left-handed hitter for?

I've noticed that Spencer pouts a lot when he doesn't play. That surprises me for a man who's been around for ten years like he has. He's usually a jovial guy, laughing, but if he isn't playing someone will say something to him, and he'll frown and say, "Big fucking deal."

Saturday, May 27   New York

Everything happens to poor Figgie. He was tied 1 to 1 in the ninth with one out and a runner on second, and Billy went out to the mound and ordered him to walk Ashby, a left-handed hitter batting .170, and to pitch to Bosetti, a righty, who proceeded to hit a triple to win the game.

After the game Figgie said he wanted to be traded. "How could he order me to walk a two hundred hitter?" he was saying. Then Figgie started complaining that when he pitches, the Yankee hitters don't give him any support. "I want to be traded to California, Boston, or Texas. Those teams would give me hundred percent support."

Because of what he said, there's now a lot of mixed emotions about him. The worst thing in the world a pitcher can say is that his team doesn't play good behind him. Goddamn, they're out there to win games just like everybody else. Figgie bitches because he can't pitch every fourth day. He also wants more money. Figgie says Gabe Paul promised him more, but George tells him, "Gabe isn't here anymore."

Graig was really pissed off about what Figgie said, and if Graig, who is really low-key, reacted so strongly, I can imagine what the other guys felt.

Figgie can forget about being traded. We would have to have a phenom in the minor leagues who we knew could hold us for five innings, and we don't have anyone like that.

* * *

Reggie strained a muscle in his left thigh running out an infield single. He could be out a week or more.

Sunday, May 28   New York

Billy's still trying to make a long relief man out of me. I relieved Clay in the third inning of the second game against Toronto, and after pitching three innings, I told him, "No more. That's it. I've had it," and I left for the clubhouse. Billy had to bring Goose in. I told Billy, "I'm not a long man. That's Rawly's job. This is my last time. I'm not coming in early anymore. Don't even call." Goose ended up having to pitch seven innings before he got the win.

In the first game, Gid won his seventh without a loss as Mickey Rivers hit a home run. Mickey also homered in the second game.

Monday, May 29   Cleveland

Andy Messersmith started his first game, and in five innings the only hit he gave up was a cheap single by some guy Norris in the first. Rawly relieved, as it should be— he's the long man, not me—and he didn't allow a hit as we won 2 to 0. The whole bullpen was really rooting for Rawly. After he finished the seventh, he came off the mound, and I was jumping up and down, waving my hands in the air, cheering him on. He saw us, and the next innings when he got to the mound, he tipped his cap to the bullpen.

When he got the last guy out, I ran in real fast from the bullpen and waited for him in front of the dugout. When he got to me, I began bowing at his feet. Rawly really enjoys the ball club now. I don't think he wants to leave here, whereas before I don't think he gave a damn.

Rawly did a super job for going two weeks without

pitching. I wouldn't have been able to do it. Now maybe
Billy will have more confidence in him and use him more.

Tuesday, May 30   Cleveland

We were playing password in the bullpen before the game,
and Holtzman was having tremendous difficulty guessing
our word, which was *timberline*. Holtzie was going crazy
trying to guess it, so Messersmith and Figueroa decided
to stay in the bullpen during the game so they could watch
Holtzman go bananas. Holtzman's very intelligent and
well read, and he has a tremendous vocabulary, but this
word had him so screwed up that it took him three innings to guess it.

Against the Indians I relieved Tidrow in the sixth, and
I was lousy again. We were losing 2 to 1 when I went
in there, and after I gave up five straight bloops, chops,
and garbage hits, I left with us losing 5 to 1.

After the game Messersmith came up to me and said,
"Nice going, asshole." I didn't know what he was talking
about. He said, "You got me in trouble all because of
that stupid, Goddamn word game you were playing." Billy
was angry with him for being in the bullpen during the
game.

We flew back to New York after the game, and after
we landed, as Andy was getting into a cab Billy started
screaming at him. Billy was in the sauce, and he was
really giving it to Andy for being out in the bullpen while
the game was going on.

Andy said to me, "I didn't know we were in a Goddamn prison. I didn't realize I had to ask permission to
go out to the bullpen." Andy seems to feel that if we
had won the game, Billy wouldn't have said anything.
Billy seems to have a hard-on for Andy, and I don't know
why that is. Maybe it's Andy's curly hair and nice tan.
Billy likes ballplayers who are aggressive, tobacco-chewing,
and hard-nosed. Sometimes when he doesn't see that in
somebody, Billy isn't quite as tolerant.

Wednesday, May 31   New York

Dick Young wrote an article in the *News* about the Martin-Messersmith incident at the airport, talking about Billy's being in the sauce. Christ, Billy's been doing that for as long as anybody can remember. Now all of a sudden, Young's trying to condemn the man for something he's been doing all along. This looks like something George would do, to build up a case against Billy so that if he decides to fire Billy, it would look justified. I don't think it has anything to do with the way things are going. We're playing badly, but Billy's doing everything he can. Christ, Boston was 23-7 in May, and we're still only three games back. Why should they even consider firing Billy? Still, Billy told me yesterday that he's probably going to get fired. He said that it looks like he's going down the tubes.

Before the game Billy was talking to a couple of reporters who told him that the Yankees had just called up catcher Mike Heath from our West Haven farm club. A few minutes later, Rosen called Billy on the phone to tell him about it. "Yeah," Billy said, "I just heard about it from a couple of newspaper guys." Then he slammed the phone down in Rosen's ear.

Figgie lost today's game when Nettles booted a ball at third, the guy stole second, and Figgie made two wild pitches in a row to let him score. Twice today Mickey didn't run out ground balls. He has a groin injury, but Billy can't rest him because Roy and Reggie still haven't come back, and he can't afford to take another bat out of our lineup. To make things worse, Thurman strained his knee real bad chasing after the wild pitch that let the run score. He may be out a couple of days.

Thursday, June 1   New York

Graig came over and showed me a newspaper article where George said he was angry with Billy for slamming the phone down on Rosen and for telling a reporter that Rawly and Messersmith are "George's boys." Billy said that because last year we won the World Series without them, and he feels we could win again without them. Billy resents the way George buys players without consulting him to find out whether those players are really needed. Then when George signs a free agent for a lot of money, almost instantaneously he becomes very close to him. That's happened with Reggie too. If anyone's George's boy, it's Reggie. But I don't think it's a good label. Nobody's calling Goose "George's boy."

Reggie has had a groin pull for almost a week, and when a player's hurt he's supposed to come to the park early for treatment. But Reggie hasn't been getting his treatment. If it was anyone else, they would raise hell, but that's the way things are in baseball. Any superstar, so to speak, has his privileges, but most of them, 95 percent of them, make an effort to get themselves ready to play. Reggie should be showing everyone he's trying to get ready.

Jim Palmer shut us out 1 to 0 on a two-hitter. Beattie pitched super but lost. Goose pitched the last two innings and struck out three of the six Orioles he faced.

Friday, June 2   Oakland

Gid was leading the A's 3 to 1 in the ninth when Goose came in with runners on first and third and one out, blew third strikes past the two batters, and went in without even breaking a sweat. Gid won his eighth, struck out 11, and his ERA is down to 1.80.

I heard that after the game Cliff walked up to Reggie and told him that another player said Reggie had been making fun of the way he batted. Cliff *should* be sensitive about it. He's 1 for 32 and hitting lower than .200. Reggie said, "I wasn't doing anything of the sort." Cliff said, "I heard you did." Reggie said, "Whoever said that is a Goddamn liar."

Saturday, June 3 Oakland

Minutes before the game was to start today, Mickey Rivers walked up to Reggie and he screamed at him, "You can call me anything you want to, but don't you dare call me a Goddamn liar." Mickey was so angry he liked to have ripped Reggie apart. Tidrow had a solid hold of Mickey and almost couldn't hold him. A few more guys moved in to hold him, but he was still almost getting to Reggie.

Rarely does Mickey get mad enough to fight. He's just not that kind of guy. He's too happy-go-lucky. But the one thing you don't call a guy like Mickey, you don't call him a liar. Anything else, but not a liar. During the game Reggie took Mickey's glove out to him just like nothing had ever happened.

Reggie and Roy both played for the first time in a while, but it still wasn't enough. Messersmith started and got bombed. Clay mopped up. The Red Sox won again, and now we're four and a half behind.

A couple of days ago I told Mary, "Gullett's coming off the disabled list and Messersmith is getting ready to come back, and we're going to have roster problems unless they put someone on the disabled list who isn't really hurt." No sooner was it out of my mouth than the Yankees put Holtzie on the disabled list. He has a bad back that doesn't let him get as loose as he'd like to, and he's been wearing a brace, but he can still pitch. Boy, was he pissed.

You know who told him? Art Fowler, and that right there is enough to piss the Pope off. Somebody with authority should tell him, like the general manager or the manager. When Fowler told him, Holtzman said, "I never, ever said I couldn't pitch." Art was shook because Holtzman said, "I'm going to sue, and you're going to court and testify, and if you get up on the stand and say I couldn't pitch, then you're a damn liar."

Ellie was shook too. He came up to me and said, "You saw how he was out there." I said, "Ellie, as far as I'm concerned, I have my own problems. As far as I know,

I never heard him say he couldn't pitch, and that's the truth."

Sunday, June 4   Oakland

Dou Gullett made his first start. He gave up three hits, walked one, allowed two runs, and retired one batter. He was trying to throw the ball too damn hard. He was trying to muscle the ball, and when you do that you don't even throw it as hard as you normally do because you're outside yourself, you're not compact anymore.

I relieved in the fifth. We were up by a run with a couple of guys on base, there were two outs, and I had two strikes on Mitchell Page and threw a pitch that started outside and broke beautifully over the outside corner. It was right there, strike three, no question. I started to walk off, and Thurman ran off too, but the umpire called it a ball.

When that happens, very rarely will the batter not get a hit. It wouldn't have mattered where the next pitch was, Page was going to get a hit, and he did. It cost Rawly, who had relieved Gullett, the game.

The next pitch was bad, and he hit it. It happens a hundred times, time and time again, and like I said to Billy, "When you're going horseshit, you're going horseshit."

Oakland beat us two out of three, and it isn't just because we're playing badly. They have some really good kid pitchers, and their manager uses them real well. If a pitcher gets hit a couple of times, he yanks him and brings in someone new. That's the thing to do when you have a young team like they do, and that's why they're in first place in the West right now. We also found out that their offense is stronger than we thought it was. You see the names in the paper, and you laugh 'cause you've never heard of any of them, but they have three or four guys who can hurt you. Page, for instance. Guerrero is playing very well at shortstop, batting fourth and hitting .280. There's no way they're going to hold their Division, but

these guys came over from other teams because they
hadn't been able to break in, and at Oakland they're getting
their chance and they're playing their asses off.

Monday, June 5   Seattle

Figgie gave up six runs in four innings to lose to the
friggin' Seattle Mariners. After a couple of things happened, someone didn't get to a fly ball, a grounder went
off someone's glove, Figgie completely gave up. He was
lobbing it in there like it was batting practice. This was
after Figgie had said, "They no play good behind me."
That's what's so bad about his having said that crap. People think maybe his fielders are getting back at him, or
they think they *really* don't play good when he pitches.
It was Seattle's first win in eight games, and unless we
start getting better pitching from our starters, we're going
right into the crapper.

The umps were really off today. Both teams were yelling
at them. Second-base umpire Steve Palermo threw Billy
out of the game for arguing and first-base ump Larry
McCoy tossed Piniella out after McCoy called him out
at first on a play where Lou was clearly safe. Maybe the
umps were tired, but they were lousy. They missed a lot
of plays, and there's no way we weren't going to bitch
like hell because we're struggling, and Boston's winning,
and Seattle's going to bitch because they're on a losing
streak.

Tuesday, June 6   Seattle

Figgie was so bad yesterday that Dick Pole, a pitcher with
the Mariners, came over to me and said, "Jeez, it didn't
look like Figgie wanted to pitch last night," which is
exactly what it looked like. When the guys on the other
team notice . . .

Before the game Gene Michaels took the lineup card
out to home plate, brought up the Piniella thing again,

and was thrown out. The game hadn't even started and already Palermo had thrown him out. We also lost the game. Goose got beat when he threw wild past first on a bunt. It's our seventh loss in eight games, and once again Dick Young is trying to wish Billy into being fired. He ran his third big article on Billy's firing. We're only four and a half back. What's the big deal?

Wednesday, June 7   Seattle

Yankees 8. Seattle 1. Another complete victory for Gid, who's now 9 and 0. He struck out ten. Roy and Bucky Dent homered, and Reggie hit two.

Billy has an interesting theory that when Gid is on the mound, our hitters feel less pressure and hit better than they do for the other pitchers. They know he's only going to allow a run or two, so they relax at the plate and hit better. Gid has 19 wins in his last 20 decisions, including postseason games. He's as close to being invincible as any pitcher I've ever seen.

Friday, June 9   Anaheim

The *New York Post*'s Maury Allen walked into the clubhouse before the game with a Xerox copy of the article Dick Young wrote in Wednesday's *Daily News,* which said that Billy is about to be fired. Dick Young and Billy don't get along very well. Why, I don't know. Next to Young's article was a cartoon of Billy in a frying pan. We all stood in the middle of the locker room looking at it. Some of us were speculating as to who the new manager might be. We were saying it'll probably be that asshole from St. Louis, Vern Rapp, who makes you cut off your hair, shave your mustache, and live in an Army barracks. If that guy comes over here, I'm not shaving off my mustache. I'm going to tell him that it makes me pitch better. But before I tell him that, I better start pitching better.

This controversy is nothing new to Billy. He got fired in Minnesota, Detroit, and Texas, and he's been through this before. It's the only way he knows. He was a fiery little red ass when he played, and he still is now. When he was real sick those couple of days in Chicago, I said to him, "Goddamn, you have to take care of yourself and start to feel better. I want to see that fiery little red ass motherfucking everybody. That's the way you are. It doesn't look right, you walking around with your head down."

What's really bothering him is that he really loves being manager of the Yankees, and he knows he's on the verge of losing it, and he doesn't know what to do about it. To him, this is the only thing there is, to manage the Yankees. He really does feel that way. If he didn't he never would have taken all the bull he's taken from George for the last year and a half. George almost fired Billy a half-dozen times last year, he publicly humiliated Billy after Billy tried to attack Reggie on national TV by making Billy agree to seven conditions if he wanted to stay as manager. Another time George was going to fire Billy, but none of the coaches would take the job. Billy knew what was going on, but he wants the job so badly, he swallows his pride to keep it.

Last year Billy and I were having a few drinks in a bar in Seattle, and Billy was in the sauce a little bit, and he said, "I can't stand it. I'm doing things I never did before, taking more shit than I ever did." I said, "Yeah, I know." He said, "I hate to eat shit." I said, "Yeah, and I know why you're doing it too." He said, "Why?" I said, "There were only two things you ever wanted in your whole life, number one, to play for the Yankees—you did that—and number two, to manage the Yankees to a pennant and a World Series. And to do that, you have to take George's shit." And that was it right on the nail.

And now that he's done that, his next goal is to surpass Casey Stengel's record as Yankee manager, and he wants that real bad too. Stengel was Billy's father almost when they were together on the Yankees, that's how much they loved each other. Casey won nine pennants and seven World Championships, and Billy wants to prove that he can do just as well. And when Billy Martin feels strongly about something, come hell or high water, no one is going to stop him. If he's willing to take as much shit as he's taking now, you know he wants it worse than anything.

If he gets fired from here, it'll be the hardest thing he'll ever go through. He'll manage again. And he'll get in hot water all over again because the reason he keeps getting fired is that he bucks the front office. He wants to do it. He doesn't want them interfering. And managers are not supposed to do that. They are supposed to say, "Yes sir, yes sir, yes sir." Billy says, "Screw you, screw you, screw you." That's it, plain and simple. And he knows that. But he can't change now. Not in the middle of the stream.

The players are at the point where they're sick and tired of the whole damn thing about Billy getting fired. They don't care one way or the other. They're down because they're not playing good, we're not getting good pitching, and there just isn't anything we can do about it. We're pressing, and we're tired of hearing all this garbage about "He's going to get fired," he's doing this, he's doing that.

The thing that hurt him most of all, and Billy realizes this, is the night he got into the shouting match with Thurman on the plane. He's apologized. That's what he's always done when he's in trouble or losing. But now he's to the point where if he does get into the sauce, he can't get rid of his thoughts. Now he gets really depressed, whereas before he didn't do that. Before, he'd be madder'n hell, but he wasn't depressed. I feel very sorry for Billy. I really do.

Figgie was his old self again. He beat the Angels, 3 to 1, with Goose pitching the ninth and getting another save.

Saturday, June 10   Anaheim

There hasn't been much fun on the bus rides. It's been dull, and the reason is that everyone's talked all their crap, given their excuses and reasons why we're not winning, and they've finally run out of reasons. They don't know why. Now they're coming to the conclusion that maybe it's themselves. They're thinking, "Why aren't I hitting? Why aren't I doing well?" and they're keeping it all inside where it builds.

Since this road trip began, I've been extremely depressed by what's going on with me. I've been going out to the same places, having drinks, doing what I usually do, but now I'm sitting at the back of the table keeping quiet whereas before I would sit at the center of the conversation and be part of it. I don't want to talk. I don't want to do anything.

We lost to the Angels today, but we shouldn't have. I was pitching in relief in the eighth with a one-run lead, a couple of guys on and two outs. Because I haven't been pitching too well, I motioned for Roy to move back a few steps. The batter hit a shallow fly ball, and Roy came in and came in, and at the last second, the ball hit the tip of Roy's glove and dropped, and a run scored to tie it up. If I hadn't waved him, he would have caught it. Roy's not getting to that ball changed the entire complexion of the game, and Goose ended up losing it in extra innings. If they hadn't tied it up, the batters then would have had to swing at everything I was throwing up there. When they can't be choosy, it makes it very easy to pitch. But when the team at bat is tied or ahead, the batters can afford to take a couple of pitches and pick the one they want to hit.

These are the breaks we've been getting: Gullett, who started, picked Lansford off first without even making a throw. As Lansford ran to second, Don wheeled and threw the ball into center field, and he scored. Later in the game Jim Spencer got up and hit a home run. The ball hit this guy sitting in the stands right on the arm. We're sitting in the bullpen, and this guy is showing everyone the stitch marks on his flesh where the ball hit him, but it must have hit him and then bounced off a chair and onto the field because by the time the outfielder who jumped and missed it came down, the ball was already back out of the stands, and after he threw it into second, the umpires ruled it a double. We knew it was a home run. Ellie went running out of the bullpen gate toward the field hollering for them to call time. Any appeal we make, you see, has to be made before the next pitch.

Once it's thrown, tough shit. So Ellie's running toward
the infield hollering, and the pitcher winds up, throws the
ball, and it's strike one, see ya.

The Sox beat the Mariners and are up by five.

During the game Thurman got hit in the throat by a
foul tip and had to leave the game, and Bucky also went
out with a real bad hamstring pull. I was pitching, the
batter hit the ball into the hole, and Bucky had to make
a big stretch for it, and pop, it went. He'll be out at
least a month. I guess Bucky'll hold me responsible like
Rivers. Rivers says it's my fault for getting the phones
taken out of the clubhouse. Mickey said, "If you hadn't
let that bastard hit that ball over my head, Billy wouldn't
have gotten pissed and taken the phones out."

This kid catcher Mike Heath replaced Thurman after
he was hit by the foul tip. Heath is a good young catcher,
has a very strong arm, and wants to play. In the ninth
inning Bobby Grich came barreling into Heath on a play
at the plate. Heath tagged Grich out, but Grich whacked
him pretty good with his elbow as he slid in. I was pitching, and Heath said, "I should have killed the son of a
bitch." Billy came out and told him, "If they try to knock
you over, hit the motherfucker right in the mouth with
the ball." Billy was right. Here's a rookie catcher, and
they're trying to intimidate him by knocking the hell out
of him. On the next play Lansford came barreling in, and
Heath smashed the hell out of him, which was fine, really
terrific. That's the way you play. Billy loves the hell out
of him now.

The kid is smart too. Heath called for a fastball. Instead of shaking him off, I just stood there, didn't brush
my glove or anything, because I didn't want Billy to know
I was shaking him off. It's better for the kid, the way it
was good how Ellie Howard protected me when I came
up. Next thing you know, Billy's going to be saying to
the kid, "What the hell is going on out there? Why is he
shaking you off?" Heath picked up what I was doing
right away. I just stood there, and he flashed me the sign
for a slider. That way nobody knows.

* * *

After the game, Billy was frustrated by our losing a game we should have won, and he was all pissed off because of the ball Roy should have caught. I told Billy, "I always have Roy playing in against left-handers, and I've been getting my ass kicked, they've been hitting the ball hard off me, so I had Roy playing back more than normal." I said, "I don't think you should take it out on Roy." That sounded good enough for Billy, and he said, "Well, maybe you're right." It made Roy feel better, and it made Billy feel better. Me? I didn't give a damn one way or the other.

Billy and Messersmith have a conflict about something. Billy said to me the other day, "That Messersmith must really hate my guts. He won't even talk to me." I know Andy won't talk to him because Andy wanted to bring his dog back with him on the plane from California, and he asked me to ask Billy for him. Billy said fine. I don't know what it is. Maybe it's because of Billy's remark about Andy being one of George's boys. Or perhaps he's still pissed off for the night Billy gave him hell for being in the bullpen.

The thing is, Andy's just gotten here, and he can't believe the crap that goes on here. He's amazed we can still play ball at all. He's new to the stuff that's said, and he takes everything said to him personally, which he really shouldn't do. Like with the bullpen incident. Andy feels Billy yelled at him strictly because it was him. Then there was the time Billy yelled at him because he didn't have his cap on. But that's just the way Billy is when we lose. He looks for something to relieve the inner tension, and Messersmith just happened to be it those two times. Other days it's other things, other people. I don't think Billy has anything against Andy, but Andy's his own person, and he retaliates and that pisses Billy off, and it keeps going around and around and around.

Sunday, June 11   Anaheim

They traded Ken Holtzman to the Chicago Cubs today for a minor league pitcher with a 7.00 ERA. I'm glad for Holtzie. Now maybe he'll get a chance to pitch again. By the time I found out about the trade, Kenny had packed his bags and was gone.

During our Series with the Angels I haven't been able to find anything in our bullpen. Neither has Rawly. But we got a kick out of the stinkbugs they have out here. They put their ass right in the air, let 'er go, and spray you. You can smell them. During the game I was following this one son of a bitch around with a toothpick. I finally nailed him, put it right through him, and I went and stuck him into a mess of ants. Rawly and I watched for a while. The ants had him for lunch.

The Angels had us for dinner. Tidrow's thumb is banged up, and today he couldn't go more than two innings. He allowed three runs. Clay, who has a good thumb, allowed four runs in two innings and took the loss. Final score: 9 to 6. Roy and Graig homered, but it wasn't enough. In our last three games, we've left 27 runners on base. Reggie, who's batting fourth in the lineup, was 0 for Anaheim. Boston won. Now we're six out.

Monday, June 12   New York

There's a lot of talk that the Yankees are trying to trade for Rod Carew of the Minnesota Twins. The Yankees are talking about trading a front-liner and a couple of our young pitchers such as Kenny Clay and Jim Beattie. The rumors can't be doing great things for their morale. Nobody wants to go to Minnesota. Nobody. Anybody who wants to go there has to be crazy. Calvin Griffith, the owner of the Twins, wants only to be respectable. His philosophy is to bring as many people into the park as inexpensively as possible. I don't really think he gives a damn whether the team wins or not. If he won, he'd have to pay high salaries. The Twins bring up good players from their farm system, play them until they become stars, and when they ask for what they deserve, they're gone: Lyman Bostock, Larry Hisle, Bill Campbell, Bert Blyleven all came up with Minnesota. If Griffith had kept these players, they'd be a contender. But he doesn't want to pay them.

It's funny. Carew used to support Griffith all the time, and now that Calvin is sticking it to Carew, it makes me laugh. Carew wants three and a half million, and after Calvin offered him two, knowing he'd turn it down, Carew turns down the offer, and it's all of a sudden "My boy Rod is a prick." Now Griffith is saying, "Screw him. I'll get someone for him before the trade deadline, the asshole." Rod's feelings are hurt because he had so much faith in Griffith, and now in a matter of three seconds after sticking behind Griffith all this time when everyone else was ripping him, Griffith's making Rod look like an asshole. I don't think there's any way Rod wants to play there anymore, even if he was offered the money.

I know that George is after him, and if there's any way, he's going to get him. The reporters asked me where I thought Rod would play on the Yankees. I said, "We'll take third base and second base and move them over to first base, and let three guys play over there."

Rod's not a bad defensive first baseman himself, and he's such a great hitter, and he can pull the ball any time he wants to. Yankee Stadium's going to be beautiful for him. Home runs will jump out of here. He'll go right in the fourth spot, no doubt about that, and with him in there, it's going to strengthen our lineup tremendously to where they're going to have to pitch to almost every one of those sons of bitches, whereas before if a guy like Nettles was hot and seventh, they just pitched around him.

I just think we're going to get Carew. George'll make Calvin an offer he won't be able to refuse. Bowie Kuhn may have set a $400,000 limit on the cash price, but I guarantee you George would give him $400,000 plus three players, plus nine players to be named later, plus $10,000 a year for the next hundred years, double the interest, and he'd cut his grass for him.

I just cannot shake this depression I've gotten into. It's driving me nuts, really's getting to me. All I want to do is sit around and sulk, and the toughest thing, the thing that drives me nuts the worst, is that I cannot bring myself out of it. I try to do other things, but I just can't.

I lose interest. Also I'm sleeping a lot more and a lot later, and I've been a real son of a bitch around the house. I don't talk. Ordinarily Mary and I play backgammon or deuces or something every night before we go to bed while we're watching TV, but I don't even feel like doing that these days.

After the last time I met with George, I told the reporters, "Listen. I'm not going to talk with you about my salary problems. I'm going to keep my mouth shut. That's the way George wants it." They said fine. So about once a week all of them, one at a time, will come over and ask, "Anything changed?" I'd say no. They'd say, "Fine. We respect you. We're not going to bother you."

Yesterday three or four writers asked me if I'm still unhappy, and I said yes, and that was that. Then Maury Allen of the *Post* came over and said, "You still unhappy?" I said, "Yeah, very." He said, "Nothing's happened so far," meaning I haven't been involved in any trades. I said, "I still have four days left." And I walked away from him. When I returned, he said, "What do you mean you still have four days left?" I said, "Before the trading deadline." I said, "I'm getting so desperate, I'd almost agree to go to Cleveland." When I said that, I meant because Gabe was there. Thank God I didn't say that. So son of a bitch, I pick up today's paper and there's a banner headline: "I'D EVEN GO TO CLEVELAND: LYLE."

I was waiting for the son of a bitch to come in the clubhouse before the game. I was saying to myself, "I hope he doesn't come in because I'm angry enough to choke him." I was talking with another *Post* reporter who said, "Our paper's tough to work for. You have to write anything you can get." I said, "I'm not saying that's right or wrong. I'm pissed off because after two months of being quiet and doing what George wanted me to do, Maury blew the lid right off of it."

Evidently this guy spoke to Maury and told him I wanted to kick his ass, because Maury later came into the clubhouse and said, "Before you say anything, I want to tell you that the only reason I wrote anything was to try to help you. I really mean that. I think you're getting

screwed worse than anyone in baseball right now." That
made me feel a little better, but the damage was done.
I said, "That's nice, but that's not the way it looked. As
far as I'm concerned, you blew it."

When Billy called a meeting today, everybody thought
we were going to get our asses chewed out. In a way
we did, but there was no screaming and yelling. He was
quiet. He just laid it on the line. He said, "You guys
are by far the best club in either league, and I'll be a
son of a bitch if I'm going to listen to some asshole making
a hundred and fifty thousand dollars a year complaining
that he's not getting enough work." He said, "I don't
give a damn about you." He could have been talking
about any one of about five guys, including me, except
that it pissed me off because he was about $20,000 a
year short in my case. Then he said, "It's up to you
guys. If you want to play ball, quit pissing and moaning
and play." He said he was shuffling the batting order
around and was taking Tidrow out of the rotation.

For a number of years, Gid had been kicking around
the minors, and last year he ripped off sixteen games,
and some people may have thought he was a flash in
the pan because he didn't finish many of the games he
started, but let me tell you, he's no flash in the pan. He's
stronger this year, and he's a much better pitcher. He
has two out pitches, a fastball and a slider, and he's in
complete control all the time now.

Thurman was joking the other night that Gid shakes
him off now and then just to show him who's boss. Thurm
says sometimes he wants to throw a pitch, whether it's
right or wrong, and it doesn't matter how many times
Thurm flashes the sign, Gid'll shake him off until he gets
the sign he wants. To me this is what a pitcher should
do because this is saying he won't throw a pitch he
doesn't want to throw. Ninety percent of the pitchers
make the mistake of throwing something they don't want
to.

When you're pitching, you're in control of the game.
The catcher is supposed to be working with you, help-

ing you, and Thurman, for instance, works extremely well
with pitchers. Nevertheless, sometimes a catcher will drop
down a sign he thinks is a pretty good pitch when the
pitcher has in mind something else. Say a pitcher has in
mind to throw a fastball, and the catcher gives the sign
and it's for a curve. Most pitchers, instead of shaking
him off, will throw it. What happens then is that because
the pitcher didn't want to throw that pitch, he won't
throw the pitch with his heart and soul in it. He's saying
to himself, "Screw it, I'll throw your pitch," and they
half-ass it up there, and the batter gets a hit. Then the
next thing you hear is the pitcher saying, "Aw hell, I
don't know why he called that pitch."

I heard Mike Torrez say that a couple of times last
year, and I told him right then and there. I said, "If that
happens, it's your fault." I can honestly say that since
I've been playing pro ball, I've never thrown a pitch I
didn't want to throw. If I'm going to get my ass chewed
out, it's going to be my pitch. And that's what Gid is
showing right now. The best thing about it is that no
one can second-guess you. If they say, "Goddamn, why
didn't you throw such and such?" you have an answer
for them: "Because I didn't want to, that's why." And
there's nothing they can say to that.

One thing I especially admire about Gid is his deter-
mination. In the minors they had wanted him to come
up with a breaking pitch, and they had him throwing both
a curve ball and a slider. I said to him, "Either you develop a curve ball or you develop a slider. You have to
make up your mind one way or the other, and shitcan
the other one." He asked me to show him how I throw
my slider. I demonstrated how to throw it, told him the
cause when it doesn't break, and told him he'd have to
work it out for himself. Now you can tell a lot of guys
how to pitch, and they still can't do it. But Gid was de-
termined, and he figured it out.

That goes back to the baseball establishment again. By
saying, "Kid, you have to come up with something," that
gets the coach off the hook. It keeps the coach from
having to decide which he should develop. Nobody said
to him: Pick one, because you cannot throw both pitches

and throw them well. Even right now, if he starts messing with the curve ball, he'll lose something off his slider and it'll be church.

Tuesday, June 13   New York

Ron Swoboda, who's now a TV sportscaster in New York, came into the clubhouse and said he wanted to interview me about how things were going with my salary dispute. I told him, "Rocky, you and I played together. You know what it's all about and that this isn't going to help me. All you're going to do is ask the same questions, and I'm going to give the same answers." So he asked me, "If something breaks, will you let me know?" I said, "Of course I will." Ten minutes later I decided to skip the game and went home.

I had been in a good mood when I got to the ball park because I've been working on the sidelines and my slider is coming around, and that in itself is enough to brighten the day. But all anyone was talking about was the trade the Yankees were going to make for Carew, how George supposedly is going to give him a half a million dollars as a bonus and three and a half million to play. It started me thinking about what I was making, and what George was paying some of these other guys, and I felt very low. I spoke to Ellie first. I said, "I can't take this crap anymore. I'm going home." Ellie told me he was on my side. He said, "You've always done what you've thought was right, and it usually worked out. I'm not saying leaving would be the right thing to do, but if you feel that's what you have to do in order to get George to talk to you, do it."

Then I went to tell Billy. He said, "I understand how you're feeling. I wish to hell I was wealthy enough to give you the money you want." I shook Billy's hand and told him that if he thought my going home would put him over the brink where George would fire him, I wouldn't do it. He said, "Sparky, I don't give a shit."

"Well, OK," I said, "I'll be back tomorrow." It was three minutes before game time. I put my clothes on and went home. As I was driving out of the stadium parking lot, I could hear the national anthem.

On the way home, I was in traffic up to my ass—it took me almost an hour to go the mile or so from the stadium across the George Washington Bridge. I was on the bridge sitting in my van listening to the game on the radio and another van pulled alongside and this kid yells, "Hey, Spark. Isn't there a game today?" I said, "Yup, sure is." The kid didn't know what to say. It made me laugh.

When I walked out, it felt so good, really good, because I was doing something for me. I've been so frustrated, and it had been building up in my head to where I felt I had no other alternative. In fact, what I had originally planned to do was not show up when we play the Red Sox next week in Boston. That would have made George come around. But I got to thinking that regardless of how beneficial that might be to me in getting more money or getting traded, the Boston series is a crucial series for us, and I felt I shouldn't do it then. I couldn't let the other guys down that way.

Before I went home, Billy told me, "George wants me to quit." He said, "He wants me to quit so he can show me he can control me."

When I got home Mary was rather surprised to see me, but not really. She knew how bad it was bothering me and she understood. I watched the game on TV in my den. Roy hit two home runs to help Figgie win his seventh, but Willie Randolph bruised his right knee and may be out. Twice he got thrown out stealing, and I can't remember when that ever happened. If Willie can't play for a while, it could be disastrous. Bucky's still out, and tonight Mickey's knees were hurting so badly he didn't play. The other night in California Mickey slid into the bag so hard that when he got up to get his helmet he was limping badly. He's so fast and generates so much power when he runs that when he steals a base, he hits that base hard and it's hell on his knees. Also, Mickey doesn't glide into the base like most guys. Mickey runs close to the base and slides, and he's hitting that base hard all the time. It's not that he doesn't know the other way. That's just the way he does it.

There's talk of a trade, Mickey for Jim Palmer of the Orioles. Defensively, we could do it because we'd have Paul Blair out there, but you'd be taking away a guy who gets on base a lot, steals bases, and makes this club go. I don't know if I'd make that trade. Palmer's going to win 20 games for you, which is always good to have. Overall, I'd say that trade would be pretty even.

Wednesday, June 14   New York

George traded Rawly to Philadelphia today for Jay Johnstone, a left-handed first baseman, and for a minor league outfielder. I don't know who's responsible, whether it was Billy or George, though from what Billy said I'm almost certain it was George, but I wish they would cut out the crap. One guy's doing everything he can to get the club going, and so's the other guy, and the combination of both of them is screwing everything up. The two of them ought to just leave us alone. That trade is ridiculous to me. I saw Rawly pitch. The guy can pitch. All you heard about him was he didn't pitch like he used to. Who cares? He was getting people out when they let him pitch, which wasn't very often. He wasn't doing any worse than anyone else. In fact, he was pitching better than most. I have absolutely no idea why they traded him. We've given up a pitcher who could get guys out and we got a left-handed pinch hitter who we don't need. Now we're going to have to use guys in the bullpen who aren't ready to throw. Dirt's finger's hurting him. Who's left out there? Me and Gossage and Kenny Clay.

Billy was complaining too. "All I have is a lot of pinch hitters and nobody to play," he said.

I guess Rawly's not going to make that sculpture out of the little things we found during the season. That's too bad. I was kinda looking forward to seeing what he would have made.

Everybody hates to see Rawly go. And he found out that he didn't want to go either. After a while, he really loved it here. Before he left, I shook his hand and said good-bye. He said he was going to try to commute between here and Philadelphia so he wouldn't have to sell his house. I told him if he had a day off and we were around to give me a call. He said he would. Then he walked out the clubhouse door and left.

Somehow everyone managed to keep it from George that I walked out before yesterday's game! I can't believe it! George doesn't even know! This morning I got a call at home. It was Rosen. He said, "Sparky, I swear to God on my life that George and I were talking about you yesterday." He said, "Sparky, you have to believe me. I told George yesterday when we were talking about the Carew deal, I said, 'You have to take care of that man first. You can't just go and do things. You have to think about things.'" Rosen said, "I can't tell you where, when, or how. All I can tell you is George said he's going to take care of you, Figueroa, and Randolph."

I told him, "I can't take this crap anymore. I don't feel like pitching. Every time I try to get my act together again, something else happens like this where I don't give a damn again. I don't want to go through it anymore."

Here I am, trying to get George so mad that he has to call me to his office even if it's just to chew my ass out, and I end up on the defensive again where I have to keep Billy and Rosen from getting fired by George. I don't know where the hell I'm at. I don't know what the hell to do.

The team's six games back, and we're kinda hurting. Thurman's cyst behind his knee bothers the hell out of him. It hurts him all the time. Some nights he'll go after a foul ball, and you'll see his leg almost go out on him. But he won't take himself out of the lineup. He'll play hurt till he drops. Dent's still out, and Randolph's hurting in both knees, and he's going to be out for a while. He made a turn rounding third yesterday, and on the way home he felt his left knee go. He said it hurt him more than his right did last year before he had it operated on.

Willie's being out will hurt us badly. He's one of the big edges we have over everybody. The kid really can

play, and his fielding and hitting are far superior to that
of other second basemen. He'll make plays where he'll
catch the ball in front of him and make it look easy,
where on the same play a lot of second basemen would
have had to backhand the ball, or they wouldn't have
even gotten to it. Another thing I love about him is that
he's gung ho. When he makes a good play, you can see
his enthusiasm. He always yells "Aw right," and he shakes
his fist if he makes a diving catch or throws a runner out
on a tough play. He's a great player, but he's quiet,
doesn't say too much. Like on plane rides, he just sits
there in his seat with his headphones on listening to
music. It's not that he isn't friendly. He's private. Even
in the locker room he sits by himself. It's his nature.
When anyone talks about him, it's always, "Goddamn,
that guy can play!"

Willie's been unhappy with his contract, too, and though
it's hard to feel sorry for a twenty-two-year-old kid making 70,000 bucks a year, Willie's one guy who should be
getting more. It took me six years to make that much,
but times have changed, and changed quickly. Sure he
should get more money. But this goes back to what I've
been going through. George can't see that. Like I said,
when he signs someone for big money, all of a sudden
they become his bosom buddies, but the players who
have been around for a year or two, he just thinks, Goddamn, they should be happy he's building the club, add-
ing players to help the Yankees win again, that he's doing
this for me, for Willie, for whoever. But it isn't that way.
No one wants to feel that he's being underpaid, I don't
give a damn who you are, whether you're a truck driver,
a secretary, or the president of General Motors.

Billy started Messersmith against Seattle, and Andy
was wild. He gave up three hits, two walks, and five runs
in two innings and was gone. Only one of the runs was
earned because George Zeber, playing second in place
of Willie, dropped a pop-up. It would have been the third
out. Craig Reynolds then hit a grand-slam home run.

Amazingly, we didn't lose it. We stole it back. With
the score 7 to 4, theirs, Billy sent me in to mop up, and
we tied it in the eighth on home runs by Graig and Cliff,

who pinch-hit. In the tenth we had two outs when Jim Spencer popped up behind the plate. It should have been the third out, but Seattle catcher Bill Plummer lost the ball in the lights, and it fell foul. Spencer then singled, Roy White singled, and Paul Blair hit a home run to win the game. More amazingly, Paul had been 0 for 23 against right-handed pitchers. Enrique Romo, the guy he hit it off, is right-handed.

Tidrow and I were talking about this kid Jim Beattie, and I said that I would rather have him in rotation than Messersmith because until Andy can get it together, he's not going to be very effective. They're not going to knock Beattie's tits off in the first innings the way they will Andy's. Beat's not going to give up four, five runs early to put us way down right off the bat. That's one of the big reasons we're losing games. In the first three innings we're giving up at least a run, and if you do that, it's tough. One reason why Guidry is winning so much is that he's not giving up that run in the first few innings. Then we score a run, and he holds them for a few innings, and before you know it, it's 8 to 0. Watch the Red Sox box scores. They almost always score in the first three innings. That's the secret.

We were in the clubhouse after the game, and Holtzman was on the television pitching for the Cubs and getting the save. I yelled, "Hey, Billy, your buddy's on TV." He looked in there, and there was Holtzie. Billy just laughed.

Billy says he has nothing against Holtzman personally. Billy says that every pitcher he had was better than he was, that's all. What the hell are you going to say to that? And for the times Kenny pitched, I'd have to agree. Yet this isn't necessarily Holtzman's fault either. A lot of times guys don't get to pitch because of situations they're in. It happened to me. When Tidrow and Grant Jackson pitched the whole second half of the 1976 season and I didn't pitch at all, it was the situation. I had lost two or three games in a row, and we couldn't afford to lose any more games, and Billy couldn't afford to let me go in and screw up anymore. Billy felt he had to do something else, so he used those two guys, and once they started rolling, he had to stay with them. That does happen. And you can't turn around and say, "Goddamn, you can't tell me Grant Jackson is as good as Sparky Lyle?" It could be yes, it could be no, but that's not relevant. The real question is "Who's hot at the time?" Holtzman got a couple of starts and didn't do well. And being hurt didn't help him either.

Holtzie had been the player rep, and with him gone, I held a meeting to elect the new player rep. I was the alternate, but I intend to stay the alternate. Player reps come and go, but alternates stay on forever. I asked for nominations, and Reggie said, "I'll take it if you'll be the alternate." I said, "That sounds fine. All in favor of Reggie being the player rep and me being the alternate, raise your hand." Everyone raised his hand and that was it.

There really isn't that much to being player rep. He mainly passes on the words of wisdom of Marvin Miller and the Players Association.

George has been staying out of everything, hasn't butted in yet, and I know it must be killing him. I just know he's dying to come down to the clubhouse and hold a meeting. Rah. Rah. Sis-boom-bah. But George said in the papers, "It's Al's and Billy's ball game. If they lose, they will get the blame." You know what that means—nut-cutting time.

Thursday, June 15   New York

Either George and Rosen have been drinking or they're up to something. We traded Del Alston and Mickey Kluttz to Oakland, and we got Gary Thomasson, who is, guess what: another left-handed hitting outfielder! I guess some people collect stamps, some people collect coins, and George is collecting left-handed guys to sit on the bench and collect splinters. Now we have Spencer, Johnstone, this kid infielder Doyle, and Thomasson. With Mickey, Graig, and Reggie in the lineup, no one throws any righties against us anyway.

Gullett got his first win, beating the Mariners 5 to 2. I don't know if my walking out had anything to do with it, but Billy had Goose pitch the seventh and eighth, and I pitched the ninth to get my seventh save. If Billy had been doing that all year long, I'd have 20 saves already, which says something about statistics. They do lie sometimes. Often, the manager has a lot to do with that.

Today's the last day of the trading period, and George wanted to trade Roy White to Oakland, but Roy's a ten and five man and he refused to give George permission to make the trade. I don't know why, but George has a tremendous dislike for Roy. I've been told that sometimes when Billy plays Roy, George calls him up on the phone and orders him to play Piniella or someone else. During one game a little while ago, George was in his office watching the game out his window, yelling, "Martin, you idiot, get that son of a bitch out of there." He was yelling so loud he could be heard in the hall.

Roy White is probably the nicest Goddamn guy on the club. He's quiet. He's well respected by everybody, and he's very classy, he and his wife both. There isn't anything bad you can say about Roy. Plus the guy hits a steady .280, he steals bases, and he's a smart outfielder. Everyone says Roy has a weak throwing arm, and it's true. When the ball is hit in the left-field corner, the batter has a sure double, whereas if you have a guy with a halfway strong arm, the runner has to make his turn right and has to do everything right to get in there. And yet if you look at Reggie on the other side, he has a gun, but he doesn't know what to do with it, and guys still take the extra base. Plus Reggie still tries to throw out the runner going from second to third—who he has no chance of getting—and the batter ends up going to second. Instead of having one runner in scoring position, you have two.

Mickey's arm in center isn't very good either, but at least Mickey tries to get the ball to the cutoff man. If you do that, you're going to get the runner going home.

Beattie was complaining that he wasn't being used right. Beat says he's a better pitcher when he goes every fourth day instead of every fifth.

When Billy heard about that, he said, "He'll pitch every fourth day. As soon as Catfish comes back, he'll pitch every fourth day in Tacoma."

* * *

Gene Michaels and I have been teammates for quite a while. When we played together, we used to fool around, try to throw balls all the way out of Yankee Stadium, stuff like that. We used to have a lot of fun with Gene.

One of the greatest practical jokes ever pulled was pulled on him. It was a beauty. Now understand that Gene Michaels is afraid of everything that moves. He's afraid of an ant. You know that a jockstrap has a little pouch in it that you snap your metal cup into. The cup protects you from being hit in the nuts by a baseball. Well, Mel Stottlemyre and Fritz Peterson took Gene Michaels's jock, took his cup out, and in the pouch they put a big green bullfrog and snapped it shut. Gene started getting dressed. He put his shirt on, and son of a bitch he puts the jockstrap on, and then he pulls his pants up and his belt, and as he puts his cap on and gets ready to grab his glove and go out onto the field, the frog starts to kick. I swear to you, Gene looked down at his fly, and he screamed, "Something just kicked my dick!" I don't know how he did it, but in one movement he jumped right out of his uniform. As his pants and jock lay on the floor, Gene was just walking around the clubhouse, looking back at the jock.

I remember one year we played a hockey game one night after a ball game. About eight of us stayed, me, Gene, Fritz, Hal Lanier, Bobby Murcer, Rich McKinnie, and a couple of other guys. We played for about two hours. We cleared the clubhouse out. I put the catching equipment on, and I was one goalie and McKinnie was the other goalie. The rest of the guys got bats and ran around in their shorts, no shoes, and whacked around a ball of tape, which was our puck. The checking was unreal. Rough stuff. Murcer hit me in the hand with his bat trying to stop a shot, and Lanier lost both his big toenails. Murcer was so sore he could barely play the next day. There was blood, but we were just having a good old time.

Now Gene Michaels is a coach, and if you've seen a Jekyll and Hyde, he's it. Now when guys are fooling around, he's saying, "You shouldn't do that. You might get hurt." All of a sudden he's become one of these company men who's telling us, "If you give everything you have, the game will allow you to play." Which is a bunch of crap. Last year Michaels was Steinbrenner's administrative assistant, and now all of a sudden he's starting to sound like Steinbrenner. Steinbrenner's always talking about loyalty. He says, "You be loyal to me. I want your loyalty." But if you give your loyalty, you expect to get loyalty back, and he doesn't give it. The day you can't get somebody out or you can't hit like you used to, screw you, you're gone. When that happens, they don't give a Goddamn about you.

They're always talking about loyalty and teamwork. Loyalty shouldn't even be involved. Teamwork is playing together, which is necessary to win, whether it's hugging and kissing like the Dodgers or fighting and brawling like the Yankees. You're still playing together. But the loyalty part they can stick up their ass. I come to the park every day, and whether it was for the Red Sox or now for the Yankees, I try to win. That's my loyalty. Nothing more. They are paying me to pitch, but that is not loyalty on their part. I don't give a damn what George says.

The old-time players believed in this nonsense, and they say we're dummies? How many of them are broke? Have the owners ever once helped one of them? You hear that so-and-so has finally won the battle against alcoholism. As soon as a player no longer can hit the ball out of the park, it's "What's your name again?" That's loyalty all right. And even the fans are brainwashed into believing this loyalty thing. They feel that you should be loyal to your team.

The owner always gets the last revenge, which is the pink slip. They say, "I hate to do it," but then they say, "but we feel you can't help our ball club anymore," and you're gone. They're very nice about it, but they just as well might say, "You bum, you're fired. Get out." Why don't they do it all that way? It's far less hypocritical. I'd rather quit than let them do that to me. I've been thinking about that for a long time. I'll be the first one to know the day I can't get them out any longer. When that day comes, that'll be it. I'm not going to give them the chance

to call me into the office and tell me to clean my stuff out
of my locker. That's my one goal in baseball, to quit before
they fire me.

Friday, June 16   New York

George called me into his office today—finally. He wanted
to know if my arm was hurt. I told him it wasn't. He said,
"I almost traded your ass today." I said, "You should have.
It would have been better for all concerned." He said,
"The only reason I didn't is if your arm is sound, I wasn't
trading you." You figure out what that means. I couldn't.
That's what he said. But he couldn't have traded me without my permission, and not only that, today is the day
after the trading deadline. Despite what he says, the real
reason he didn't trade me is he's scared to. He doesn't
want to trade me and have me come back and haunt him
like I've haunted the Red Sox.

I'm sure he could have made a trade with the Dodgers.
And Texas wants me real bad, but he's not about to let
me go there. He knows Texas has a better chance of beating Kansas City if I go over there, and that the Yankees
have more trouble with Texas than they do with Kansas
City. All Texas is lacking is relief pitching. They lose their
games in the late innings.

George told me to get some realistic figures into my
head and he'd talk in a week as soon as the team came
home from Boston. Well, I have realistic figures in my
head, the same ones I had when I went in. I want $200,000
a year. That's realistic. I can write them down in black
and white if they aren't real enough for him.

Tito Fuente, who has been one of the most renowned
hot dogs in baseball history, came to the stadium today to
work out. He hit and fielded, and I guess he's looking for
a job. Willie's out and we need a second baseman. Brian
Doyle can't hit his weight, and we have this kid Garcia,
who looks like a good ballplayer but he doesn't have experience either. Fuente, I understand, wants $180,000 to
sign. If George signs him, that's going to be it for me. I'm
going home—for good.

* * *

I heard from a Yankee employee that they were talking about trading Billy to the White Sox for Bob Lemon. He said, "We're going to trade managers. Billy's going to Chicago, and Lemon's coming here." Later it got back to them that the guy had been talking, and when Rosen found out, he told him to keep his mouth shut from now on. I won't mention the name of the guy who told me because if it gets back to George, George might fire him. I don't want this guy to lose his job.

Reggie had a good game, went 4 for 4 with three RBI's to keep us in the game, but Beattie and Messersmith each gave up five runs, and California won 10 to 7. Beat hit Downing and Baylor, and Angel pitcher Dave LaRoche hit Mickey Rivers and broke his hand. Mickey has a hairline fracture. They put him on the disabled list. First Dent, then Randolph, now Rivers. If the heart of a team is up the middle, like they say it is, we're in trouble.

The Red Sox scored two runs in the bottom of the ninth to beat the Mariners. We're seven back. If Boston doesn't start losing a few soon, it's going to get mighty tense around here.

Saturday, June 17   New York

Gid has been ab-so-lute-ly phenomenal. Tonight he won his eleventh game without a loss. He shut out the Angels, 4 to 0. He allowed four dinky hits, and he struck out 18!

I've been saying all year long that Guidry's the most impressive pitcher I've ever seen. He's more impressive than Seaver or Palmer or Ryan. Gid hasn't been here long enough to have that kind of reputation, but he's building it up in a hurry. He goes out there with two pitches, plus a pretty good change-up that he doesn't even use. If he ever dropped one of those on somebody, the guy would screw himself into the ground swinging at it. Gid throws so easy, and he's in complete command out there. Even if he gets into trouble, he knows that there's no way they're going to score. He just adjusts his style of pitching, goes to whichever pitch is working best. He throws so hard the hitter can't stand in there and say, "I'm going to hit this slider," because his slider is too good. And he can't wait for his fastball because it gets on you too quickly. He's really got them. As long as he can get his pitches over the plate, he's going to keep right on winning.

Tonight the guys in the bullpen were pulling for him like hell to break the major league strikeout record. Seaver, Carlton, and Ryan have the record at 19. Gid was one short, but it was a hell of a try.

If you see Gid pitch, you watch him, and you know he's throwing hard, but I don't think the spectators realize just how hard. The batters either swing and miss, or they hit a fly ball way up in the air, but it never seems to go anywhere. You're sitting there watching the guy, and he's just winding up, throwing the ball, and the catcher's throwing it back to him, like they're playing catch, and before you know it, Jesus Christ, the ballgame is over, they've got three hits, and he's won 2 to nothing.

The greatest thing is to hear the fans chanting and clapping for that strikeout after he gets two strikes on the batter, and when he strikes the guy out, they go crazy. And what's making the year so tremendous for Guidry is that he's becoming famous for something he loves to do. It's not only self-satisfaction. He's also getting the recognition that goes with it. It's gonna make him feel so good and so confident that he might come back and be even better next year.

The only thing I was worried about as I watched him strike out all those guys was that I hope the effort didn't take too much out of him for his next start. When you strike out so many, it takes so much strain and energy that sometimes you need a fifth day to come back and throw good again.

Gary Thomasson played in his first game as a Yankee. He got a single and a triple, drove in two runs, and scored a run. The kid looks like he really wants to play.

This other kid Brian Doyle, who's playing second base in place of Willie Randolph, signs his autograph, and under it he writes "John 5:24." I asked him, "Is that a little prayer you go over before you play a game?" He said,

"Yeah, something like that." He said he always signs his autograph that way and asked me if I knew John 5:24.

I told him I'd have to look it up, that I didn't remember what it was. "I can't tell you right off what it is," I said. "It seems to have slipped my mind right now." Jeez. Let me think now. Could you start it for me?

Sunday, June 18   New York

Figgie went into the ninth tonight tied 2 to 2. He got the first two outs, and with Ron Fairly, who's a left-handed batter, up, Fowler called time and went out to talk with Figgie. Fowler told him to throw Fairly all fastballs outside and that it didn't matter if he walked him because right-handed batters were hitting next.

Figgie threw a fastball on the black outside and got a strike, and then he threw another one and got strike two. Cliff Johnson, who was catching, then called for a curve, and Figgie threw one down and in, and Fairly jerked it out for a home run. Now I don't know why Figgie did that. All I can think of is in Toronto, Fowler told him the same thing, "If you walk him, I don't care," but as soon as he walked the guy, they took him out of the game.

This had happened once to Holtzman too. Fowler told Holtzie, "Pitch around the guy. Don't give him anything good to hit. We don't care if you walk him." So Holtzie pitched him careful, ended up walking the guy, and Billy took him out.

Now I'm not saying this was on Figgie's mind. All I'm saying is this happened before, so it could have been. Or Figgie figured he had been throwing outside and figured he would fool Fairly with an inside pitch. At any rate, Fairly hit it out, we lost 3 to 2, and Billy went crazy. And now Figgie's demanding to be traded again, saying that Billy's a second-guesser. Among all the things Figgie said, the one that made the most sense was "If they want me to walk him, why didn't they just order four balls. They tell me to pitch carefully. What the hell does that mean?"

What it means is that the manager and pitching coach are passing the buck. To me it makes a hell of a lot more sense to go out to the mound and tell a pitcher, "Pitch to the son of a bitch and get him out" or tell him, "Walk him intentionally." That leaves no room for error unless you throw the ball away while you're walking the guy. To say to a pitcher, "Pitch the guy away and I don't care if you walk him," that doesn't tell the guy a damn thing. Are you supposed to nibble at him or throw the ball five feet outside, or if you get ahead of him, should you try to get him out?

And the worst thing was that Figgie had his momentum going. He had two outs, was rolling along, and then all of a sudden time is called, the game is stopped, and they walk out and tell him this. That's the worst Goddamn thing you can do to a pitcher. I know this from experience. This is what makes Thurman such a good catcher. He never comes out to the mound and says stuff to you when you're having trouble. He might motion that your arm is down, but he'll never break your rhythm, never break your momentum. It's just terrible when you're pitching out there, going and going, and some friggin' guy comes running out, and there you are, you're stopped. Now you have to start all over again.

If you want to tell your pitcher something like that, tell him in the dugout. They knew Fairly was the third batter. Tell him in the dugout, not in the middle of the inning. And if you can't tell him in the dugout, then leave the guy alone. You have just as much a chance, even more of one, of getting the guy out. Just leave him alone. He knows what he's doing out there.

We're seven out, and we have a three-game Series with Boston starting tomorrow night. Before today's game I went to Billy and told him that he should pitch Goose in relief up at Fenway because I haven't pitched well there in three years and because it's to our advantage, until I start throwing good again, to pitch him instead of me up there.

Even though Kenny Clay's going to start against the Sox tomorrow, he was in the bullpen tonight. He had told Billy he could go an inning or two if he was needed, and as the game went on and he saw he wasn't going to get in, he got up and started to warm up for tomorrow's start. He must have been throwing for fifteen minutes, and he really aired it out, and as I was watching him, I was thinking that he was throwing too hard for too long. He has good stuff, and he throws hard, but he has no experience, and tomorrow his arm is going to be tired, just wait and see.

Monday, June 19   Boston

Sorry to say, I wasn't wrong about Kenny Clay. He wasted it all in the bullpen yesterday, and the Sox hit him for four runs in three innings. He told me that when he got up to throw yesterday, his arm felt sore and crummy, and he got worried and decided to throw it out, which isn't what you do. You have to have the discipline not to pitch, to wait. He had three whole days to rest his arm, but he didn't take advantage of them.

Goose relieved in the fifth and held them at 4 to 4 until the bottom of the eighth, when he tired and got bombed for five runs. The last batter Goose faced hit a ball to Reggie in right, and with runners on base, Reggie looked at the runners instead of looking at the ball, and he booted it, which is something he's done numerous times, and it caused Gossage to go out of the game. It used to piss me off, but Reggie does it so often, it doesn't bother me anymore. I know he's going to be that way, so there's nothing you can do about it. I walked a couple and gave up a couple of hits and was lousy.

I've never gotten my ass kicked consistently like this before. Not during my entire career. I've given up at least one run in eight of my last nine appearances. And what makes it worse is that when I go into a game, my mental attitude goes right South. Lately when Billy puts me in, it's never when the game is on the line. It's the third inning or the fifth inning, and there's no hope for getting the save, and it's depressing. The other day Rosen said to me, "When you're on the mound, it doesn't even look like you want to pitch." My mental attitude just isn't there, and I don't know what to do about it.

Tom Burgmeier relieved for the Sox in the fourth after we scored four runs off Luis Tiant, and he just stuck it up our ass. Burgmeier has a big breaking curve ball and a change of pace, and he has good control, and as long as our guys stand up there and swing at his crap, he's going to get them out. Guys saw him and wanted to hit him so bad they jumped at whatever he threw up there, whether it was in the strike zone or not.

Steinbrenner was really pissed after the game because Burgmeier's a lefty, and Piniella, who bats right-handed, sat on the bench until the ninth, when he pinch-hit and singled. The Sox had scored six in the eighth and were winning 10 to 4 at that point, and Lou's single didn't mean squat. George loves Lou and hates it when he doesn't play. Lou is also George's son's idol. Last year when Burger King put out a set of baseball cards with the pictures of the Yankee players on them, they forgot to include Piniella, and George called them up, reamed their ass, and made them print a special Piniella card to add to the set. So today, in a game that would have been a natural for Lou to play, when he didn't, George was burning.

After the game Lou was also second-guessing Billy for not putting him in sooner against Burgmeier. Lou said that when we rallied for four runs in the fourth Billy should have used pinch hitters to get us more runs. "You can't win with a tie game if you play thirty innings," Lou said.

We're now tied for third place, eight games behind Boston.

Tuesday, June 20   Boston

George called Kenny Clay on the phone last night after his bad outing and told him he wasn't trying hard enough. When I heard this, I said, "Holy Christ, I can't believe this. You can't call a kid on the phone and tell him something like that. What in the world is wrong with him?" When George sees someone who throws as hard as Clay, he feels Clay should go out there and not get hit. Why, that's ridiculous!

I just can't understand why Rosen is doing the things he's doing. He says he's a man who's played the game. He's always talking about "When I was a player this, when I was a player that." But he's starting to learn that baseball has changed. It's not like it was before, which is something all the old-time players resent very much.

You've got to be out of your tree to call a kid on the phone and tell him he's not trying, especially after he just pitched against a team like Boston. All that does is make the guy go out the next time, thinking, "Jesus Christ, if they don't think I'm trying, I can't afford to let them hit the ball hard off me," and it takes away your whole concentration. The next thing you know you're three and two on a batter and you don't know what the hell to do.

Rosen goes around making statements like, "Competitiveness between two ballplayers makes them both play better." Personally, I think that's a big crock. I think it hurts ballplayers. When he came out with that statement, he was talking about me and Gossage, that he felt we'd both have better years than ever because of the competitiveness between us. But it's not like that. It'll never be like that.

There's talk that Rosen's going to take over as manager of this ball club. If he gets the chance, he will, but I don't think he'll be able to do it. The first time he makes a move that everybody thinks is wrong, that'll be the end.

In the fourth inning, we were losing 4 to 0 and facing the prospect of being nine games back when Chicken Stanley got up with the bases loaded in the fourth and hit a grand-slam home run off Mike Torrez. We scored three more in the inning, Reggie homered in the ninth, and we won 10 to 4.

Chicken's home run was funny because the night before, he pinch-hit against Burgmeier, and he flew out, but he said, "Goddamn, I just missed hitting the son of a bitch out there. If he had hit one then, it would have put us ahead in the first game." Tonight we were sitting in the bullpen, and Torrez's first pitch came in and it was a high curve ball. I said to Tidrow, "He better not be throwing Chicken that pitch again. If he does, Chicken's going to take him into the net." And son of a bitch if Torrez doesn't throw him another high curve ball, which Stanley put right into the net for a grand slam.

You have to give Fred Stanley a lot of credit. He works out, tries to make himself stronger so when he does hit the ball, he gets everything. He's a solid shortstop with a lot of range, and Billy likes him because he can do everything. He plays all three infield positions, he can bunt, he can hit and run, and these are the things players like him have to do to keep their jobs. He's not going to hit a lot of home runs, but it was Fred Stanley who hit the last grand slam in the old Yankee Stadium, and I remember he once won a game for me in the ninth with a home run. When he hits one, it's usually right down the line and goes in about the third row, but what's the difference. It still counts.

Rookie Jim Beattie started against the Sox tonight, couldn't get through the second inning, and before the game was over, George had shipped the kid back to Tacoma. Fred Stanley told me that from where he was at shortstop, he could see George in his box screaming at Bill Kane, his assistant, as the Sox were scoring five runs against Beat in the second. Kane got up and left the box about the same time Billy took Beattie out of the game. Apparently George was screaming at Kane to send the kid back to the minors.

Last week against Seattle George Zeber screwed up a pop-up, and the next day he was sent down. By the time he got to the park the next day, Brian Doyle had already been called up and was walking around with Zeber's uniform on. That's as quick as you can be. You can't be any quicker unless you get the guy on the CB on his way to the ball park. "Ah, breaker 19, breaker 19, Zeber, don't bother coming to the ball park. Somebody else is already wearing your uniform." The other night Doyle screwed up a ball, and now this kid Garcia is playing second. When Randolph's knees get better, Garcia'll be gone too.

Cat pitched the ninth and gave up two long back-to-back home runs to Lynn and Scott. Cat's arm was hurting. He's not ready to pitch yet, and it's a shame because he's such a competitive person and it's just eating him away. He's a great pitcher, and to see him go through this is terrible. It hurts me to see what he's going through. Cat told reporters after the game, "I hurt from the shoulder all the way to the arm. I wish someone would cut it off." Nevertheless, he would keep going out there if he got the chance, hurt shoulder or not. I imagine he'll be put back on the disabled list. The one question nobody talks about is whether this means the end of Cat's career. I really would hate to see that happen. We would miss him very much around here.

It's easy to see how badly our pitching staff is riddled by our having to pitch Beattie tonight in the first Boston game. He hasn't been pitching well lately, and if our regulars weren't hurt, he wouldn't be there. We had to throw the arms that were the healthiest because you have a better chance with a healthy arm than with somebody who's hurting. Some people thought that Guidry should have started tonight, but it would have been a day early for him, and he still might have gotten his ass kicked, and it also might have hurt him for the next three starts. I think Billy did right there. You shouldn't pitch the guy before he's ready. They didn't want to start Tidrow because his thumb still hurts him. Besides Beattie, all they had was me and Goose. The guy I would have started instead of Beattie is this kid at Tacoma named Larry McCall. He has a real funky motion, but the important thing is he keeps the ball down. Still, it's not much of a choice, rookie A or rookie B.

Boston has a super lineup, and they can really hit in Fenway. They're a patient team, they wait, play perfect ball until someone on the other team screws up, you make an error or you walk a guy, and they take advantage of the opening you give them. That's the way the Baltimore teams used to do it. And Boston has the kind of lineup where they're going to score runs, with Yaz, Rice, Lynn, Fisk, Scott, Burleson, Remy, and Hobson. Every one of those guys makes good contact and hits the ball hard.

This year Boston's also getting good pitching, with Torrez and Eckersley added to their staff. When the Yankees let Torrez go last year, I didn't think anything of it. He was a .500 pitcher who did real well in his last seven or eight games, but there are a lot of guys as good as he is, so I didn't think it was any big deal letting him go. Still, he's got ten wins this year, and he's pitching very well. Eckersley won his seventh game today. He used to be a strictly fastball pitcher when he was with the Indians, but this year he seems to be throwing more off-speed stuff than before. Whereas before he was a thrower, now he's more of a pitcher. Last night, the guys weren't very impressed with Eckersley. They said he was hanging his sidearm curve, but we weren't even offering at them. It's been like that lately. Boston has the momentum right now, and I'd rather have that than anything. For a while we were keeping up with them, but we have so many guys out, when they went on a rampage, they just opened up the gap.

Our backs are to the wall after losing two out of three to the Sox. Eight games is a long way back. Still, Billy firmly believes we can beat these guys. Everyone does. We're not down so bad. If we can stay within five or six games of them by the All-Star break, we can catch them—unless they play this well all year long. If they do, they're going to break a lot of records.

Thursday, June 22   Detroit

George called Beattie gutless for the way he pitched yesterday. Can you imagine? What a terrible thing to say about one of your ballplayers. If George had any class, he'd apologize to the kid. But no owner, not Walter O'Malley or any of them, would apologize in such a situation. But O'Malley would never say such a thing to a ballplayer.

I'll tell you something about George. He'll tell a kid, "You're not trying," or "You're gutless" and he'll send him down, and then he'll turn around and bring the kid back and smile at him and say, "Do a job for me, son." How can you respect somebody like that? It's like taking your ordinary everyday working person and telling him, "I don't know why I keep you. You never do a job right," and then turning around the next day and saying, "Would you do me a favor?"

Beattie throws harder than most pitchers and he's got an average breaking ball, but if he doesn't keep the ball down, he gets hurt. His biggest problem is that he's always behind the hitters. You can't always be 2 and 0 on a hitter and expect to win. But Beattie's a good kid, and I expect to see him back here soon—if George hasn't quit on him.

* * *

On the road the coaches are supposed to dress together, but Gene Michaels now has to dress by himself. Billy thinks Gene is a spy for George, that he's one of the guys telling George stuff. Billy doesn't know for certain, but he knows that he doesn't like him. If Billy can keep his job to the end of the year, he'll fire Gene at the end of the season.

I walked by Gene before the game, and he was sitting on a table in the clubhouse. Here in Detroit the coaches have their own little room with the manager. Gene was dressing outside around the corner with the players. I said, "Well, here you are, not allowed in the coaches' room. What's going on?" Gene said, "I don't know what's wrong. They just don't like me anymore."

That would be George's way, to have spies. That's why he's so arrogant, because he gets to know so much about people, it's unbelievable. I'm sure that he knows everything that everyone does. I'm not condemning Gene either. It's a good example of what the love of baseball can make a person do. He loves the game so much that this is what he'd do to stay in it.

I'm sure Reggie goes up to George's office and pops off every now and then too. Reggie a little while ago came up to me in the outfield and asked me if anything had been done about my money. I said nothing had. He said, "What are you going to do?" I said, "I don't even feel like pitching anymore. It just doesn't matter if I pitch." Reggie said, "You're not that way." He said, "You know that George made me promises that he never kept." I said, "Yeah, but there's one difference. You have a long-term contract, and I don't." He said, "You can't expect to get the money I got." I said, "Hell no, I don't expect that, but I do expect a little more." So Reggie told me, "You just go out and pitch your ass off, and I'm sure George will take care of you." I swear he sounded just like Rosen. I don't know whether that came right from Reggie or through George. It makes you wonder.

Billy held a meeting tonight before the game. He said he wanted us to go out and try to forget all the crap that's going on. He said, "I know we're playing bad and we have a lot of injuries and our pitching staff is hurting. Just go out there and try to play as aggressively as you can, and let be whatever will be." And that was the end of the meeting. He didn't chew anybody's ass out. You can't do that when you're playing badly. It's different when guys aren't hustling or aren't doing the things they should be doing, but that isn't the problem. Not having Dent and Rivers and a healthy pitching staff—that's the problem. Making things worse, it looks like Randolph has a cartilage tear behind his left knee and will be out for a long time. He's on the twenty-one-day disabled list. Catfish was also put on the disabled list. He can barely raise his arm high enough to shave. Also today, Thurman bumped ump Jim McKean after McKean called him out on strikes, and he may be suspended for a few games. What we need is Guidry and three days of rain.

I shouldn't have worried about Gid straining his arm after his 18 strikeout game. He pitched very well tonight, giving up six hits and one run to win his twelfth. He was behind 1 to 0 in the ninth, but Reggie hit one out, and we scored three more to win it for him. It would have been terrible for him to lose his streak with a 1 to 0 loss. And I like what he said after the game: "I wouldn't have felt bad if I had lost a game like that." He made a good pitch to Ron LaFlore in the first, but LaFlore just hit it out. When you lose a game, you'd rather lose it that way rather than lose it on a shitty-ass pitch or on an error, anything where you shouldn't have lost it. It was a good win for Gid and for us.

Piniella's been hitting the hell out of the ball. Tonight in the ninth Billy sent Lou up to pinch-hit, and he told him to bunt. "Bunt?" Lou said. "I'll go up there and hit a line drive up the middle. The hell with bunting." Billy said, "OK, go ahead." The second pitch, bang, a line drive up the middle scored the winning run.

Roy's starting to hit the ball pretty good now too. He's been in a slump, but in order to do well, he's got to play regularly. Roy's been around so long, with his stats, there's no denying he's a steady ballplayer. A player can accept the fact that he's not hitting because he's getting old and can't do it anymore, but that's not the thing with Roy. Roy hadn't been hitting because he wasn't playing, and that was frustrating because it was out of his control. It's the same thing with me, except it's happened to me before, and I can take it because I realize what's going on. This is the first time it's happened to him. Every year you read where they're going to trade Roy White, but they can't, they can't afford to trade the guy until they can come up with someone who's going to be as consistent as he is, and there are very few of those around.

The Yankees called up Larry McCall to replace Beattie on the roster.

Friday, June 23   Detroit

Billy called me into his office before the game and told me he was going to take Goose and me with him to the All-Star game. I said, "OK, yeah, fine," even though I don't think I deserve to go.

In our locker room here, there's a big Pepsi case with a glass window, and in it there was a watermelon. Johnstone took it, drew a face on it, put a Yankee hat on it, and laid it on top of two shoes inside the cooler. Then he took Thurman's uniform shirt and put it under it alongside Thurman's glove. It was funny. It really was. It had sideburns and a little fat face. Looked just like Thurman.

Figgie got some support tonight, but it didn't help him. Chambliss hit a grand slam in the first off Wilcox, but Figgie couldn't get the five innings in to win it. I came in after four and two-thirds, shut 'em out, and after Blair hit a three-run double and Roy hit a three-run homer, I was the beneficiary of an easy 12 to 3 win. I'm now 5 and 1, which is embarrassing because I've been pitching so badly. After the game Nettles said to me, "You're five and one?" I said, "Yeah, everyone thinks I'm one and one or one and two. Keep quiet about it. I don't want anyone to know I'm doing so well pitching so badly."

* * *

For the first time in several weeks I've been able to shake the depression that's been hanging over me. I finally sat down and told myself that this thing is no different from being under pressure. See, to me pressure doesn't exist. Pressure is something that a person creates for himself. It comes from within. When I pitch, I never feel it. I pitch my way, and I say, hell, this is the way it's going to be, and nothing's going to change that. I figured out that depression is just like pressure. I thought to myself, "Jesus, I'm doing this to myself, and it's something that may turn out to be a positive experience because this never happened before, and it's something to learn from." And when I decided that it was something within my control, as fast as I went into it, that's how fast I snapped out of it. I'm fine now, glad that it's over with.

I don't know how true this is, but Maloney, one of the umps doing the Detroit games, called Ellie over and told him he had heard that Steinbrenner was talking to Walter Alston about managing the Yankees. Ellie and I were talking it over. He said, "I can't see how they could possibly hire that guy. He's too old, too set in his ways, and he'd never be able to handle our guys." If they hired Alston, we'd never win, that's for sure, and I don't think he'd last a month. He wouldn't make it to the end of the season mentally or physically. If they fire Billy, there is nobody who can take his place aside from Dick Williams, and he isn't available.

It isn't good for contenders to change managers in midseason, especially on this club. It will only create more conflict. When a manager gets fired and the players on the whole don't feel he should have been fired, they're not going to play their best for the next manager. And in this case, even if Billy gets fired and no one cares that he got fired, they'll just wait for the next manager to screw up so they can say, "Christ, they never should have fired Billy."

This club would be the hardest one for any manager to take over. These guys are great ballplayers, but they're different because they take losing in stride. To us, winning and losing are the same. You play the best you can, and if you lose, well, there's no sense in crying about it. The new manager is going to have to be able to handle that.

Dick Williams can do it. If he came in, everyone would listen because they know he's a great manager and he's not going to mess with anyone. Williams doesn't give a damn who you are either. If you screw up out on the field and there's no excuse for it, Goddamn, you're liable. He'll give you hell. And if you mess with him, he's going to say, "Piss on you. You can go sit on the bench and I won't even know you're here." Nobody wants that to happen, so they toe the line.

If we bring in a passive manager like Bob Lemon of the White Sox, the only way he'll be able to win with this club is to show the players right away that he knows how to manage and manipulate this club to the best of our advantage, and that means to win games. If he tries to lay down the law and treat us like kindergarten children and change a lot of things by saying "A rule's a rule," that is going to be tough with the personnel we have here.

Amid all the talk that Billy's going to get fired, he came to me and asked, "How much pension can I get?" I said, "I think it's about two grand a month." He said, "I just might quit and live off my pension. Screw it. Let the bastard fire me." I said, "You want to keep your medical and dental coverage?" He laughed.

Saturday, June 24   Detroit

The pressure that George puts on his managers has taken its toll on Billy. It's tough enough to make decisions on the field, and when you're the manager, you're the only one who can make them, whether they're right or wrong. You have to make them without hesitating. But when another guy comes along and says, "Why did you do this? Explain to me why you did that. Why did you use this guy instead of that guy?" everything gets screwed up.

That's the main reason Rosen and Billy were supposedly going to run the club this year without interference from George. But George just is not going to stay in the background. He never has.

Ralph Houk, who's now the Detroit manager, managed the Yankees when George bought the Yankees. During George's first season Ralph held a meeting. He told us, "This guy," meaning George, "is very difficult to play for. But I'm not going to let him beat me. I promise you. I'm not going to quit. I'm going to stay right here until he fires me." We were glad to hear that because we loved Ralph as our manager.

I'll tell you what kind of manager Ralph was: even the guys who didn't play liked him, which is about as big a compliment as you can pay a manager. He made you want to play for him because he was so nice and because he treated you like men. Plus Ralph was an excellent judge of talent, and he always tried to protect his players.

We had a player by the name of Ron Blomberg. Blomberg was always criticizing Ralph because Ralph always platooned him. Blomberg was a left-handed hitter who could not hit lefty pitchers, and Ralph knew it. But Bloomie would always tell reporters, "I can hit left-handers. I can do this. I can do that. I can hit home runs. Blah. Blah. Blah." But Bloomie wasn't a home run hitter. In batting practice he'd hit ten balls up in the upper deck, but in the game nothing. He was good for maybe ten home runs a year, if that. Mostly his complaint was "I can hit left-handers." But Ralph knew he couldn't, and Ralph tried to protect him for as long as he could. When Bill Virdon replaced Ralph, Ron started dropping his crap on Virdon, and Virdon put him in there against left-handers, and the next thing you know he couldn't hit left-handers or right-handers, his swing was messed up so much.

Blomberg was something. Once he got mad at himself and said, "I should quit baseball and become a doctor and a lawyer." And a lawyer. Jesus, he was something.

I remember we got a big pizza pan, one of those great big pans that go in the oven when the pizza is being cooked, and we took it and hacked the hell out of it until we folded it in half, and then we hung that thing in Blomberg's locker with the sign on it, "BLOMBERG'S GLOVE." That's about how hard his glove was too. He was a first baseman, and in Texas one day I knocked down a line drive barehanded for what would have been the last out, and I threw it over to him and he dropped it. Clank. He said the ball sailed. Another time we were playing in the stadium and Yaz was on second, and there was a ground ball and we got the guy at first, and Yaz kept going right around third and headed home. Bloomie was playing first, and everyone was hollering, "Home. Home." Bloomie looked home, looked again, made a double pump, and threw the ball straight down into the ground, about a nine hopper. Yaz slid, but he didn't have to. And how in the hell he ever got a big contract from Bill Veeck of Chicago is beyond me. For two whole years Blomberg was out with injuries. What makes Veeck think it'll be any different with the White Sox? Maybe he figures he'll be strengthening his team by buying him and writing him off as a tax loss.

We had the Alou brothers when Ralph was here, and one night toward the end of the season, they each popped up in a crucial situation and it cost us the ball game, and George called Ralph and ordered him to release both of them. Ralph told George, "Give me a few days to trade them." They were making big money, around $100,000 each, and they were in their thirties, and if the Yankees had released them, they would have had to take a big pay cut to sign with another team. By trading them Ralph kept them from losing a lot of money. But Felipe—or was it Matty?—got mad at Ralph for trading them so late in the season. He didn't realize that all Ralph was trying to do was protect them. It's too bad. I don't think they ever knew that.

That was the type of thing Ralph did. One day, I remember, we had a pitcher who lost a really tough game, and he got so plastered he was still drunk the next day. We were scheduled to play a day game, and his wife called me and said, "Sparky, he's out cold. What am I going to do?" I said, "Whatever you do, keep him there. Don't even wake him up. I'll take care of it." I went in and told Ralph, and Ralph said, "Well, hell, I can understand that. It was a tough one he lost last night." He said, "I did that a few times myself in my younger days. We'll just tell everyone he has a cold." And that's what he did. I called his wife back because she was real worried. She was afraid her husband was going to get released. She thanked me, her mind was put at ease, and he was able to lie around and get better.

When I accepted the Cy Young Award at the baseball writers' dinner last winter, I said, "I'd like to thank everybody in the Yankees, and most of all I'd like to thank Ralph Houk for giving me the chance to pitch the way I wanted to."

What hurt Ralph more than anything was that he finally had to resign. He told me that he couldn't take any more from George, that he couldn't manage the team looking over his shoulder all the time. George was hollering at him continually, always asking Ralph why he did something, and it was affecting Ralph's managing. Finally Ralph said, "Screw it, I can't stand it anymore," and he resigned. He held a meeting before the last game of the season and told the players he was resigning.

I wasn't at that meeting. The night before, Ralph told me what he was going to do. I was kinda close to Ralph, and we confided in each other. I told him, "I'm not showing up for the game tomorrow." It was a one-game protest to show Ralph how I felt. No one else knew about it—until now.

Before tonight's game Nettles went up to Kenny Clay before he was scheduled to start against the Tigers, and he said, "I don't know if I should be telling you this before the game, but remember what happened to the lassssssssst guy who started and didn't win," meaning Beattie.

Clay went an inning and a third, gave up three runs, and we lost 4 to 3.

Sunday, June 25   Detroit

Goose was pitching in relief of Gullett, who looked sharp beating the Tigers tonight, and toward the end of the game Billy calls down to the bullpen and tells Ellie to get me up as a decoy. He figured that if the Tigers saw me up, they wouldn't bring in a left-handed batter to face Goose. I told Ellie I couldn't figure this one out. If I was managing the other club, and there was a guy on the mound throwing 100-miles-an-hour, and you got another guy in the bullpen throwing 70 or 80, who would you want in that game? What did Ralph do? He sent up three straight left-handers to the plate. Goose struck out two of them and got the other to fly out. The game was televised, so when I started warming up, I knew I wasn't going into the game, so I started throwing pitches behind my back. I had a great time and the crowd out there went wild.

Being in the Yankee bullpen these days is craziness. During the game Art will call up and say, "How much time does so-and-so need to get ready?" This is before the guy has even started to warm up. Ellie'll ask me how long I need. I'll say, "How in hell do I know? Do you want me to get up or not?" Sometimes he does, sometimes he doesn't.

There's so much pressure being put on Billy that he's doing things he ordinarily wouldn't do. One night he called up and said, "Just get up and soft-toss. Throw easy." A minute later he called back and wanted to know if I was ready. His mind is whirling about a hundred different things, and sometimes I think he forgets what he's doing. You can't expect a man to manage with the pressure George puts on him, and I don't even think George realizes this. His answer would be "He can't be a professional manager if he can't take the pressure."

Reggie hasn't been hitting, so Billy decided to DH Reggie and bat him sixth. When Reggie saw that, he took himself out of the lineup. Billy told the reporters he was resting Reggie, but why would you rest Reggie Jackson when a right-hander is pitching? Reggie's ego won't allow anything less than for Reggie to bat fourth and play right field, even when Billy is right. Reggie is 4 for 27 this week, and outside of his home run, he has exactly two RBI's. What makes it worse is that he strikes out two out of three times he gets up.

When the club is playing well, Reggie will hit. When it isn't, the pitchers never give him anything good to hit and he starts swinging at bad pitches. After a while the pitchers will bounce it up there and Reggie will swing at it. When you have a guy hitting fourth striking out so much, it's one of the big reasons why a team will stay in a batting slump for so long. Our other guys get on, and maybe we'll have an out or two with men in scoring position. Reggie comes up and strikes out. If before there was one out, now there're two, and now you need a base hit to score a run where before a long fly would have gotten the run in. That hurts you.

After the game Reggie came into the trainer's room and threw a couple of beer bottles against the wall and smashed them all over the place. We had just won the game and he was carrying on like a maniac. I hollered at him, "What time does Act Two come on?" I thought he was just putting on an act. He said, "What did you say?" I said, "What time does Act Two come on?" Three times he asked me and three times I told him. He didn't say anything more to me after that.

There's no room for that crap, smashing beer bottles against the wall in the trainer's room. Christ, people are running around in their bare feet. What if someone had been around the corner and walked in just as Reggie was throwing a bottle? To me that stuff is uncalled for.

George wants to fire pitching coach Art Fowler. Supposedly George is blaming our problems on Fowler. I also heard that after the last Boston game when Beattie got bombed, he was going to fire Billy. Billy told him, "Shit or get off the pot," that he was tired of hearing all the rumors about getting fired. Rosen was there, too, and Rosen supposedly made the statement that Fowler and Billy were on thin ice. Billy told George, "If you fire Fowler, then I'm quitting."

Art feels bad because he has no control over the injuries that have hit the staff. He really has no control over who pitches well and who doesn't. I told Guidry yesterday when I heard they were going to fire Art, "If they fire him, you go to the papers and raise hell. Tell them, 'Goddamn it, the only reason I'm pitching well this year is Art, and I'm not pitching anymore if he goes.'" I told Gid, "Watch how fast they hire him back." But Gid wasn't going for that. He said, "Nah, nah, nah. I don't think so."

At the airport yesterday, Figueroa and a couple of

other guys came over and shook his hand. Art was in
the sauce and was really down.

I don't know who our new pitching coach would be.
Fred Stanley seems to think it would be Eddie Lopat because Eddie hangs around the clubhouse and always tries
to give little tidbits of advice to the pitchers. Or it could
be Hoyt Wilhelm. He's in our organization now.

Fowler wasn't a bad pitching coach. You'd hear moans
and groans like "Ahhhhh, he doesn't know squat," but
when it came down to the nitty gritty, the guy who made
the statement would eventually go up to Fowler and ask
him something. To me a pitching coach in the big leagues
has to be able to know what you look like when you're
pitching well, so that when you're not, he can say, "You
aren't doing this" or "You aren't doing that."

We won three out of four from the Tigers, but we still
dropped a game in the loss column to Boston, which has
won 14 of its last 16. Don Zimmer, the Boston manager,
made the statement, "We're twenty-nine games over five
hundred, and that means we could play five hundred ball
the rest of the season and still have ninety-five wins.
Maybe that won't be enough, but I guarantee you we
won't play five hundred ball the rest of the way either."

Monday, June 26   New York

With Randolph and Dent out, our defense is hurting and
it's costing us ball games. Today Hobson hit a pop-up
behind second base. Damaso Garcia, that rookie we called
up from Tacoma to replace Randolph, went over and
called for it, and Fred Stanley, playing for Dent, also
drifted under it and called for it. Apparently neither heard
the other 'cause when Garcia tried to catch it, Stanley
hit his arm and the ball dropped for an error. Messersmith
got the next two guys out, but Rice homered and we
were dead. They catch the pop-up, the two runs don't
score, and we're still in the ball game.

With all the rumors floating around about Billy getting
fired, when he brought the lineup card out before the

game, the 50,000 fans gave him a two-minute standing ovation, which really must have burned George's ass. As big an ego as Billy has, George has a bigger one, and he deeply resents the fans' love for Billy. George has spent a lot of money bringing the Yankees back, and George can't figure out why the fans don't love him for that. But the fans aren't dumb. If the guy's a prick, he's a successful prick. It's still Big Daddy George picking on Little Billy, and George should realize that the fans will support Billy until the day George fires him. Maybe even after.

George made the statement that Reggie has let the team down. Christ, Reggie knows he isn't playing well, so why should George go around and say something like that? That's the way George is. Immediately when he signed Reggie, Reggie and him became great friends, and now George is saying, "You've let me down personally." But the interesting thing is when George says something like that, Reggie may get mad at it, but at the same time it's building up what Reggie has been trying to show everyone, that he's the stick that stirs the drink. It's like Reggie's statement, "If we lose, it'll be my fault. If we win, it'll be my doing." That's ridiculous.

Reggie won the final game of the World Series with one of the best performances I've seen since I've been in baseball, but screw it, it's over, and during the course of a season there isn't one man who can make or break a ball club, I don't give a damn who it is, including Babe Ruth. Even Guidry, as great as he's going right now, can't do it. You couldn't ask for a better performance from one man than from Gid. He's got 12 wins and no losses, but what are 12 wins in the midst of what we're in? No one could put forth more of an effort for a team than Guidry, and if you compare that to what Reggie's done, Reggie looks like a peon.

Fowler was still with the team today. I don't know what his status is.

Tuesday, June 27   New York

George, Rosen, Billy, and Billy's agent Doug Newton met for two and a half hours, and after it was over Steinbrenner issued a statement that Billy will be the Yankee manager for the rest of the season no matter what. When we heard that, we said, "He'll be gone in two days." When George says things like "You'll be here as long as I am," as he told Bobby Murcer before trading him to the Giants, the next thing you know you're gone. As soon as we heard that, we said, "Goddamn, he doesn't have much time left." The last time George said something like that was when he told Dock Ellis, "You're going to be here all year. You're not going anywhere." All of a sudden, bang, he's gone. It's almost a sure thing. It's like when a player finally buys a home and gets traded the next day. It's like the kiss of death.

It looks like Fowler's going to keep his job too. Art was really hammered coming off the plane from Boston, knowing he was going to be gone. What stopped it is that Billy told George, "If he goes, I go." It's hard to say exactly what happened at that meeting. There was some talk that George offered Billy money to quit and go run his boys' camp. George supposedly was worried about Billy's health. All I know is that Billy and Art are still here.

I keep telling Billy not to make me a long man. If only he'd listen. Like tonight, Goose relieved Gid in the sixth and held the Red Sox through the eleventh, and then Billy brought me in and I held them scoreless till the fourteenth, when Graig hit a home run off Dick Drago to end it. It was the best I've thrown all year. Now if only a couple of starters would go all the way and give us a little rest for a day or two.

Wednesday, June 28   Milwaukee

Thurman began a three-game suspension for bumping
umpire Jim McKean in Detroit last Thursday, so our
lineup for a doubleheader against the Brewers did not
include our starting catcher Munson, our double-play
combination Dent and Randolph, who are hurt, and center fielder Rivers, who is also hurt. In the second game
Billy gave Graig a rest, and with Brian Doyle playing in
his place, we fielded a starting infield of Chambliss, Garcia, Stanley, and Doyle. With so many pitchers hurting,
we started Larry McCall, who did fine until the seventh,
holding them at 2 to 2. Sixto Lezcano singled, and after
umpire Rich Garcia called a balk on him. the kid really
became unglued. It was the kid's first start, and after that
call McCall got really shook up. After that the Brewers
bombed him, and it was all over for us.

In the first game we got a grand total of six hits, all
singles, and zero runs against Mike Caldwell. Roy White
got three of the hits, and since he started playing regularly two weeks ago, he's hitting over .300. But that's
typical for Roy. They always want to trade him or keep
him on the bench, but when they finally have to put him
in the game, he's the best guy out there.

The Red Sox won again, putting us ten back. Things
are not exactly looking up, and I'm sure George is getting
more and more impatient with the way things are going.

When I came into the clubhouse and saw Billy, I said,
"Goddamn, are you still here?" He just laughed. "Yeah,
yeah," he said.

Friday, June 30   New York

It looks like Billy is going to get his way as to playing
Reggie the way he wants to. Today's lineup had Johnstone and Spencer leading off, with Fred Stanley, who
usually bats ninth, third. Nettles batted fourth, Chambliss
fifth, Piniella sixth, and Reggie seventh. All Reggie did

was go 3 for 5, hit a grand-slam home run, and drive
in five runs in a 10–2 win over Detroit. Reggie called
Steinbrenner a fool for saying he had let the team down.

Reggie's ego is going to continue to take a beating,
though, if George allows Billy to keep batting Reggie
seventh. At least Reggie is still playing right field. If it
was up to Billy, Reggie would bat seventh and be the
DH.

Gullett won his fourth without a loss, and if he'd stay
healthy we'd have a chance to catch Boston.

Saturday, July 1   New York

Messersmith started, walked five in an inning and two-
thirds, gave up a few hits, and allowed three runs. That
was the good part. The bad: from the other end of the
clubhouse I was watching him get dressed after the game.
He was holding his right arm flush against his body, trying to put his pants on with one hand. I said to myself,
"Holy Christ." There was more. Kenny Clay relieved him,
allowed three runs in an inning and a third, and he also
hurt his arm. After the game his arm was in a sling. I
figured it was time for the M.A.S.H. helicopters to come
down, drop two off, pick two up, see ya.

I feel so bad for both of them. Kenny's worried like
a son of a bitch. He hurt himself in a new place, and
when that happens, it's a very traumatic experience, especially for a pitcher.

After they pitched, I came in the third, got 'em out
through the fifth, and gave way to Dirt, who finished up.
After Billy took me out, I got dressed and figured, "Screw
it, I'll beat the traffic." You're not supposed to do it, but
I left the ball park before the game was over and went
home. On the way I was listening to the end of the
game on the radio, and Phil Rizzuto announces that Jim
Spencer is warming up in the bullpen. I almost turned
around and went back. I figured I would see this. With
Eastwick and Holtzie gone, we only have three guys left
in the bullpen: Goose, me, and this kid Kammeyer, who's
a rookie. Tidrow mopped up, and Spencer wasn't needed.

Sunday, July 2   New York

Mickey Rivers returned after being out two weeks with a hairline fracture of his hand. He hadn't been able to swing a bat, and after being away, it'll be a while before he gets his stroke back. Once our ball club starts playing a little better, once a couple of guys get hot, you wait, a couple more will get hot, and they won't be able to pitch around guys. Right now they're throwing righthanders against us and beating us. When that happens, you know we're in trouble.

Goose relieved in both games of our doubleheader against the Tigers. He saved the first one for Gid, who is now 13 and 0, and he was the winner in the second game when Thomasson hit a home run in the bottom of the ninth. We brought this kid Dave Rajsich up from Tacoma to pitch the second game, and he went four and two-thirds. Who do you think relieved him? Billy still wants me to be the long man, and even though our staff is a disaster, I still cannot accept that role. I will not accept it. I just won't.

I went to see Billy after the game, and on his desk I noticed the list of names for players going to the All-Star game. I told him to take my name off the list. I said, "You're going to get a lot of static if you take both Goose and me. I haven't exactly been setting the league on fire." Even though I'm 6 and 1 with seven saves, I'm really not doing that good a job. My ERA is way over three, and it doesn't look good to pick me when there are other pitchers with better stats. There's no reason for me to go. Billy said he understood and said he'd pick someone else.

We're eight behind the Sox and fly to Boston tonight for two games.

Monday, July 3 Boston

More bad news. Figgie left in the fourth with a painful elbow after giving seven hits and six runs, and in the sixth Thurman injured his knee running the bases and had to leave the game. Thurm'll be OK, but Figgie'll be out for at least a week. Art is just devastated by what has happened to our pitching staff. He says he's never seen so many sore arms at one time on one club.

I was telling reporters about a clipboard we ought to have out in the bullpen. When you go there, they should make you sign one of three columns: Old, New, or Departed. The list for "Departed" is the longest of the three. On that list are Holtzman and Eastwick, who were traded, Messersmith, Catfish, and Clay, who are on the disabled list, and Beattie and McCall, who were sent back to the minors. Now Figgie's hurt.

After he went out, Long Man Lyle got the last out in the fourth inning and pitched the fifth, and Kammeyer finished up. Kammeyer pitches pretty well. He moves the ball around a lot. The bad thing is, if he misses, he gets hit pretty hard. Let me put it this way: I don't think he's our savior.

Eckersley, who beat us June 21 and June 26, beat us again. When Gabe traded Eckersley from Cleveland during spring training I didn't think too much of it, but you gotta admit, the guy isn't doing too badly for himself. We're nine back again.

After the game I walked into the trainer's room, and on the wall was white adhesive tape about three feet long in the shape of the letter P. I don't know what the hell that's all about. I'm afraid to ask.

Wednesday, July 5 Arlington

Billy has a rule that we have to wear coats and ties when we're on the road. Today we flew into Texas, and when we got there it must have been 100 degrees out. It was so hot that I refused to wear a coat and tie and sweat my balls off to walk through an airport. I don't see why if you want to wear a suit and have your shirt open without a tie, you can't. To me, that's just as presentable.

Because of the injuries, we've been shuffling the lineup around more than ever, and that really hurts the ball club. Monday Garcia forgot to cover first on a bunt, and it cost us. He's a good athlete, but he's not yet experienced enough. Today we lost when he made another rookie mistake. We were tied 2 to 2 in the eighth, with Richie Zisk, a pull-hitter, up. There was a runner on third, and Goose was pitching, when Billy noticed that Garcia wasn't playing close enough to second base. Billy was yelling his lungs out over the crowd noise and Zisk hit the ball right where Billy wanted him to play to drive in the winning run.

It isn't just Garcia. I've never seen balls screwed up between infielders and outfielders so many times, because nobody knows what the other guy is doing, and that puts a mood over the club where everyone says, "Goddamn, it's so easy not to have that happen." The outfielder calls off the infielder. It sounds so easy, but there's a lack of communication between the players because they haven't been playing together. Johnstone and Thomasson have been in the outfield and Stanley's at short and Garcia or Doyle at second, and these guys never played with one another before. Most people don't realize the teamwork that's needed to play baseball. Teamwork isn't a tug of war where everyone's pulling together, the old rah-rah crap that George likes. It's communication, working together in the field, hitting the cut-off man, knowing what the other guy is going to do, and this comes from playing together for a long time.

That's been the difference between Boston and us. They have a set lineup, and those guys play every day. With us, no one ever knows what the lineup's going to be from one day to the next, except Chambliss, Nettles, and Thurman. Nobody else knows what their job is right now. When you know you're going to play, and where, you can get ready for the game. When you don't know if you're going to play, what do you have to look forward

to? There's no sense psyching yourself up. It begins to
reach the point where you get to the park, see your name
in the starting lineup, and say, "Great, I'm playing, but
I'm just not ready to play today."

The way we're playing, it's bad when a kid makes a
mistake because it gives everyone the chance to say,
"Goddamn, that cost us a ball game." But that isn't what
cost us the game. We're playing badly. We don't have our
first team out there, and it just gives everybody something to put the blame on.

John Matlack, a tough left-hander, started against us
tonight. Billy benched Reggie. Piniella played right, Cliff
DHed. It didn't help.

Thursday, July 6   Arlington

Billy held a meeting before the game and complained that
some of the guys weren't wearing their ties and jackets on
the road. I was one of those guys. Yesterday I wore an
open sports shirt and a pair of jeans. I wasn't defying the
manager, and neither were the other players who didn't
wear ties. It's not that at all. It was too un-fucking-com-
fortable. Billy said, "If you keep doing this, I'm going to
have to fine you, and I don't want to fine you." Hey,
I'm willing to accept a fine. Fine me the $50 and quit
bullshitting about it. When I walked off the plane, if he
had said, "That will be fifty dollars," I wouldn't have been
pissed. Take it out of my check, but quit hemming and
hawing about it. That's half our problem. There are rules
that, when they're broken, nothing is ever done about it.
Why make rules? That's one of the things that caused
us to get off on the wrong foot this year. The rule is
no card playing before the game. Little by little they
started to get the cards out. Never once did Billy come in
and say, "Knock off the Goddamn card game." It was
always, "Art, tell them no more card playing." Billy never
did it himself. So it became an everyday thing.

Ever since Billy took over as manager in 1975, he's
been setting down rules and not enforcing them. It was
always "All right, Goddamn it, there's not going to be

any more of this" or "I'm taking your money. I don't
want to take it, but I'm going to take it." Then the player
would do it again, and still nothing would happen. He
still didn't fine him. Then Billy would hold another meeting and he'd say, "All right, I said I was going to take
your money, and I didn't. I was lenient 'cause I thought
maybe you'd learn. *Now* I'm going to do it. If you don't
want to obey, I'm going to take your money for sure."
Still, nothing would happen. After he cried wolf like
that, you started not to believe him.

The other thing is, you begin to get the feeling that
Billy has one standard for the regulars and another for
the guys who sit on the bench. A bench guy makes a
mistake out there, and you get the feeling, "Christ, he'll
yell at Fred Stanley, but he doesn't yell at Lou Piniella
or Thurman or Reggie, or any of the other starters. The
shit bums, as we call them, they know they're going to
be ridiculed if they do something wrong. Billy jumps on
their ass all the time about little mistakes. Like he jumped
on Brian Doyle's ass the other night because he didn't
catch a ball. The kid tried, but Billy jumped on his ass
about it. This hurts the little player because he says to
himself, "I can see why he jumps on my ass, but when
so-and-so does the same thing, he doesn't say squat to
him." And that little guy, he isn't going to open his
mouth. He's afraid to for fear he'll be sent down or won't
be allowed to play the 20 games he would have.

And when the manager's always jumping on the little
guy, it keeps snowballing to where you start noticing every
little thing that happens. It's like a person who you hadn't
realized was a stutterer. Then all of a sudden you notice
it, and it becomes an obsession to where you hate to talk
with the guy because he stutters so much. You just notice it more and more. That's what's happening here. You
start noticing every little, weak thing that goes on—
things that don't mean a damn thing to winning or losing
ball games, things that just add to the dissension on the
club.

The Rangers are a team with problems of their own.
They made four errors tonight and handed us four unearned runs, as Tidrow went all the way to win it. Reggie

batted seventh again as DH and got a couple of hits.
Thomasson was in right and also got a couple of hits.
I'm surprised that George is letting Billy play Reggie this
way, and I'm also surprised that Reggie hasn't said anything.

Saturday, July 8   Milwaukee

I finally talked with Billy about his using me as a long
man. He never puts me in the game in a situation when
I could get a save. Either I go in when we're behind or
I pitch the middle innings and Goose picks me up and
gets the save. Last year I won the Cy Young Award as
a short reliever, and this year I have seven crummy saves.
It's humiliating. At this point I don't know what I'm
going to do, but Billy's buried me and I won't let him
keep doing that. When I told Billy about it, his answer
was that I'm the only one who can do the long man job.
Well, hell, let someone else pitch the middle innings sometimes, and let me finish. But George would never allow
that. Goose got almost $3 million, and George would
never allow me to have a better record than Goose. I
gotta get out of here.

Rajsich started against the Brewers, got his hand ripped
open by a line drive, and it's back to the minors for him.
Graig had strained a muscle in his left big toe yesterday
during Gid's 6 to 0 loss to the Brewers, and he didn't
play, and in the second inning Bucky, who was making
his first start at shortstop since early June, came back
too early and reinjured his hamstring, and it's back to the
disabled list for him. For the second night in a row Larry
Hisle hit two home runs. The second one beat Goose for
the eighth time. With the Red Sox winning, we've sunk
to eleven and a half out. Milwaukee's now in second, ten
back.

What we desperately need is a couple of well-pitched
ball games to bring the team around. We need to win
a game 1 to 0 or 2 to 1 to take some of the pressure
off the hitters. Our pitching hasn't been good, and the
hitting hasn't been good enough to make up for it. The

hitters are tired of hearing they aren't hitting enough. They know it. But there's nothing that can be done about it.

Sunday, July 9 Milwaukee

For the third day in a row the Brewers went out and really kicked our ass. Don Gullett couldn't get through the first inning, and his arm is hurting so badly he can barely lift it. Gullett may be finished for the season along with Cat. Jim Beattie pitched a no-hitter for Tacoma today, and I guarantee you that you'll see him back in a Yankee uniform real soon. A healthy arm is a healthy arm.

Reggie and Billy are at it again. Bill Travers, who is left-handed, started for Milwaukee today, and Reggie spent the game on the bench. Reggie is now saying that Billy makes up excuses for not playing him, which I can't understand. Reggie once went up to Billy and said, "I don't want to play because so-and-so is pitching." Then after the game when George wanted to know why he didn't play, Reggie turned around and said, "Beats me."

Reggie hasn't been talking much around the clubhouse, but he keeps telling the press how humiliating it is for him when Billy benches him against lefties. Reggie was saying, "If I don't produce, I don't play." Well, hell, how many weeks does he expect Billy to leave him in there before he starts doing something? Reggie has always said, "If Reggie Jackson doesn't hit, the Yankees don't win." Well, no kidding. When he's in the fucking number four spot and he's striking out all the time, that's the truth—we're not going to win with him not hitting, which is one of the Yankees' big problems right now.

Piniella was complaining to reporters about how bad the atmosphere in the clubhouse is, that there are people who don't want to be there. That's true. I'm one of those guys. You could probably find out the same thing from almost everyone in this club. They wouldn't give a damn if they were traded or not. We know we have a good ball club, but when you're eleven and a half games behind and you're losing and things are happening to you like what's been going on on this year, you don't bother looking for the bright side. You don't even think about it. Every little thing that goes wrong is intensified. You think, "Aw Jesus, not again," and everyone starts saying, "I have to get the hell out of here and get a new start, play with another team where I don't have to put up with this crap that's going around, where I can get my mind back on baseball and playing well again. That's why I want to leave. I want to go somewhere where I can pitch and be effective again. At least if I get my ass kicked then, it'll be because I'm not pitching well enough.

Lou says guys are unhappy and want to go. Hell, Lou's one of those guys too. He's always pissing and moaning. He's always saying, "Ah crap, I wish Billy and George would leave me alone to do my job." And just about everybody on the club is guilty of that except maybe the new guys like Thomasson and Doyle. Thomasson wants to play baseball, and if we could get that attitude back, we'd go out and play better. But George is pissing everyone off with all this crap between him and Billy, and Billy's pissing the players off, and those things alone are enough to destroy a ball club.

George feels that the only way to be successful is to push and press his employees, including his manager and players. You cannot push a player to do more than what he is capable of doing, I don't give a damn who he is. God couldn't do it that way. When you keep harping and pushing, pushing, pushing, the ballplayer says, "Screw it, I can't take this crap anymore." But it's the way George runs his team. It's his obsessive personality that pushed George to bring in all the free agents, which has created a lot of unhappiness among some of the players.

Figgie was telling reporters today how happy the Yankee team had been before the free agents. Our '76 team was the nucleus for a very together ball club. It wasn't our most talented club, but it was the best all around. Everybody knew exactly what his job was, and everyone had a specific job. Oscar Gamble knew that when a left-hander started for the other team, he wasn't playing, and he knew that if it was a righty, he'd be playing. And he'd be ready to play that day. There was no guessing. Our '76 team had gotten its ass kicked in the World Series, but we were proud of what we had done and we knew that in '77 we were gonna be the ones who were going to do the ass kicking, and we also knew it was going to be a lot of fun.

Then George started buying all these free agents. He paid a ton of dough to guys like Gullett, Jackson, and Goose, and he got guys for the bench like Bob Oliver, Jimmy Wynn, Cliff Johnson, and Jay Johnstone, guys who had been used to playing every day. You can't sit these guys down and expect them to pinch-hit a home run every time. It just doesn't happen that easy. When they're not playing regularly, they don't play well. And when they found themselves sitting on the bench, there was a lot of bitching and moaning. The guys want to play. So there is such a thing as having too much talent on a club. It can destroy a ball club. It can destroy the careers of some guys. Sitting on the bench takes the drive out of them because regardless of how well they do when they get in there, they still know that they're not going to play every day. All they start thinking about is "I have to get out of here."

The '77 team may have had more talent, but I think the guys on the '76 team could have repeated without the free agents, which isn't a knock at the free agents. You have to sign them, or you're not going to keep winning. But after paying them all that money, George then had an obligation to take care of the people who had been helping him all along, people like Willie Randolph and Figgie and me, and he didn't do it. All of a sudden these other people are brought in, and they become George's close friends, which is another bullshit thing, and you feel like a schmuck when they tell you to go out there and give 110 percent. You start wondering, "Why the hell should I do that anymore?" There's no sense in it, outside of pride in yourself, which makes you play the game the best you can. But what I'm talking about is how you feel, and you feel like it's a wasted effort when you're not appreciated. It's like working ten hours overtime and not getting paid for it.

George always tells his ballplayers, "If you don't win, heads will roll." Well, we won two years in a row, and they couldn't have rolled any more heads than if we had come in last. We don't have five Goddamned guys left from the '76 team. But again, that's George. To him it's cutthroat. It's a business. Like what happened to Bobby Murcer. George told Bobby he'd be with the Yankees as long as George was there. George had Bobby to where he felt they were such good friends that George would never do anything to hurt him. Bobby became sort of a spokesman for George. When I was having contract trouble one year, Murcer came to me a couple of times and spoke to me on George's behalf, and the next thing you know, George stuck it right up Bobby's ass, traded him to the Giants for Bobby Bonds. And this is what George is going to do to everyone sooner or later. You may be friends, but when the time comes, it's "Gee, Sparky Lyle can't help us anymore."

Yet I don't condemn George for this. I really don't. I don't think guys should be pissed off at George for what he does to them. If they're mad at anyone, they should be mad at themselves for believing his crap. It's a business to George. You can't sit there and take in everything he promises you and believe it and think that it's going to be as he says. It won't be. And it never will be.

Tuesday, July 11   Lake George, New York

I'm really glad I didn't go to the All-Star game. Mary and I have been camping out in the woods, and we're having a wonderful time away from the madness. Goose went to the game, Billy brought him in, and he ended up getting his ass kicked and losing the game. Just like what happened to me last year.

You can pitch during the regular season and not have your good stuff and get by, but in the All-Star game you have no chance. I don't care who goes out there. If you have the good stuff, you'll be all right. But if you don't when you're facing one tremendous hitter after another, boy, it's very scary. Goose still hasn't gotten sharp, and he didn't have a prayer out there in San Diego this evening.

I remember my first All-Star game. It was in '73, and I was very happy to have made that team because I never dreamed I'd get a chance to play in one. I thought I should have been named after some of the years I had had before that, but I wasn't, so I really hadn't counted on ever playing in one. Managers rarely pick relief pitchers anyhow. Ordinarily they use starters in relief. The game was in Kansas City, and I remember pitching to Willie Mays, who had announced that it would be his last year. I struck him out on three pitches.

The writers asked me if I felt bad striking Willie Mays out in his last All-Star game. I said, "Hell no. Why should I feel bad?" They said, "It was his last All-Star game." I said, "I don't know what you're getting at, but I felt real good about striking him out. Real good. I'm sorry I didn't get the chance to strike him out twice."

I went to the All-Star game three times, in '73 and the last two years, but I don't want to go again. The All-Star game is a popularity contest, a matter of being in the right place at the right time. Take Mark Belanger, for instance. He played for years before he got into an All-Star game, and he's been the top fielding shortstop every year. He plays as well as anybody, but the fans don't even look at him. The ballplayers should pick the players. We play against the guys. We know who's hitting the best and who's having the best years. Some of the best guys sometimes don't even get on the ballot because they're rookies or they got traded, and another guy who's on the ballot, he may be having a lousy year, but he's going to get votes. It's so ridiculous.

Graig hurt his toe in our last game against Boston and, as a result, missed the last couple of games before the All-Star break. Graig had been elected to be the starting third baseman for the American League in the All-Star game, but the Yankee management called him up and told him he couldn't go, which made him mad as hell. They said it was for his own good, which made him even madder. The game was played in San Diego, Graig's hometown, and he wanted to play in front of his family and friends. Jeez. How could they do that to him after the way he's played for the New York Yankees?

Graig has been jerked around more than anyone on this team. He had a contract problem last year, which they could have taken care of in a matter of minutes, but no, they had to mess with his mind for three-quarters of a season before straightening it out. The front office gave him a lot of grief about his contract, and they didn't give a damn about him. You know, the old "You play third base and shut your Goddamn mouth" sort of thing. It's unbelievable what George did to him.

When Graig signed a contract in July 1976, George and Graig agreed that Graig would get some deferred compensation. Graig asked George the best way to do it, and George set it up in such a way that Graig would be able to take the money any time he wanted. The only problem with that was that the IRS doesn't see it as deferred compensation if you can take it any time you want. George had given him the worst possible advice.

What made things complicated was that in August the owners and players agreed to a new contract, one that gave the players the right no longer to be bound to the reserve clause after a certain number of years, and when Graig discovered last spring that he had tax problems, when he went to George and asked him to change the contract to get him a better tax break on his deferred compensation, George refused to do it. George was afraid to change it because he didn't want Graig under a new contract. When Graig got mad, as he had every right to be, and walked out of camp, George made him look bad in the press. George came out with this: "If Graig realizes he made a mistake by leaving this team and he learns from it, I'm willing to sit down and help him. But he has to stand up like a man and admit he made a mistake." The next day Graig handed in a printed statement saying he was sorry.

And now all of a sudden the tide has turned where they need him. They're afraid he's going to hurt himself worse by playing in the All-Star game, so now it's "For your own good, Graig, we feel . . ." They're acting real concerned. And what really pissed him off was that they weren't concerned about him as a person at all. All they

cared about was a void that they might not be able to
fill. It just proves one more time how management dicks
you around, dicks you around until they need you, and
all of a sudden they turn around and look you in the
eye and act real sincere and expect you to believe them
and buy what they say. It's like a guy sticking you in
the back with a knife and then turning around and putting a bandage on and fixing you up. Graig just said,
"Go screw yourself. I'm playing."

The only way Graig got to play was that the day before the game, Reggie called in and said he had a tem-
perature, and they put Graig on in Reggie's place.

The second half of the season began today, and before
the game George held a meeting. I knew he wouldn't be
able to go through an entire season without jumping in.
He couldn't stand it. He's done everything he could to
stay in the background, but he can no longer stand by
and watch this crap. It's not his nature. I will say this
for him: when he makes up his mind to do something,
he'll do it come hell or high water. He'll get a lot of
flack for this after his promise not to interfere, but he
won't give a damn. That's what makes him so interesting.

You can usually tell when George holds a meeting.
When it's Billy's meeting, it's "Meeting in five minutes."
When George holds a meeting, it's "The guys better get
over here. We're having a meeting." This afternoon
George was in Billy's office, and Billy came out and
started to say, "Will you gather round here, please," and
right in the middle of the sentence, we heard, "Can I
have your attention? Can I have your attention?" It was
George. He said, "We've done it your way for the first
half of the season and it didn't work, and now we're
going to do it my way. I still believe we can win the
pennant, but we're going to have to try harder. I've had
a talk with Billy, and there are going to be some changes
made, and if you don't like them, come and see me, and
I'll try to accommodate you."

He said, "There are going to be some changes made in
the lineup, some players aren't going to be playing as
much, but there's no sense in getting mad. This is the

way it's going to be. It's my ball club. I sign the checks and I'll do what I want."

Under George's lineup, Thurman will play right field, rookie Mike Heath will catch, Reggie will DH, and Gary Thomasson will be in left. George is also bringing in Clyde King to help coach the pitchers. Lou and Roy end up on the bench, or Lou may end up DHing against lefties, which means that Reggie's the DH against righties and nothing else.

It wasn't one of those "Rah rah, you have to have balls" meetings that George likes. It was short and sweet. Still, you can shuffle the guys around all you want, and you still can't play Randolph and Dent 'cause they're out, and you can't start Messersmith or Clay or Cat or Gullett 'cause they're out. We have exactly three starters left: Guidry, Dirt, and Figgie, and Figgie's forearm has been hurting. That leaves Beattie and this kid Rajsich. They're good prospects. Plus, nobody's going to make any trades with us 'cause Rosen refuses to trade unless it's a steal for the Yankees. I do not mind telling you that we are in a shitload of trouble.

After George left the clubhouse, Billy finished the meeting. He told us we are going to get a list of dos and don'ts, and he brought up the tie thing again. He said he was now going to enforce the tie rule. It's going to be $25 for the first time, and it escalates up. I just can't see bringing this up time and again. Just fine me and get it over with. Saying, "We're going to do this, we're going to do that," that's half the trouble. They set down rules, and when we break them, nothing's said. Everybody's guilty of not wearing ties, not just one or two guys. But not wearing ties isn't why we're not winning.

After the meeting was over, Mickey Rivers was talking about George's moves. He feels they're horseshit. "He shouldn't be screwing around with a team that won the World Championship," he said. "It ain't right to panic. All Steinbrenner has to do is wait until the hurting guys get healthy. Then we would have started to win. There isn't any need for this crap." Mickey's right about George, but George doesn't have the patience to wait for the guys to get well. He wants to start winning now.

* * *

To me the worst part of George's shuffling the lineup is with Thurman in right field, they have to alternate Thomasson and Lou in left. I don't agree with that because I don't give a damn who's pitching, when Lou gets hot, he can hit anybody. All they're going to do now is screw up Lou's stroke. And I don't know why Thurman's not catching anymore, unless his legs are hurting so much he can't catch. I'd rather see him behind the plate, Thomasson in left and Lou in right, with Reggie DHing. That's our best ball club. Thomasson's good. He's an aggressive ballplayer. He wants to play. He's hit a couple of home runs that have helped us, and he's a steady outfielder. One game he slid into the fence and caught the ball to save the game. That's what we need. A couple of more plays like that could turn this club right around. It happened last year. We came from behind a couple of times, and it fired up the whole team, and there we were, playing good all of a sudden. Right now, we're far from that. It's going to be a long, hard road. Today Garcia made an error that let in two unearned runs, and we lost to the White Sox, 6 to 1. Fortunately, the Red Sox also lost. We're 11 games out, and we're going to have to play better ball to have a chance at catching the Sox.

Friday, July 14   New York

Gid's arm finally may be tired. He gave up six runs in the nine innings he pitched, but he didn't lose because Cliff hit a pinch-hit home run in the bottom of the ninth inning to tie it. Goose won it in relief in the eleventh when Graig drove Reggie home with a single. Willie Randolph played his first game since mid-June, and it was great to see him back. It's nice to win every once in a while when you're playing poorly.

There haven't been many funny things happening. It's been very quiet. I didn't think I would ever see this on the ball club, but it has a lot to do with what Billy's been through. He looks awful, and he hasn't slept much, and George is giving him a rough time 'cause we're so far back, and nobody wants to intimidate him any more than he has been already. Billy doesn't like us to carry on, especially after we lose, so we haven't been. Not that anybody really feels like carrying on. We're getting tired of losing. This may sound like the players want to keep Billy, and I believe they do. After you play for him awhile, off and on you hate him and like him, but that's his way of sparking a ball club. Some of the guys have been saying, "Maybe they should fire him," but when they start to talk about who would replace him, they say, "Christ, keep the man."

I saw Catfish today for the first time in a couple of weeks. He's been through so much this year, and a lot of people think he may be finished. He even might think that. If he does, he's not going to hang on. He'll just say, "Screw it. See ya." He has too much pride to hang on.

As a last resort Cat was put under anesthesia, and the Yankee orthopedist, Dr. Maurice Cowen, stretched his pitching arm back farther than Cat could have by himself. By doing this, Dr. Cowen broke the adhesions in his arm which were causing him pain and keeping him from throwing naturally. What's hard for me to understand is how they know just the right amount to bend the son of a bitch. Do they bend it this far? or this far? or this far? How do you know what when you wake up your arm won't fall off?

Saturday, July 15   New York

George has been saying all along that he would call me up to his office when he was ready to talk about my contract, and today he made the call. I told Mary, "If he offers me close to what I want, I'll sign." I'm not the type of guy who harps on something and fights, and then at the very end when the other guy makes an offer, says to himself, "Well, hell, if he'll give me this much, I'll try and get a little bit more." When I arrived at George's office, he said he would give me $200,000 a year for the next three years, and it's their option whether they want to pick me up for the 1981 season. I agreed to that because if I can't pitch by 1981, what the hell, nobody's going to want me anyway.

It's a fair offer, and I'm satisfied. I really hadn't been expecting anything like that from George. I had learned to cope with my depression over the money and was at peace with myself. I had lost my fire and had quit trying to piss George off. I just accepted what was as what was. If he had called me and said tough shit again, I probably wouldn't have said a thing. I might very well have said, "Okay, screw it," and been satisfied with my $135,000 a year.

Figgie made his first start since July 3 and gave up eight runs in four innings. Dennis Leonard beat us 8 to 2. In the second, Figgie had Pete LaCock 0 and 2, and threw him a curve. It was the same sort of thing that happened with Ron Fairly. LaCock hit it out, and the Royals had a 5 to 0 lead. Me and Kammeyer mopped up.

For the second game in a row Billy had Reggie DHing and batting sixth. The way he's been hitting, he's lucky he isn't lower in the order. We're a better team when Reggie's not playing the outfield, and we're a better team when he's not hitting in the number four spot because he strikes out too much. Billy has known this all along. Unfortunately for Billy, George puts pressure on Billy to bat Reggie fourth and play him in right. When Reggie's in a slump like he is now, he strikes out a hell of a lot with runners on base. We lost a lot of games 'cause of that this year, and as long as he does this I guess we're going to lose a lot more. And what makes it bad is that when he strikes out, he doesn't put any pressure at all on the opposing pitcher. The pitcher just throws the ball anywhere. That's all, just throw it up there 'cause he's not going to touch it. With men on base, it's important to put pressure on that pitcher, to make him throw a wild pitch or make him pitch in and out, up and down to tire him out. If they would put someone who doesn't strike out a lot in there, you're gonna have a different ball game. Some of those runners would score.

Billy batted Munson third, Chambliss fourth, and Nettles fifth. It's a smart move on Billy's part.

Sunday, July 16   New York

We were losing 3 to 1 with the bases loaded. Lou Piniella
got up against Larry Gura, and he hit a ball 430 feet—
where it was caught by Amos Otis in the deepest part of
Death Valley. Lou couldn't believe it! He thought he had
a home run for sure, that he had won the ball game, and
all he ended up with was a long out. After the game he
was moaning and groaning about Yankee Stadium. Piniella was saying, "To hit a home run here you need help
from Superman, Batman, Robin, Spiderman, Wonder
Woman, Godzilla, King Kong," and he kept naming more
and more comic book characters. We've lost eight out
of ten, Boston is 13 games in front, and the way things
are going, we'll be watching the play-offs this fall on
Channel 4.

Gura, who's now 7 and 2 for Kansas City, played for
the Yankees, but one morning last spring Billy saw him
and Rich Coggins in their whites going to play tennis.
Billy, who calls tennis a pussy game, went right up a tree.
You have to understand, Billy was seeing this guy who
hadn't been pitching well going out to play tennis. Billy
said to himself, "What the hell is he playing tennis for
when he isn't pitching worth a crap? Swinging that racket
can't be doing his pitching any good. No wonder he's
horseshit." Gura, on the other hand, is thinking, "I'm
keeping in shape playing tennis." They're looking at it
from different standpoints. But the manager, of course, is
going to win out. Billy said, "I'll get rid of them fuckers."
And that's just what he did.

Reggie didn't play tonight. Gura's a lefty, and Billy
benched Reggie in favor of right-handed Cliff Johnson, who
is making the situation worse by going 0 for 4 every
time he plays. These days when Reggie plays, it's only
to DH, which I know he doesn't like. Even so, Reggie
hasn't said very much. He told reporters, "I'm not talking anymore." Who knows what's lurking in the heart of
Mr. October? I'm sure we'll find out soon.

On the surface it seems that Billy's sitting Reggie down against lefties is bad on Billy's part, and yet Billy isn't treating Reggie any different from the way he treats anyone else. A number of guys like Piniella, Thomasson, and Roy White were even hitting the ball and found themselves sitting. Spencer was one of the hottest hitters on the team for a little while, and all of a sudden he stopped playing. When you're struggling like we are, you have to try things, and Reggie hasn't been swinging the bat very well, and that's the reason Billy takes him out. Not for any other reason.

It's hard to tell what's running through Reggie's mind. Billy has finally been allowed to keep Reggie out of the outfield because he hurts us too much out there, but any time a manager does that to a ballplayer, especially a ballplayer with an ego as big as Reggie's, the ballplayer is going to go into a tizzy. No ballplayer likes to be told he sucks, even if he knows it's true, and what makes it worse is that because it's New York, the Yankees, the team of controversy, Reggie Jackson, Billy Martin, George Steinbrenner, it gets magnified way out of proportion, and everyone makes a big deal out of it. The writers are now going to run over to Reggie and ask him provocative questions like "Is Billy deliberately showing you up?" or "Do you think you're good enough to play right field?"; questions like that, and Reggie's going to say something bitchy, and then the writers will go back to Billy, and after the writers get finished with them, there's going to be some shit flying.

Billy didn't want Reggie on the Yankees. Billy wanted Joe Rudi, a right-handed batter who hits in the clutch and who's an excellent defensive outfielder. Rudi, however, isn't very colorful, and he isn't a draw. Reggie, with his big mouth and his big swing, puts people in the park. Plus he's a home run hitter and he makes a good play in the field once every once in a while. George knew this and spent almost $3 million to sign him. What George didn't know was that this guy is a real piece of work.

After George signed him, when he told the papers, "I didn't come to New York to become a star. I brought my star with me," right then I knew. I said to myself, "This guy is going to be trouble." He's always telling everybody

how great he is, and you never know whether he believes
the stuff he says or not. This spring he told a TV reporter
how important it was that people respect him. Then he
said, "But to be respected, you have to be godly." Godly?
Is he kidding? I respect plenty of people, but not one of
them looks like the Pope, or Charlton Heston even.

Reggie's a mystery to me. He's a very intelligent guy.
I've watched him on TV when he announces for ABC's
Superstar competition during the offseason. He ad-libs,
jokes around, uses the right words, and you can see that
Reggie's a really smart person. If you listened to Reggie,
you'd think he was the only intelligent guy on the whole
Yankee team. That's what Reggie says—over and over.
He told that to Carlos May once. May didn't give a
damn what his IQ was and told him so. Reggie said, "You
can't even spell IQ." Another time Reggie was giving
Mickey Rivers the same jive. "My IQ is 160," he told
Mickey. Mickey looked at Reggie and said, "Out of what,
Buck, a thousand?" Cracked everybody up. Reggie's always trying to show Mickey how much smarter he is. One
day he asked Mickey, "What am I doing arguing with
someone who can't read or write?" Mickey replied, "You
oughta stop reading and writing and start hitting."

Another thing I noticed about him. When Reggie was
taking so much heat after his article in *Sport* magazine, he
told a reporter, "The guys don't like me 'cause I'm black."
The guys didn't like him 'cause he came to our team,
and he wasn't here three months when he attacked Thurman in a magazine article and told everybody how great
he was. Then we got pissed, and he said it was because
he's black! Why did he have to say a thing like that?

Reggie isn't one personality. He's several. Some days
he's real happy and friendly and nice, and other days he's
nasty and surly and always growling at everybody. Then
on other days he sits by himself and doesn't talk.

Reggie doesn't usually talk much with the other players anyway. Mostly it's with the press. We get to read the
bull he says in the papers the next day. I don't pay attention to anything the guy says, never, and I'll tell you why.
We were in Oakland for a game, and after it was over
Reggie was being interviewed on the radio. Radios were
on in the clubhouse, and we could hear what he was say-

ing. Reggie's talking away, and he says, "You can't believe most of what the New York writers are saying about this team." Well, the New York writers are listening to him say this, and when he comes back to the clubhouse they are pissed. They ask him exactly what he meant by that. Reggie for a few seconds didn't know what to say, and then he said, "You guys heard that? If I knew you were listening, I wouldn't have said it."

When Reggie started playing with the Yankees last year, Billy discovered that Reggie wasn't nearly as good as Reggie thought or said he was. Billy started batting Reggie fifth, instead of fourth where he was used to batting, and George went crazy. George ordered Billy to bat him third or fourth. Billy told the press, "It's no big deal. Reggie's just not used to playing the way other people want him to." But it was a big deal because Reggie's George's boy, and for the two years Reggie's been here, Billy rarely can play Reggie the way he wants to, which is frustrating for Billy 'cause he feels a team should do everything it can to win, regardless of whose feelings get hurt.

Billy almost got fired last year over Reggie. We were getting our ass kicked by Boston, and George was on Billy's back because we weren't in first place, and in the middle of the game Jim Rice hits a pop fly to right field. The ball fell in, and Reggie trotted after it like it didn't matter at all, and he took forever to throw it back in. Billy walked out to the mound to take out the pitcher, Mike Torrez, and as I was walking in from the bullpen to relieve him, Billy also sent Paul Blair out to right to replace Reggie, who had without a doubt loafed after that ball. Billy was so angry he wanted to embarrass Reggie. If you lose, Billy always wants you to go down fighting, and Billy had been pissed off because even though Reggie had been winning some games for us, he was costing us a lot of ball games with his fielding.

Let's face it, Reggie's a bad outfielder. He has good speed to get to the ball, but the catching part is shaky. Before the game, Billy had wanted Reggie to shag fly balls during batting practice, but Reggie had refused. See, if Reggie had done that, I don't think Billy would have been as angry as he was. And Billy's taking Reggie out

of the game embarrassed him in front of all the people
in the park and all the people watching on national television, which really hurt Reggie a lot. Reggie hates to be
embarrassed, especially in front of 50 million people. So
when Reggie came in to the dugout, Reggie said, "What
did I do? What did I do?" Billy said, "You know what
you did." Reggie said, "You have to be crazy to show me
up in front of all those people," and then Reggie made
the mistake of calling Billy an old man.

When Reggie said that, something in Billy snapped. Billy
hates to be embarrassed as much as Reggie does, and
when he said that, Billy went for his throat. Ellie, Howser, and Yogi had to wrestle him to the bench to keep
him from reaching Reggie. Reggie was yelling at Billy,
"You better start liking me," as if to say, "If one of us is
going to go, it isn't going to be me."

George had not been at the game. He was at a funeral
someplace, and he had watched the game on TV and
he saw the whole thing. A couple of days later he decided
to fire Billy for losing his temper, but when Milt Richman
of UPI leaked the story, the reaction of the fans was so
hostile, George changed his mind.

When I heard that Billy was going to get fired, I went
to him and told him, "I want you to know something. If
you get fired because of this incident, I'm going home.
I'm going to pack my bags and go back to New York
for the rest of the road trip, and I'll show up when the
team gets back." What I would have been saying was, if
you fire Billy over an incident like that, where Reggie
was loafing and Billy was punishing him for it, then you
might as well have made Reggie the manager. "I can't
see the manager taking the consequences when he's right,"
I told Billy. Not so much that it was Reggie and Billy.
If it had been any manager and player I would have felt
the same way.

Monday, July 17   New York

Before the game tonight Reggie met with George for more
than an hour, and they must have discussed Reggie's bitch
that Billy's been batting him low in the order and has

been DHing him—against righties—because tonight Paul Splittorff, who's a lefty and a good one, started for Kansas City and Reggie played. Splittorff had been the opposing pitcher when Billy benched Reggie in the final game of the play-offs last year. Tonight against Splittorff, Reggie DHed and batted fourth in the lineup. Reggie ripped Billy about that before the game. He told the reporters, "One day I won't play. The next day I'm the cleanup hitter." The way he's been hitting, he's lucky he's ever the cleanup hitter.

Billy really burned my ass tonight too. Billy told me I was going to pitch the sixth and seventh innings and then he was going to bring Goose in. In other words, it was Long Man Lyle again. It didn't matter how well I pitched. He wasn't going to leave me in there. Billy keeps telling me he understands how I feel about going into games early, and yet it keeps happening again and again. So tonight Catfish made his first start since May, and he pitched well. He left with a 5–3 lead after five innings and a third. Billy sent me in and I got out of the inning, and I shut them out in the sixth too. I walked in from the mound, went into the dugout, and said, "That's it, my two innings," and I left. I walked up the runway to the clubhouse to get dressed. When Fowler came after me to pitch the seventh, I told him, "I'm not a long man, and you're not going to put me in that job. Two innings are two innings, and now the other guy can take over." I showered, dressed, and went home.

He's made me the long man, and now, when I go out there to pitch, I can see Goose behind me in the bullpen warming up. If I give up one or two hits, the manager's walking out to the mound to take me out. Leave me out there, for Christ's sake. I'll get out of it. I got in it, I'll get out of it. But Billy doesn't do that anymore. With Goose back there, he doesn't feel he has to.

After I left the park, I was driving home in my van listening to the game on the radio. Goose had given up two runs in the top of the ninth to tie it, and in the bottom of the tenth Thurman leads off with a single. Phil Rizzuto then starts talking about Reggie bunting. The first time Reggie tried to bunt, I thought, "That's good. Reg-

gie's trying to move the runner over." After he fouled
off another bunt for strike two, I said, "Well, hell, at
least he tried. Now he'll have to hit away." But when he
bunted with two strikes and struck out, I thought, "Holy
shit. I can't believe this. There is going to be hell to pay."
Just listening to the radio and knowing how the game is
played, I knew Reggie wasn't bunting to move the runner. He was bunting to get back at Billy.

I don't know. But I didn't feel it was entirely my fault
that we lost. Thurman dropped a fly ball in right to help
load the bases in the eleventh. With two outs, Goose went
to 3 and 2 on Willie Wilson, and on the next pitch Heath
and Goose both started walking off the mound, knowing
it was strike three. Umpire Marty Springstead, however,
called it a ball, the winning run came in, and Goose got
so mad he got thrown out of the game. Kammeyer came
in, gave up a two-run single to Patek and another run to
make it 9 to 5, and when we scored two in the bottom
of the eleventh it was too little too late.

Tuesday, July 18   New York

It's too bad Reggie and Billy had to clash, but the way
both of them are, that's something that's going to go on
forever. Neither one of them is going to let a dead dog
die. No way, and neither one of them is gonna get any
good out of it.

I can see why Billy got so Goddamn mad at Reggie.
Reggie was telling everybody, "I bunted because I thought
that was the best thing to do since I wasn't swinging the
bat so good." To me that's a weak excuse for doing what
he did. He got himself into trouble he didn't count on,
and now he's trying to get himself out of it. When a
manager gives a sign, and the third-base coach tells you,
"Reggie, swing away. Don't bunt," and he bunts anyway,
you might as well not have a manager.

And what gets me is that Reggie can make a statement
like "I bunted because I thought it was right to bunt,"
and the reporters accept it. They don't give it a second
thought that "Hey, wait a second. Is this guy bullshitting
us or putting us on?" They don't force him into a corner.

Why doesn't Steve Jacobson ask him the type of question he asks everyone else, where you have to give an answer: "You mean to tell us, Reggie, you honestly weren't mad at Billy? You expect us to believe you really were interested in moving the runner over?" But they don't do that 'cause why should they? This way they go over to Billy and tell him what Reggie says, and it gives Billy an opportunity to call Reggie a liar, and they go back to Reggie and tell Reggie what Billy says, and Reggie says something nasty back, and it is on.

The Yankees have announced that Reggie has been suspended for five games, which is right. Mickey Rivers, though, was angry that he was suspended. Mickey thought they should have just fined him and let him play. "We need a big bat in the lineup right now," Mickey said. But Reggie's been 2 for 16 since the All-Star break.

We needed the day off today, but Boston won again and is 61 and 28, 14 games in front of us. Forget this season. The rest of the year is just playing out the string.

Wednesday, July 19 Minneapolis–St. Paul

Minnesota moved the visitor's bullpen, so we had to sit in the dugout with the rest of the team, which is a pain in the ass for me. It's hard for me to watch what goes on on the bench during a game. The hollering at the umpires and guys striking out on bad pitches and coming back makes me jumpy. Billy getting on someone's ass. I don't want to hear it. It just makes the game tougher.

Piniella came back to the dugout after making an out with a guy in scoring position, and he whizzed his helmet against the dugout wall. That's part of the game, but I'm not exposed to it when I'm in the bullpen. Maybe batters have to do that to get themselves up for hitting next time. Maybe it's their way of getting it out of their system. It's so tough for these guys to get so frustrated and then have to go out and play defense. That's what Graig Nettles and Chris Chambliss do. You never see them standing out in the field pissed off, looking up at the sky. I'm not condemning Piniella, or the other guys who lose their temper;

it just seems to me that it's so much easier to play the other way.

I didn't want to hear the crap, so midway through the game, I walked into the clubhouse, and on everyone's stools in their lockers was a typewritten sheet of rules. Billy had put them there. They're no different from the rules we've had all year long, except now they're in writing. There's no excuse for anybody saying, "Goddamn, I didn't know."

Figgie pitched himself a shutout, we won 2 to 0, and we didn't even miss Reggie. He went back to Oakland during the suspension. The *New York Post* is running a poll, asking their readers to call in and say whether they think Billy was right in suspending Reggie or whether Reggie was right. After the game Billy gave it to Reggie some more. A reporter asked him about the rules he had given out, and Billy said that all he asks his players is that they hustle and obey orders. Now just who do you suppose he was talking about?

After I walked off in the middle of Monday's game against the Royals, Chuck Hiller, Kansas City's third-base coach, asked Graig, who was playing third, "Where's Sparky?" Kiddingly, Nettles said, "He's not a long man. He went home." Hiller just laughed, but apparently Hiller was talking about it on the Royal bus, and a reporter must have overheard him, and this reporter must have talked to a New York writer 'cause Henry Hecht of the *Post* came over and asked me about it. I refused to talk about it. Henry said, "Well, I hope I don't hurt you by what I'm going to write." I said, "I hope you don't either. I wouldn't want to hurt you either."

Thursday, July 20   Minneapolis–St. Paul

Henry Hecht wrote an article in the *Post* saying that there's a double standard on the Yankees, that Reggie was suspended for five games for what he did because he's black, and no one said anything about what I did because I'm white. What the hell! Why bring that up? There was no reason to bring any black-white stuff into it. And when he wrote that, the whole controversy flared up all over again.

I'm not saying whether what I did was right or wrong, but I was standing up for what I felt are my rights. I had to walk out there and then or face getting buried. And I'm not going to let that happen.

Hecht had no business writing an article like that. There was no basis in fact, and it's so incredibly irresponsible. Christ, this had absolutely nothing to do with black or white. It was just two guys—Reggie Jackson and Billy Martin—like it's been all year. That something happened with me had nothing to do with it. How was I supposed to know something was going to happen after I left?

Billy wasn't mad at me. He understood why I left. There was no big fight. I left and that was that.

Gid pitched a four-hit shutout over the Twins, his fourteenth win against just one loss. It was the first time since the end of May that our pitchers put together two consecutive complete games. After the game I got Henry in a corner and I told him, "If you ever write any other thing about me, I'm going to kick your ass. I promise." That's how mad I was.

In his little squeaky voice Henry said, "Don't you threaten me." I was pressing Henry against the wall with my body, and Henry's such a little guy that when Cliff Johnson came up behind me, he didn't see him. Cliff was just screwing around, and he gave me a hard slap on the shoulder. Without even looking to see who it was, I spun around and threw a hard right that missed his face by maybe an eyelash. His eyes got real big, and I just glared at him and turned back to continue yelling at Henry.

Later on, Cliff came over and said, "Goddamn, I didn't even see little ole Henry back there. You damn near knocked the shit out of me." I told him, "I was so mad right then that I didn't even know who you were."

Friday, July 21   Chicago

Because of Henry Hecht's article, Steinbrenner really got on my ass. I had to call him from Chicago at ten o'clock in the morning to tell him exactly what had happened. He asked me, "Did you say to Billy on the bench that you're not a long man and you're not pitching anymore?" I said, "No, I didn't." Which I didn't. I didn't say it to Billy on the bench. I said it to Fowler in the clubhouse.

After I answered his questions, George said, "From now on, you don't leave the bench when you're pitching unless you get permission from the manager." I said, "OK, that's fine."

Later on, Catfish came over to me and said, "They're really screwing you after what you did last year." I said, "Yeah, but what are you going to do?"

I went to Billy and I said, "Screw it, just suspend me and get this crap over with. I don't want to hear about this double standard anymore. Suspend me, fine me, I don't give a damn what you do. If that's what they want, do it." Because Billy had understood why I walked off, Billy told me to calm down and not to worry about it.

Beattie started and couldn't get through five. He has a big windup, and it hurts his control, and after Billy took him out he suggested that Beat start using a no-windup delivery. Billy figures it'll keep Beat more compact so he'll be in better control of himself. We were losing 4 to 3 when I relieved Beat in the fifth, but Roy hit a home run and drove in a couple of more runs, and I had my seventh win.

After the game Jim Spencer was griping that after he struck out three times against the Red Sox two weeks ago, he hasn't played since. I don't know what he's bitching about. Jay Johnstone NEVER plays.

It sounds funny, but every time George holds a meeting, we end up winning a bunch of games right afterward. We've won three in a row, and I can't say it isn't because of that meeting. Why it is, I don't know and I don't care to know. The thing is, we're winning again, and that's what matters.

Saturday, July 22   Chicago

The reporters stand around waiting and listening. The
other day I saw Henry Hecht taking a piss and writing
at the same time. You don't know what it is. It could
have been nothing, but why was he doing it back by the
pissers? Henry stands around and listens to what the
players say to each other and writes it down. I've seen him
running around to other writers, asking, "What did he
say? What did he say?" because he doesn't get it himself.
It sounds like I'm picking on him. All right, I'm picking
on him, but it's because he's done somthing I think was
wrong.

Granted he has a job to do. That's what he told me.
Well, good, but do your job right. Don't write any old
thing. You can always rationalize by saying, "That's my
opinion, so I wrote it," but when you write about a black-
white double standard on a major league ball club, it can't
be your opinion. You have to know for sure.

I was watching Cat warm up before the game, and I
said to Goose, "Goddamn, he really is throwing good."
Because Cat, when he throws, is very deliberate. Everything is the same. The windup is nice and smooth, and
then bang. Before he went on the disabled list, you could
see that he was pushing the ball. His arm would be lagging
because his shoulder was hurting so bad, but today, boy,
he was throwing the hell out of the ball. That's the hardest
I've seen him throw in a couple of years. Cat went five
and two-thirds against the White Sox, allowing three hits
and an unearned run.

Billy used me as the long man again today, and again
Goose came in after me and got the save. The reason
Billy gives me for using me the way he does is the old
righty-lefty crap, where if we start a right-hander, the other
manager starts a lot of lefty batters, so when I come in,
he has to substitute righties, making it easier for Goose
when he finally comes in. I say bullshit to that. I can get
righties out as well as lefties and so can Goose. But that's

'the way the man is playing it, and there's little I can do about it.

Today some of the guys were looking at me when I relieved Catfish in the sixth. They were looking to see whether I'd be pissed off when I came in. Fowler asked me, "Are you all right?" I'm so tired of his asking me that. For as long as I've been playing, I've told coaches, "Don't ask me that. I don't want you to ask me how I feel. Screw it. When I'm pitching, just leave me alone. I'll try to do the best job I can. I don't want anybody treating me like a prima donna like they do some of these other people. Hell, leave me alone." I finally told that to Art. I said, "Hey, I'll let you know if I don't feel good or if I don't have enough stuff to get them out." I'm not afraid to say, "Hey, I don't have it today." That's how you win ball games, you tell them when you don't have your stuff so they can warm up someone else. So I'm just going along with it now, but I am going to try to get out of here. I'm not going to go up and holler and scream. I'm going to go up and have a very serious talk with Steinbrenner after the season's over. He said he'd try to accommodate anyone who doesn't want to be here. We'll see if he keeps his word. Of course, I'm not going to leave here for the sake of leaving. If I don't better myself, if I can't go to a club where I'm the only short man, I'll stay here. But if I have a chance to go to a club like Texas—bye, y'all.

With Reggie suspended, the crap has stopped. Cold. We've won four in a row with him gone, and the talk has shifted from the bitching and moaning to "Goddamn, we're playing great." A lot of the players feel that it's quiet with Reggie gone. Mr. Controversy isn't around with his shadow hanging around everybody, and everybody's been feeling better mentally. Still, his being gone isn't the reason we've won four games. We've won because we're playing hard, and we know we'd better make a move. At 11 games back, we're still a long, long way from catching Boston, but at least we're getting closer to them, rather than dropping further back like we had been doing.

Sunday, July 23   Chicago

Figgie had a little tenderness in his arm, but again he was sharp and we won our fifth straight, beating the White Sox 3 to 1. Goose pitched the ninth and got his fourteenth save.

Reggie came back to the club today. When he came into the clubhouse, the writers were waiting there in a pack. They had been asking the other players what they thought about it and couldn't get a good quote from anybody. When he came in, they started interviewing him. For a long time he was standing there talking, saying he didn't feel he did anything wrong and he wasn't getting out of his clothes, wasn't getting ready to work out, and Billy got pissed at him.

"We're winning without you. We don't need any more of your crap. We don't need you coming in and making these comments," Billy said. Billy was beside himself. Billy screamed, "If he doesn't shut his fucking mouth, he won't play, and I don't give a damn what George says. He can replace me right now if he doesn't like it. We got a good thing going and I don't want him and his mouth coming along and breaking it up." Billy was ready to fight. He still hadn't forgiven Reggie for what he had done and then not admitting what he did. "It's like a guy getting out of jail and saying he's innocent after he kills someone," Billy said.

Later Reggie complained to reporters that Billy hadn't talked to him in the year and a half they were together. When Billy heard that, he was flabbergasted. "It's a flat-out lie," he said, and of course it was. The reporters should know by now that Reggie says a lot of stuff that isn't true. But even though they know it's just Reggie, they still go right to Billy and ask him to comment on what Reggie says. If either of them would just stop commenting on each other, we wouldn't have the problems we have, but neither of them will do it. I am so sick of hearing and reading this bull, you wouldn't believe it.

The players are to the point where they don't give a damn who's arguing. They just want it to stop. We're tired of the bullshit. We want to play baseball and see if we can pull this thing out. I think we have a chance, but we have to be able to play without all the distractions and bullshit.

Why Billy and Reggie hate each other so much is beyond me. That's something that goes with Billy Martin. You either stand behind him 100 percent or you don't stand behind him at all. That's the way he manages. I made the statement on a TV show the other night: "If you can't play for Billy Martin, then you can't play for anybody." Billy Martin treats you like a man. If you do your job, he leaves you alone, whereas most managers don't.

Monday, July 24   Kansas City

As usual I slept until about two-thirty this afternoon, and when I came down the hotel elevator, the door opened at the lobby, and in front of me was a mob of people standing around, including some players and reporters. "What happened?" I asked Tidrow. He said, "Billy quit." I was sorry to hear that.

From what I was told, last night at the airport Billy went to the bar to have a few drinks. Billy had a few Scotches, and when he left, he ran into Henry Hecht and Murray Chass. Billy was still mad at Reggie and was in the sauce, and he told them that Reggie and George were made for each other. "One's a born liar, and one's convicted," Billy told them. When George found out about it, it was church.

Billy then denied that he ever said that, but those guys aren't going to make up something like that, and when he denied it, he had no alternative but to resign. Billy must have finally said to himself, "Screw it, I can't take this crap anymore." He's taken more than he has from any other owner since he became a manager, and that was the thing bothering him the most.

Billy was becoming very drawn. He wasn't feeling good, and it hurt me to watch this thing drive him crazy. That's the part I thought was sad. He's not a bad guy. He just has his own ways in which he does things. He wants to control the club, which a manager should do, but I never knew one who had complete control. And when there are 25 guys, you're bound to have a conflict of personalities.

Billy's just happened to be with the guy George paid $3 million for. And when you're managing a club like ours with so much talent in it, there's also bound to be trouble from the guys sitting on the bench. It wasn't an easy job, and with all the added pressure, it finally got the best of him.

This team could never have become what it did without Billy Martin managing it. Billy had that fierceness. He had that competitiveness that oozed all over him. Ralph Houk couldn't stand how George kept interfering. Ralph got to the point where he finally said, "Screw it, I can't manage like this." It was just a matter of time before he quit. Billy, though, fought and argued with George, which in a strange way was good for the team because everybody saw how Billy stuck up for himself, and they respected that. I think if Billy hadn't come, the team would not have been capable of doing things we now can do. Before he came we knew we were good, but it was Billy who taught us how to come from behind and win. It isn't an accident that no team can come from way back and pull it out like we can, whether it's one game or a whole season. Look what we did last year. We finished something like 41 and 13 to win the pennant. And I don't care how far behind we may be now. We'll see who's in first when the World Series rolls around. Someone else will be the manager, but it will still be Billy Martin's team. We know we're winners and can play hard-ass ball. We have a scrappiness, and it's from him that we got it.

I remember in the 1976 play-offs against Kansas City, Billy was yelling and screaming like he always does at the other team. Being fiery and alert and keeping us in the game, and that's great because everybody feels that way, but it's Billy who lets it out for you. Just by him screaming, whether he's yelling at somebody in their dugout or at the pitcher or at the umpire, or when he goes out to argue for you, it just pumps you up. We were scoring, and we saw we had a chance to win the thing and it was getting really frantic and Billy was releasing his thing, screaming and yelling, helping everybody out. He got us so fired up, we just kept going and going and going until we won. Chris Chambliss hit that dramatic home run in the bottom of

the ninth against Mark Littell, and when he swung and
that ball soared toward the right-field bleachers, the feeling
was unbelievable! What made it so fitting was that it was
Chambliss. Not that he doesn't hit home runs, but if you
had to pick one guy to win the game with a homer, would
you have picked him? But with a different guy winning a
game each day down the stretch, it showed us that we, as
a team, could do it.

Dick Howser managed the team tonight, his one shot at it
until Bob Lemon comes in tomorrow. Howser blew it. We
were winning 2 and 0 in the seventh when with two outs
and two guys on, Steve Braun hit a liner at Munson, who
waited for it, ran in, caught it, and then dropped it.
Thurm, not being an outfielder, stepped on it, kicked it,
and two runs scored on what was ruled a double. It was
really funny to watch. We laughed our asses off. Howser
brought me in and again I was lousy. I allowed three hits
and three walks in an inning and a third, and we lost 5
to 2.

Tuesday, July 25   Kansas City

Remember the rumor that New York and the White Sox
were going to switch managers? Though they didn't exactly
switch, we did end up getting Lemon. Lem and Rosen
played together on the Indians in the fifties and are good
friends. Billy seems to think he's going to manage the
Denver team next year. It sounds like Finley's finally going
to sell the A's, and the new owner's going to move to
Denver.

Gid made Lem's debut as Yankee manager a piece of
cake. He pitched a six-hit shutout against the Royals, striking out eight. Splittorff started for the Royals. Reggie didn't
play. Lem said he was rusty. Reggie didn't say anything.
The Red Sox have lost six of seven, and though we're only
in fourth, their lead is down to nine and a half.

Now that Billy's gone, Reggie's going to be very passive
about this whole thing. On TV today Reggie said that if

he ever got in trouble, Billy Martin would help him out if he asked. The type of guy Billy is, he probably would too. Billy doesn't carry a grudge. But what Reggie is saying is really a crock. Reggie's glad that he's gone, and I'm sure there are other players glad too, especially the ones who didn't play. I had my differences with him too, as far as how he used me, but I never wanted to see him go.

I had only been angry with Billy once while he was manager. It was early in '76, and in a game against Detroit, Figgie was pitching and he was tiring. He had been in trouble the last couple of innings, but Billy, like most managers, hates to change pitchers. He figures, "Shit, he got out of jams before," and he'll go to the mound to talk with the pitcher, and the pitcher will say, "I'm all right," and unless Thurman comes out and says, "Take him out," the pitcher has a good chance of staying in there. So Billy left Figgie in, and there were a couple of hits, and we lost the game.

The writers asked Billy, "Why didn't you bring in Lyle or Tidrow?" Billy said, "I didn't think I had anybody out there with as good a breaking ball as Figueroa." Billy could have said, "He talked me into leaving him there" or "I left him in there too long." No, he tried to put the blame somewhere else by saying we weren't good enough. I went crazy. It really burned my ass.

I saved the next game I pitched, and when Billy came out to shake my hand, I gave him the cold shoulder, busted right past him without shaking his hand. I went to the trainer's room and told him to get the hell away from me. The next day I thought about going to see him, but I decided not to until he asked me first, because I felt that he knew why I was mad.

It was two weeks before we talked. One day he walked by my locker and said, "All right, red ass, I want to see you in my office." And I went in there and told him exactly what I was mad about. Ever since then, we've been friends. I enjoyed playing for Billy even though I had my differences with him as much as anyone else did. I was sorry to see him go, but I guess it was inevitable, and wherever he goes, whatever team he manages, it will happen again, you can be sure of that.

Wednesday, July 26   New York

I'm not going to give up on getting traded. You can reason
with George if you use the right approach. You gotta be
honest with him, and you gotta say what's on your mind.
If you don't, you might as well not go up there. Some like
to use agents because they don't have confidence in themselves or they'd rather the agent get in the argument. I negotiate myself, and I've been in many arguments with
Steinbrenner, I mean real beauties, and it's never caused
us to hate each other. I know George when it comes to
business, and to him, that's business, and I understand that.
We can scream and holler at each other, but when I walk
out, it's over with. Away from the ball park, he's a pretty
nice guy.

It seems that every team we play throws as many lefties
as they can against us, and Cleveland is no exception. They
started Rick Waits, who was winning 1 and 0 until Lou
Piniella hit a three-run home run in the bottom of the
ninth to beat him. Again Lemon kept Reggie on the bench.
Some writers were saying that maybe Lem didn't play
Reggie because he was afraid of the fans' reaction. Lem
isn't the type of guy to worry about fan reaction. He's
gonna field his best team. He just wanted to give Reggie a
couple of extra days' batting practice. As for the fans, they
boo the hell out of him and yell nasty remarks every single
day anyhow, and at any one of us. Him they holler at the
most. That will always be there. You always have people
who pay their money to come to the park and holler
something at you. That will last forever. It's part of the
job.

Beattie used that compact delivery Billy suggested and
was outstanding. The kid has poise and good stuff and is
going to make a hell of a pitcher when he gets a little experience. Texas beat the Red Sox, and their lead is down
to eight and a half.

Thursday, July 27   New York

Figgie, who has been solid and reliable, pitched a three-hit
shutout for seven innings, I got through the last two, and
we breezed past the Indians in the first game of a doubleheader, 11 to 0. In the second game Cat started and was
throwing good, but he was wild, so he didn't get through
the first inning. In fact, he didn't get an out. Gave up three
hits, three walks, and six runs. The important thing, though,
is that he says his arm doesn't hurt. A healthy Cat will
make a big difference in our chase to catch the Red Sox.
Kammeyer relieved him and allowed nine more runs.
Everything the Indians hit fell in. Reggie returned to the
lineup, batted sixth, and went three for three with a home
run in the first game and two for five in the second, which
we lost 17 to 5.

Reggie was back in right, Thurman back catching.
Thurman hasn't said anything, but though he went to the
outfield because his legs were hurting him, he found out
that he had to do a lot more running playing right, and it
wasn't any easier on them. After a while I think he wanted
to go back to catching. If he's going to play this game, he'd
rather play it behind the plate.

The last month's been so Goddamn serious. Every time
it seemed that we were getting back to normal, something
else would happen. By the time you got up mentally, bang,
something'd happen, and you'd be back down again. It's
been a bitch. The best thing they did was hire Lemon. The
guy is so easy to play for. He knows all the fundamental
moves, and he knows about pitching, which is going to
help our ball club a lot. Even if you're getting guys out,
he can tell whether you have something left or not. I think
he'll get our pitching staff rolling pretty good.

There's such a difference in the bullpen, too. The phones
ring, and someone gets up, and when the pitcher is ready,
Ellie calls back. Sometimes they'll call and ask how close
you are but the phone doesn't ring ten times. What's great
too is that you know exactly what you're going to do. Like
in the second game, Lem called down. He said, "How

'bout you and Goose splitting up the eighth and ninth inning? Kenny Clay pitched two innings and he's supposed to pitch Saturday." So I pitched an inning, Goose pitched an inning, and that was it. I knew when I was going in, Goose knew when he was going in. None of this "Warm up, buddy, you're going in," and you warm up, and the phone rings, and it's "Sit down. He's going to go another inning."

Also, the atmosphere isn't so uptight anymore. It's hard to get mad at Bob Lemon. His philosophy is "All I ask is that you hustle." He told us, "When I played, I played the game as best I could. I hustled, and that's all I ask you people. If you can't hustle, come and see me, and I'll take you out of the lineup. When you're ready to hustle again, tell me, and I'll put you back in again." You can't ask for any more than that. That's what he did when he managed Kansas City. He did it to Amos Otis. He told the press, "Otis is not going to play until he walks through my office door and tells me he's ready to play." And when Lem says something, he sticks by it. There are no exceptions to his rules, which is the way it should be.

"We're struggling right now, but we've closed the gap from 14 to 9. Plus Boston's been hurting. Yaz has a bad back and Hobson's arm is bad. Right now we're worrying about how quickly we can close this gap. In August last year we were five games out, and now we're nine out and it isn't August yet. If we can narrow it down to where we were last year, we feel we're going to win it. All that's on our minds now is playing baseball and winning. The club is closer-knit—maybe not as far as friendships, but as far as teamwork on the field. During Reggie's suspension Willie Randolph returned to the lineup, and that's made us stronger, and guys are now starting to talk to each other, trying to help each other out. Guys are becoming more critical of themselves too. The other day I was pitching, and Thomasson made an error in left to let a run score. At the end of the inning he came over and said, "Goddamn, I should have thrown the guy out at the plate. I'm sorry. I bobbled the fucking ball." He didn't have to come over and tell me that. Yeah, I'm the pitcher, but I knew the man was trying his best. But stuff like that had not been happening this year. We did it last year and now we're starting to do it again. And when guys are saying, "I should have done this, I should have done that," you know that mentally they want to play good baseball and that they'll do anything they can to win. That's why we feel we have a shot at this thing. Before, it was, "Aw fuck," "Goddamn it," "We're snakebit." It was never, "Well, I won't do that again tomorrow."

Friday, July 28 New York

A reporter asked me whether fewer guys will want to leave the Yankees now that Billy's gone. Nah. The ones who wanted to go still do. It's a combination of money, not playing, and George. We'll get rid of five or six guys before next spring training, no doubt. Maybe even more than that. That's the way George is. He believes in new faces all the time. Hell, from the first year we won the pennant, it was bang, bang. Then we won the World Series, and he went and did it again. We're going to keep changing and changing. We're never going to show up with the same ball club two years in a row. That's as true as the sun coming up.

Lem brought me into the game in the fifth inning today, with the Twins winning 5 to 2, and son of a bitch if Nettles didn't hit a two-run double to tie it up. Then in the tenth, after I was pitching so good, one of their guys got a hit and Willie Norwood hit the ball out of the park to beat me.

Saturday, July 29 New York

It was Old-timers Day today, and after I got into my uniform and went into the dugout, the clubhouse boy gave me a message that Billy wanted to see me. Billy was hiding in a boiler room under the stands. I went in there and we hugged, and he told me that George had hired him to manage the Yankees again in 1980.

Knowing this, I sat in the dugout waiting for Bob Shepard to make the announcement. I was watching faces as he

said, "May I please have your attention, ladies and gentle-
men, I have an announcement to make. In 1980 Bob Lemon will become general manager, and in 1980 the Yankees
will be managed by Number 1 . . ." and before he could
say the name, the crowd let out such a roar that you
couldn't have heard it if you were sitting right next to him.
It was bedlam. Billy ran out onto the field, and there was
a standing ovation that went on forever, which must have
really burned George's ass. George hates the fact that the
fans love Billy so much, but when Billy ran out there, he
cried. He was happy for Billy.

In the dugout, the players looked at each other in amaze-
ment. The thought had never even crossed anyone's mind.
Some guys just stood there shaking their heads. Other
guys were staring out into space, saying, "What do you
think of that?" No one, and I mean no one, could believe
it. Reggie walked around like he didn't know a thing about
it. He was saying, "What happened? What happened?" I
don't believe him because you can't tell me Steinbrenner
didn't tell Reggie before it was announced. As close as
they're supposed to be, George isn't going to do that. The
announcement was a surprise, but after all the crap that's
gone on, it was anticlimactic. Everyone felt, "Oh well, let's
get the game started."

When a reporter asked me about it, I was surprised as
hell. George has a knack of doing things like that, though.
Hearsay from the front office was that the day Billy was
fired, thousands of people called the Yankee offices to complain. He said that the calls were in favor of Billy by a big
margin. By noon George was so upset by the reaction of
the fans that he closed the office early to keep any more
calls from coming in. He told the PR department to tell
the press that the calls were running about fifty-fifty. The
next day he also closed the switchboard. If George says
that public opinion had nothing to do with his hiring Billy
back, don't believe him.

Nevertheless, I'm still skeptical that Billy will manage
the Yankees in 1980.

Reggie told me that the Yankees had put him on waivers
yesterday. He just laughed. I don't think he cares whether
he gets out of here or not. The Royals and Orioles were

two teams that claimed him. The Yankees, of course, withdrew his name immediately, but now they know who's interested. Teams get ready to make trades that way, instead of having to make a hundred and fifty telephone calls.

We staked Kenny Clay to a 6 to 1 lead, and with Goose saving his fifteenth, we beat the Twins. Boston lost. Eight back.

Sunday, July 30   New York

I read in the papers that Billy is obligated to take care of himself more and has to get himself straightened out physically if he's to come back as manager in 1980. George can get out of his contract with Billy by saying Billy didn't uphold his end of the bargain. If George says, "We don't feel he's ready to manage again," he's out of it.

I can't really see Billy agreeing to George's conditions, but on the other hand managing the Yankees is the only thing he wants to do for the rest of his life, so maybe he will be back. And if Billy goes along with the conditions, it's going to be rough for George not to have him manage in 1980. Billy's just liable to follow that baby and get back to managing the Yankees again.

I thought Mike Farber of the *Bergen Record* had the best line of the day about Billy's return in 1980. Farber wrote, "Billy Martin rose on the fifth day, the greatest return in almost 2,000 years."

Steinbrenner hired this guy named Lucky Lester to prance around the infield while the ground crew cleans up the field in the fifth inning. This guy has a great time dancing around. He's performing in front of 40,000 people every day. When we saw this guy, we said, "What the hell is this? Goddamn, we really need this to embarrass us. George is always talking about looking like Yankees, acting like Yankees, and winning like Yankees, and he goes and hires this guy running around with a broom and doing his funky." He really wasn't doing much. A couple of shuffles here and there. He'd act like he was sweeping the bases with a broom, but it would be two feet high off the ground. The reason George hired him is that in Detroit there's this one little ground crew guy who comes on the field, a regular member of the ground crew, and he struts around shaking his derby, highstepping it, and the fans just love him, and he loves it too. So George musta said, "We gotta get someone like this too." But there's a difference. The guy in Detroit was just into his own fun. Lester was hired to act that way, and we thought it looked stupid. We signed a petition saying it's in the best interest of the New York Yankees that he quit doing it. I'm sure some players didn't give a damn, and other guys probably said, "Screw it, leave the guy alone." I don't care if Lester is a professional clown. We thought it was best.

Loused up another one today. In the first game of the doubleheader against the Twins Goose pitched super, struck out four in a couple of innings, and got the win, his seventh. In the second game I relieved Beattie in the ninth with the score tied 0–0, men on first and third, and I gave up a hit to this guy Morales for a run. Then when Butch Wynegar bunted, I threw the ball past first for another run, and Beat lost 2 to 0. Fortunately, the Red Sox keep losing, and we gained another half game on them.

Another good omen: Bucky started at shortstop today. It's the first game since June 10, 49 games ago, that we had the same starting lineup that beat the Dodgers in the Series last year.

Tuesday, August 1   New York

We picked up pitcher Paul Lindblad from Texas today. He's the left-handed long man we've needed all year. If we had had him from the beginning, maybe I could have stayed as short man a little longer. He's been around, knows how to pitch, and is real tough on left-handed batters.

Lindblad supposedly came in a straight waiver deal, but the first thing on my mind when I heard about it was that perhaps it was part of a bigger deal at the end of the season. The Yankees had to have given up something for him. Maybe it's me.

* * *

I brought my two kids to the ball park today about three o'clock. They always tell you if you want to bring your kids to the park, bring them early. We went out onto the field, it was five hours before the game. I was pitching to them, and they were hitting. Dane is ten, Shane five, and while I'm out there playing, one of the stadium guards ran out onto the field and ordered me to get my kids off the field. Boy, am I tired of this weak crap. The Yankees have more to worry about than two little kids hitting a baseball on the field. The guy said, "Are you getting off?" I said, "Why do you want to know?" He said, "Because they . . ." I said, "Screw 'em. Tell them if they want to say something to me to come down and tell me themselves."

I took my kids out to the bullpen and they threw off the mound for a little while.

When I got back to the clubhouse, the phone rang in the manager's office. Billy was on the phone. He said, "Goddamn, I told you you're not allowed to let your kids on the field." He was laughing. Billy's been at the park. I don't know why, but it looks like they're serious about his coming back.

Before the game, everyone was talking about the pennant race and how Boston has lost 12 of its last 15 games. Still, no one seems to think we can win this thing unless we come up with another consistent starting pitcher to go with Gid and Figgie. Everyone is hoping that Cat will be the guy.

Cat pitched a three-hit shutout for eight innings today to beat Texas 8 to 1. Reggie was 2 for 2 with a homer, and since his return eight days ago has hit .571 with seven RBIs.

I'll tell you what: Cat threw the best ball I ever saw him throw. He threw *hard*. It was amazing. He's been on and off the disabled list two or three times. Dr. Cowen manipulated his arm, he came back and threw real well, and then hurt his arm again. Dr. Cowen manipulated his arm again, really popped it this time to break the adhesions, and since then Cat says he feels great. Believe it or not, Cat could reel off ten wins in a row the way he's throwing.

On the other hand, I saw Don Gullett in the clubhouse. I said, "How're you doing, buddy?" He said, "Just hanging around." That's all he does is hang around. He comes to the ball park every day and sits, doesn't even dress, just gets treatment for his arm. I don't know how he does it. If it was me, I'd be as far away from here as I could. Gullett's had so many different treatments for his arm, the other day I walked into the trainer's room, and he had this thing on his shoulder with little strips of tape. It looked like a target. I thought he was going to have to run through the woods and have guys shoot at him. He wants to pitch so badly, and it's driving him nuts that he can't. I feel sorry for him.

After the game Piniella was watching the mob of reporters crowded around Catfish. Piniella yelled over, "What's the big deal? Even a blind hog finds an acorn sometimes." Ha. Ha. Ha.

I pitched the ninth inning. Bonds hit a home run that's still going to ruin Cat's shutout.

Two weeks ago, the Red Sox had a 14-game lead, and now it's six and a half. The White Sox beat Boston tonight, Rice and Scott haven't been hitting, a couple of other guys have been hurt, and Boston comes to town tomorrow for two games. With this team, who knows what could happen.

Wednesday, August 2   New York

We were ahead of the Red Sox by 5 to 0 tonight, but we couldn't hold it. In the fourth they scored two runs on a wild pitch by Tidrow and an infield out. Then in the sixth, they loaded the bases and Goose came in after throwing only 15 warm-up pitches in the bullpen. He walked Yaz on four pitches for another run, and then he walked Jack Brohamer after going 1 and 2 on him.

In the eighth the Red Sox tied it up when Rice doubled. With a 0 and 1 count on Yaz, the rains came. Boy, was it miserable—cold, windy, and damp—and the game was delayed a half-hour. When it resumed, Goose threw another wild pitch, letting Rice go to third. With Yaz up, it's almost an automatic run when a guy's on third. He hit a sacrifice fly to center to tie it. After 14 innings, the curfew stopped the game. I pitched the last two innings, didn't have squat, but they didn't score.

Thursday, August 3   New York

We blew our big chance today. We could have been four and a half out. Instead we're eight and a half out. Boston got four hits and two runs off Clay in the seventeenth to win the game that started yesterday, and Mike Torrez beat us 8 to 1 in the second game in a game the rain ended after seven. It was Torrez's thirteenth win of the season.

Because of all the trouble we're having with our pitching staff, you could say that it was a mistake to let Torrez go, but when he left, quite frankly I didn't think we'd even miss him. Without him we had more than enough pitching. Except that Hunter, Messersmith, Gullett, and Clay have been on the disabled list at one time or another.

In the two games Reggie was 0 for 10 with six strikeouts. When he gets hot, he's tremendous, but when he's in a slump he's so bad it's unbelievable. His slumps make up for his streaks, and he comes out about even. What hurts us more than anything is that because Reggie is a star, the manager won't pinch-hit for him like he would somebody else. Everybody knows he might go 0 for 40 before he breaks out of it, hoping the next hit will be gone. Granted it's a blow to his ego, but if there was some way the guy could understand how much he was hurting us, that it's in the best interest of the club for him to be sitting down, we'd be a lot better off and win a lot more games.

The two losses today were a real setback for us. It may take us two weeks to make up what we lost today, but even though we're eight and a half back, we still have a chance because all the Eastern Division teams have to play each other at least one more time. Anything can happen. The way it's set up, the team that gets hot at the end will win it.

Friday, August 4   New York

Lemon's doing a pretty good job. We're eight and a half games back, but everyone's playing pretty good, so we're still hopeful. It's a really big change from all the contro-versy. Lemon is quiet and happy-go-lucky, and nothing shakes him. Still, the crap hasn't stopped completely. How could it? Reggie's still here.

In the seventeenth inning of yesterday's game, the score was 5 to 5 when Dwight Evans fouled the ball into the stands near the foul pole. Reggie, in right, chased after it. As he was jogging back to his position, Kenny Clay didn't notice Reggie, pitched, and Evans hit the ball for a single right at where Reggie would have been if he had been in position. Two runs scored, it turned out.

In the papers today Reggie said it was the catcher's fault for not looking to make sure all the fielders were ready. Cliff Johnson was the catcher at the time.

Before today's game, Cliff came over to me and said, "Ain't that a bitch they blaming me for losing that game." I said to Cliff, "Hey, screw it, of all people Reggie shouldn't be blaming anyone for anything." He said, "I'm a lame duck, and they're pinning it on me." I said, "Yeah, that's the best way to put it." It's all well and good that Cliff wanted to get it off his chest, but you can't keep thinking about it and talking about it because it just makes you madder and madder. The important thing is today's game, not yesterday's. I said to him, "I've been seeing that sort of thing for fifteen years now. Everywhere you go it's always the guy who doesn't play very much or the guy who has to go in and play when someone gets hurt. Those are the guys who are always getting their ass chewed." Cliff just happened to be in that spot at the time. I told him to forget about it. Yeah, it hurts a little, especially when you see it in black and white because now he's going to get more static from the fans: "Ya lost the game, ya bum," that sort of thing. But still, you have to forget about it. We have more important things on our minds.

Guidry lost his second game against 15 wins tonight when we made an error and DeCinces hit a home run. In 29 innings, we've scored exactly two runs, including one tonight. Mike Flanagan won it for Baltimore.

Saturday, August 5   New York

I relieved Figgie with the score tied and one out in the ninth, got the last two batters, and got an easy win, my eighth, when Roy singled in Nettles with the winning run in the bottom of the ninth. A record of 8 and 2 doesn't look too shabby, but I still have only seven saves, and I'm still pitching for beans. I was hoping Lemon would use me differently than Billy did, not make me the long man anymore, but it looks like Lem really can't do anything because they're dictating to him what to do. I've just resigned myself to that now and to the fact that I definitely want to leave the Yankees. I've made up my mind. I can't rebel anymore because it won't do any good. I might as well not even do it. It's not that I'm giving up and putting my tail between my legs. It's just that it's more important to win the pennant, and if that's the way they want to use me, then I'll do my darndest to help.

After the game, all the writers crowded around my locker, and I told them, "Before you ask any questions, just go ahead and write whatever the hell you guys want to write 'cause I don't have anything to say, good or bad. Do whatever the hell you want to do."

Thurman was really pissed off today at an article Dick Young wrote in the *News*. Young said that even though Billy Martin was gone, the problem between Reggie and Thurman still remained, that Thurman still hated Reggie for the article Reggie wrote in *Sport* magazine last year. Maybe Young is right that Thurm's never forgiven Reggie for all that shit he said, but why bring that up now?

Sunday, August 6   New York

The Cat is back. Catfish threw a five-hit shutout and beat Palmer 3 zip. It was so good to see him do that 'cause having a guy like that who goes from winning 20 games four, five years in a row, to not being able to do squat, that hurt him a lot. It was really hell for him when he'd go out there, give up four or five runs in a couple of innings, and then come back to the clubhouse and not be able to lift his arm. Today, though, he must have really been feeling good about how he pitched. He's not the type of guy who turns somersaults or cartwheels when he pitches good, but he had to be happy. We're giving him a little static because after the last game he pitched, they were writing, "The Cat is back." Guys walk by his locker and say real slow, "The Cat . . . is back." It's funny when you see seven or eight guys coming by and saying, "Did you hear? The Cat . . . is back."

After the game Mickey Rivers was teasing him. "Damn," he said, "I oughta get ten cents a mile out there for running over here, running over there, running, running, running after balls when you're pitching." Cat just laughed.

Tuesday, August 8   New York

Dirt held Milwaukee to three hits and no runs for eight innings today, and we beat the Brewers 3 to 0. Goose pitched the ninth and got another save. Two of his three outs were strikeouts.

Everybody's talking about how much better Dirt has been pitching since the Yankees brought up Clyde King to help coach the pitchers. Clyde was going to take Art Fowler's place when Art was about to be fired, but when George decided to keep Art, he decided the Yankees should bring King up anyway. The reason Tidrow's pitching better has nothing to do with Clyde King. It's because his right hand has healed, not because of Clyde King.

Since Billy's left, Art's been feeling worse than ever. He knows he's just here for the ride and that he'll be gone as soon as the season's over. The only reason he's here now is that Billy still stays in contact with George. We keep ribbing Art. We say, "Where's your buddy at?" He says, "Who?" "Clyde King." Art goes crazy. "Well, screw him, the son of a bitch," Art says. Or we're out in the outfield and we say to him, "We're not running unless

Clyde throws the balls to us." He says, "Well, screw it then, I don't give a Goddamn." It's so quiet around here. Fowler's not even funny anymore.

Wednesday, August 9   New York

Billy called Mickey Morabito, the head of the Yankee PR department, yesterday and asked him to set up a press conference for him, so Morabito did. Billy called it to explain what his job will be until 1980, but some reporter asked about Reggie, and Billy aired it out. Billy said that Reggie wasn't a superstar in his eyes 'cause he doesn't play like a superstar, and he said that sometimes he even rates Fred Stanley above Reggie. Billy said that if Reggie was here in 1980, he'd be treated no better or worse than anyone else.

When all the shit hit the fan about Billy blasting Reggie, George told Morabito, "You're responsible for this, and if the papers come out tomorrow, you're fired." But Morabito's still here. Today the newapapers went on strike! I told Mickey, "Talk about having luck. You could have been fired. But now, lucky you, you get to stay here with George." George is punishing Mickey by not letting him go on the four-day road trip to Baltimore starting Friday. He's sending Mickey's assistant, Larry Wahl. I said to Morabito, "He did you a favor by not sending you. Wahl is the guy he's punishing, not you."

We were losing to the Brewers by four runs in the bottom of the ninth and scored five runs to win it! Bucky singled with one out, and Rivers hit a home run. Yount booted a grounder, Thurman walked, Chambliss got a double to drive in a run after their center fielder knocked the ball backward after it went over the fence. Puff was walked intentionally to load the bases, and this guy McClure, the Brewer pitcher, hit Reggie in the arm to tie it up. The bases were still loaded, and Lou got up and laid down the worst bunt you've ever seen. The ball hit the plate and went a mile into the air. As Chambliss was running home, their catcher tried to barehand the ball and step on the plate at the same time, but when it finally came down, he booted it and Chris scored to win it. Boy, were they pissed. The win moves us back into second place, seven and a half behind Boston and a half a game ahead of the Brewers.

Rookie Larry McCall pitched the top of the ninth and got a Christmas present early. It was a nice present before he goes back to Tacoma tonight. The guy has really traveled around lately. The Yankees called him up from Tacoma August first. He watched the game from the bullpen, and after it was over, he was told about our getting Lindblad and that he was going back down. He drove his car to West Haven to leave it with a friend, and when he got there, the Yankees told him to come back because Spencer got hurt. Now Spencer's better and McCall's gone again.

The other day Lem saw him carrying his bags. He said, "Every time I see the guy, he's got a bag. If he was paid by the mile, he'd be making a lot of money."

Thursday, August 10   New York

Lemon calls everybody Meat. Before the game, he called me over. He said, "Hey, Meat, I'd like to talk with you." I said, "OK," and we went into his office. He said, "Do you think the guys are kinda ticked off at me because I don't run out on the field and argue all the time like Billy?" I told him, "All the players like to have their manager out there fighting for them, but the players in my opinion know that you don't do that as much as Billy does. I don't think they expect you to do that. When the time comes, if the call is bad enough or close enough or important enough, I guarantee you you'll be out there. That's really all you have to do. You don't need to run out there every time one of the guys starts bitching. Most of the time they're wrong anyhow."

Gid struck out the first four Brewers, struck out seven of the first ten batters, and beat Milwaukee 9 to 0. In the last forty-something innings, he's allowed three, count 'em, three runs. Reggie didn't play today. His right forearm is very sore from his getting hit by a pitch in yesterday's game.

Friday, August 11   Baltimore

We were leading 2 to 1 in the middle of the sixth when it started raining buckets. The sky opened up, and after about two hours, the ump had to call the game when the ground crew said it couldn't get the field back in shape. Catfish won his sixth, allowing only four hits.

Saturday, August 12   Baltimore

Beattie gave up four runs in the second inning, and we lost to the Orioles 6 to 4. It was Beat's seventh loss in a row, and we're not going to catch Boston unless he can stay ahead of the hitters better. If you can't throw strikes, you're going to get hurt, no matter how hard you throw. That's all his problem is, control. He throws hard and he keeps the ball down. He's gotta be more consistent.

Piniella's been hitting the ball good. He's hitting around .320, so you know he's been hitting, but when he has one of those nights when he doesn't hit the ball hard or hits it right at someone, that just drives him crazy. Tonight, Lou hit a ground ball, and the infielder just did throw him out at first. Gene Michaels, the first-base coach, threw his hands up in the air as if to say, "Oh, Goddamn, he just did nip you," but Lou saw him and thought he meant, "Goddamn, the ump blew the call." Lou got so mad that his eyes were bulging when he ran up to first-base umpire Dave Phillips and started screaming at the top of his lungs at him. Lem came running out of the dugout and had to wrestle Lou to the ground to keep him from attacking Phillips.

From the bullpen we could see that he was out, and when he started screaming, we were laughing our asses off out there. In the clubhouse after the game I said to Lou, "Jesus Christ, it's hard to tell what you'd have done if you'd really been safe." He got kinda pissed. He was saying, "Arrrrgh, grump, moan."

When I was with the Red Sox I used to love to get Lou out and then just wait. I'd stand on the mound, and when he got to the dugout, I'd listen, count to about five, and then boom, bam, boom, motherfucker, mother, fucker, fuck, fuck, throw the fucking ball, boom, boom, boom, and you could see his teammates. They'd be standing up, watching him. They'd be saying, "He's going down the runway. There he goes. He's going." And then you'd hear, boom, boom, boom, bam.

When Lou first came over here, to see him do that was the greatest thing I ever saw. I mean he just went crazy. He'd take a bat and beat the water cooler or the bench or whatever he was beating to the point where you were ready to put the restraints on him. Then just as suddenly, he'd turn around, smile, throw up his hands, and say, "Aaaaaaaaaaaah. What the hell?" He'd smile at you so nice and pleasant, and then he'd lay his helmet down, sit quietly, and watch the game as though nothing had happened. He'd say, "You just have to get that crap out of your system."

In the runway from the dugout to the clubhouse, there is a row of lightbulbs, and the man who invents something to keep Lou from breaking those lights is gonna have a hell of a product on his hands 'cause Lou'll take his bat and really beat the hell out of those lights. Lights, water coolers, it just doesn't matter. He just has to do it. I'm not saying whether that's bad or good. I know I wouldn't want my kid doing it. From Lou, though, you kind of expect it.

Sometimes when he strikes out or gets jammed, he'll come in, and he'll have his batting helmet on, and the guys on the bench know that he's gonna throw that helmet somewhere, and the guys are sitting there trying to figure out where to maneuver to avoid getting hit by the helmet. If he's going left, you go right, and vice versa 'cause you know he's gonna fire that helmet somewhere, but if he's coming straight at you, you don't know which way to go 'cause when that helmet hits, it bounces crazy like a football, and it's tough to get out of the way of it. Everyone gets hit once in a while, but it's nothing. I really enjoy

watching him. When he goes nuts, he just lets it all hang
out.

The fans love it too 'cause they know how mad he gets
and they love to agitate him. He's been fined a few times
for yelling stuff at fans. On the road they get on him,
"You're a bum, you're this, you're that," and he takes it
for just so long and then he starts screaming at them,
"Screw you, you motherfucker." Before a game this guy
was getting on him, "You can't hit anymore. You're a
bum." Finally Lou screamed at him, "If you keep your
wife out of my bed at night, maybe I'd get some rest and
I'd be able to hit better."

Three times during the game the lights behind home
plate short-circuited and went out, delaying the game for
more than an hour. I pitched the last three innings and
gave up a run. Boston won twice and leads by eight again.

Because Reggie hasn't been hitting for shit, Lemon
batted him eighth on the lineup card. Reggie must have
gone in to Lemon and said, "Hey, I'm not gonna hit in
the fucking eighth spot. If I am, I'm not playing." They
must have just left it that way because Reggie didn't play.
They told the press he was ill, had a stomach virus. After
the game, when the writers asked Reggie if he was ill,
Reggie kept saying, "I'm sick." They said, "What do you
mean, are you sick or are you ill?" He'd say, "I'm sick."
For Reggie, the home run hitter, batting eighth was too
big a blow to his ego.

Sunday, August 13   Baltimore

The Orioles were beating us 3 to 0 when we scored five
runs in the top of the seventh. But then before the Orioles
could get up again to finish the inning, it started raining
like hell. Boy, was it wet, and in minutes the field was
like a swamp. Figgie was out there waiting to pitch, but
Weaver was doing his best to stall so the game would be
called. Christ, the field had been unplayable *before* the
game. There was so much water that it was lying in huge
puddles in the outfield, and when the umps finally called

time, the Baltimore ground crew took the tarp out and dumped it into left field where the puddles were already lying there instead of putting it over the infield the way they should have. It took them so long to cover the field, it was unbelievable. The umps then waited about a minute and a half to call the game. Because the Orioles didn't get to bat in the seventh, our five runs didn't count, and Figgie ended up losing 3 to 0. We protested the game immediately. We won't win the protest, but we were so pissed off about losing that we had to do something. In the clubhouse after the game all the players were saying, "Goddamn, we can't let this happen. We gotta retaliate. We gotta do something. Let's not play tomorrow. Screw it, we won't play."

It wasn't anyone in particular. It was the tone going round the clubhouse. Reggie came over and said to me, "Let's hold a meeting and put not playing tomorrow to a vote." I didn't want anyone to get in trouble, so I said to him, "I want you to understand that if we do hold a meeting and put it to a vote, and the majority votes not to play tomorrow, it's majority rules, and we're in trouble." I said, "There's gonna be some mess if that happens. MacPhail's gonna intervene and make us play, and Marvin Miller's gonna be here as soon as he can hop a plane, and he's gonna be screaming at MacPhail, 'You can't make them play.' And here we are, trying to win a pennant." I said, "It won't do any good, one, because it's not going to change things, and two, because it's not good to get Mac-Phail and Marvin Miller at each other's throats with our contracts running out at the end of the year." I told Reggie it would be better to let Lem take care of it, and I told him I'd go in and talk to him.

I went in and told Lemon, "I'm probably looking at this thing more tragically than it could ever be, but that's the way I like to see things. I like to look at the worst possible thing that could happen," and I told Lemon what I told Reggie. I said, "The thing is that during a meeting most of the guys don't even listen to what you're saying. They say, 'Yeah, OK,' and then later they come over and ask questions. Half of them wouldn't even know what they're voting on." I said, "I think it would be better for you to explain to them exactly how far this thing can go, and that if it comes from you, instead of me, they'll listen a little bit more closely," and Lem agreed to do that.

I told Lem, "If you just let the guys know you're thinking about it and trying to do something, that'll hold everyone for two or three days, and after that they'll forget about it completely." There isn't a thing we can do. Sure we're pissed off because we battled back and scored five runs, and they were taken away from us. We were victims of circumstances. We got outmaneuvered by Mother Nature.

Monday, August 14 Baltimore

Before the game tonight Lemon called a meeting and said, "Hey, I know it's been tough and we got screwed last night, but the same thing happened to them two nights ago when they called the game, so there isn't much anyone can do about it. I want you guys to try and forget about it and go out and win this game." Everyone said OK, and that was the end of it.

The lights went off twice more tonight, causing a delay of about an hour and a half. Poor Mickey Morabito. It's a shame he had to miss all this. In the eighth inning, Eddie Murray came up to the plate. Goose, who'd been wild all night, was throwing his smoke, and with the count of 3 and 2, Goose wound up, Murray got set for the pitch, and he must have heard the lights go click because just as Goose was about to let go, they went off again. Before you could blink, Murray was 20 feet from the plate. Jesus, that was funny.

Before they went out, Goose had had him 3 and 0, and he had worked his way back to 3 and 2, and Murray then fouled off three or four pitches. Then the lights went. Because they're mercury lights, they take fifteen or twenty minutes to come back on, and when a pitcher is 3 and 2, he hates to have to wait a minute, never mind twenty minutes, before throwing because it throws off his rhythm. When the lights went out, I said, "Son of a bitch, it wouldn't surprise me if them bastards deliberately shut them off. Three and two and Gossage being wild, and the damn

lights go. No way that was an accident." I said, "That's a
dirty Goddamn trick."

Finally they came back on. Goose was warming up,
throwing his heater, and Murray had to have been sitting
on the bench, thinking, "How many more can I foul off?"
He got back into the batter's box, and Thurman called for
a change-up, which was beautful. It was "see ya" for
Murray.

Dirt was sharp again, allowing one run in six and a
third. It was tied when Goose went in, and after Mickey
Rivers drove in a run in the eighth, Graig put it away with
a two-run homer off Palmer.

Tuesday, August 15   Oakland

Gid 6. A's 0. Reggie batted seventh and hit a two-run
home run. Gid is 17 and 2 with an ERA of 1.79. He allowed four hits and K'ed nine. Angels 5. Boston 2. Tanana
beat Eckersley. We're seven out.

Wednesday, August 16   Oakland

Cat won his fifth game in six starts since coming off the
disabled list last month. He beat the A's 5 to 3, but not
before Rico Carty hit a home run nine miles. I relieved in
the seventh after Bucky hit a homer to put us ahead. The
mound was so screwed up, I couldn't throw the ball hard,
and I more or less flipped the ball up there, almost like
batting practice, because I didn't want to injure myself.
In the dugout after I got out of the seventh, Fowler came
over and said, "What's wrong? Did you hurt your arm?"
I said, "No. I just can't throw off this Goddamned mound."
I went back there in the eighth, struck out the first guy,
and Lem came and took me out. I admit I wasn't throwing
very hard, but I was getting the sons of bitches out. That's
the first time I struck out the first hitter of an inning and
got taken out of a game. Goose relieved and got his seventeenth save.

Friday, August 18   Seattle

Figgie pitched a four-hitter and beat the Mariners 6 to 1.
Mickey Rivers, who hit in his seventeenth game in a row,
tripled, drove in a run, and scored a run. As Mickey goes,
we go. Graig had a double and three ribbies.

Saturday, August 19   Seattle

Bucky seemed really down after the game. He's a very
quiet guy, tough to get to know, but I do know his legs
are bothering him quite a bit, and when the manager pinch-
hits for him late in the game, like Lem did tonight, he gets
very down on himself 'cause Bucky worries a lot about his
hitting. When Billy was here, if we were behind and we
had runners in scoring position the second time Bucky
came up, Billy would pinch-hit for him. That's embarrassing to a player, yet at the same time Bucky's never had a
very high batting average. And every time he goes through
a period where he's not hitting the ball, not getting hits, he
starts worrying that maybe he's going to be benched, and
what happens, it worries him so much, he ends up saying,
"Screw it, if that's the way it's going to be, I don't want
to play here. Trade me somewhere where I can play."

I hate to see him down on himself about it, but sometimes a manager has no other choice, especially when you
have people like Cliff, Thomasson, and Spencer on the
bench to hit for him. Lately, Lem hasn't been pinch-hitting
for him much, except when he needs someone to go up
and hit a home run. That Bucky doesn't mind so much.
The thing is, the way our club is going, we have to take the
runs whenever we can get them. That's all a manager is
trying to do. He's not trying to belittle Bucky.

Sunday, August 20   Seattle

Bucky went in to talk to Lemon about Lem's pinch-hitting
for him. You can usually tell when Bucky's going to go in

there. Bucky will mope around the clubhouse for three days. Then when he comes to the park, if he's still moping the fourth day, you know he's ready to go in there. Today was the fourth day and he was moping.

We were playing a night game, and this afternoon Mickey and Roy went to the local track. They didn't leave the track until the card was completed, and they arrived at the park at about a quarter to seven. Lem scratched Mickey from the lineup and probably will fine them. Lem has only one rule. He told everyone about it when he took over. He said, "The only thing I will not tolerate is not being here three hours before the game." They told Lem they got caught in traffic, but Lem didn't buy it. "Yeah, they probably left at six-thirty," he said.

Once again we lost to the Seattle Mariners, with Goose getting beat in relief of Guidry. As far as I can remember, we won only one game in the Kingdome all last year and we lost two or three in June. When you're not used to playing here, it's a bitch. Take what happened to Chris tonight. Some guy hit a high pop that got up in the air in a hurry. In this park, if you don't watch the ball the whole way down, you're in trouble. Chris never saw it, it fell, and it cost us.

I relieved Goose after he got banged around, and the first guy up hit a line drive right back at me. I tried to barehand the ball, and the ball got me right on the ends of my middle and pointer fingers of my pitching hand. The fingertips went completely numb to where I was afraid to look down at them. I thought one of them was split for sure. At first I thought I'd try a couple of pitches, but the game was out of hand, and I thought, "Screw it, there's no sense in it. I can't throw the ball," and I walked off the mound. I didn't say a word to anybody, just walked into the trainer's room, sat down, and put my fingers in ice. Beattie had to finish up. Fortunately for me, the fingers weren't broken, and I'll be OK in a few days.

Monday, August 21   Anaheim

Yesterday Lem fined Mickey and Roy $250 each for being
late to the park, and today in the papers Mickey was complaining that he's unhappy playing for the Yankees because
George isn't giving him "extra money." If this is true, I
don't blame Mickey. I blame the person who gives him the
money. He shouldn't have given it to him in the first place.

Tuesday, August 22   Anaheim

Black widow spiders are all over the place in Southern
California. You can tell a black widow by its coarse web.
There was one crawling up the wall in the john of our
bullpen, so I went and caught a moth, which is easy to
catch at night—they flutter around the lightbulbs—and I
fired it into the web and watched the black widow slowly
crawl over to it and go to work on the poor son of a bitch.
Beattie came in and watched her for a couple of innings.
They are something to watch. Oh Jesus, are they vicious
looking. Cat, meanwhile, won his fifth game in a row,
going all the way to beat the Angels, 6 to 2 on six hits.

After what Reggie did tonight, all the mustard in the
world couldn't cover him. He hit a single to right, and as
he rounded first, he gave one of his stares at Bostock in
right as if to say, "Go ahead, challenge me, motherfucker."
Bang, Bostock fired the ball in and picked him off first
base. Challenge me, my ass. It made me so sick because
there is absolutely no reason for that. And what I thought
was interesting was that nobody said a word. It used to be
"Look at that crap." Everyone would bitch and moan to
each other about it. Billy would go crazy. Now everyone
goes "Oh." Ellie said, "Did you see that?" I said, "Yep,"
and that was all there was to it. I went back to the john
and fed my black widow another moth.

Reggie's problem always has been that he wants to do
things that everyone will notice. If a batter hits a ball to
him and then looks like he wants to go to second, Reggie'll
hold the ball and stare at him as if to say, "I dare you to

run on me," instead of just picking the ball up and throwing it to the cutoff man like everyone else. Sometimes the runner'll stare back at Reggie and just run right to second.

Last year, against Kansas City, I was on the mound late in the game losing 3 to 2 when Hal McCrae hit a ball into the right-center field gap. Reggie went over for it, and he couldn't pick up the Goddamn ball because he kept looking at the runner. McCrae, who can run, ended up with an inside-the-park home run. I was pissed. At the end of the inning I waited for Reggie at the top step of the dugout and told him he'd better start giving his best, only I phrased it a little differently. Actually a lot differently. My exact words were "Get your head out of your ass." I told him, "When I'm in the field, sometimes I get beat and sometimes I don't, but at all times I give a hundred percent and expect it from everyone else, too."

Well, I guess he thought I was mad about my earned run average, which is ridiculous. I was mad because it was the eighth inning, and the run put us out of the game. Reggie said, "If you don't want me out there, get somebody else." I told him, "That's fine with me." When the writers came over and asked me about it, I asked, "Whoever told you that?" It wasn't bad enough that Reggie had done what he did. He then had to go and tell the writers about it.

I was talking to Chambliss in the hotel after the game. I said, "We don't even have anything going on on the bus anymore." He said, "Yeah, because the club has changed so much over the last couple of years." We started talking about when we had Oscar Gamble and Carlos May, guys who were fun because they knew exactly what their jobs were, and you could harass them, and they'd harass you back without anyone getting hurt or angry. With these new guys, they're a lot more sensitive about things because they're upset that they're not playing, and so sometimes guys'll be ripping each other and having fun, and then all of a sudden someone makes a remark that hits a little bit too deep, and the guy thinks to himself, "Goddamn, maybe he meant that." As a result, you can't rip like that anymore during the bus rides, which is also too bad because our ripping sessions were also useful. You could kid a guy about something he did wrong on the field, and

maybe he'd think about what you said and better himself.
But no more, and it'll be dead until we get through the
year. We really don't think we can do it. We're seven and
a half back with 39 games to play, and even if we beat
Boston all seven games that we have remaining with them,
if we lost a couple of games and they won, it would be
church. If Boston went 20 and 20, to win we'd have to go
28 and 11, and Boston's not about to fold with the club
that they have.

Wednesday, August 23   Anaheim

While we were in Anaheim, Andy Messersmith, who lives
here and who is recuperating from his arm miseries, came
to visit us. The doctors told him that if he had an oper-
ation, there would be a fifty-fifty chance he'd never be able
to pitch again. He's upset about that because he has to sit
out the rest of this season and hope to come back next
year. I felt sorry for the guy. I felt bad for all the hard
work he went through getting himself prepared for spring
training, and then after he worked himself into great shape,
he fell on his shoulder, tried to come back again, and now
his arm is really screwed up. That's gotta be a tremendous
mental strain on him. He worked so hard and got nothing
to show for it.

Chris Knapp beat us and Boston also lost. Status quo.
Seven and a half out.

Thursday, August 24   Oakland

Thurman's been very quiet. He's just going out, doing his
job, trying to win every day. He's happier catching. He
never wanted to play the outfield anyway. Yet I don't think
anything's changed as far as his wanting to leave the
Yankees. He's just fed up with the aggravation. I told one
writer, "If you had to do the job Thurman does and get
harassed for it by all these fans, you wouldn't like it either."
I know that everyone has to put up with fans who come to
you and say, "Lyle, you suck," when you won't sign an

autograph, but with Thurman you're dealing with a different personality. He's a very sensitive guy, and you can't change that. That's the way he is. So he's resorted to the only thing he could to keep those people off his back, and that includes not getting any publicity in the press. He's made it plain and clear that he doesn't want to talk to them. The newspaper strike has been a help, too.

Friday, August 25   Oakland

It was our first day back from the road trip, and Phil Pepe of the *News* came running down the hall leading to the clubhouse to ask me about my walking off the mound in Seattle after the line drive hit me in the hand. He said, "They were saying you didn't want to pitch, that you weren't hurt at all." Boy, did that piss me off. Who's "they"? I asked him, "Why'd they say that?" He said, "Because you didn't take a warm-up pitch to see if it was better." I said, "Who's to judge? I don't have to take a warm-up pitch to know I have no feeling in my fingers, for Christ's sake." Some writers will write anything, whether it's true or not, just to be controversial.

The umpires went on strike today, so the league had to hire some college and semipro league umps to take their place. Luckily, we didn't have any plays that were that close. Before the game I was in the bullpen looking out at the field, and I said to Goose, "Holy Hell, look at that guy at second base. He's so Goddamn nervous he can't stand it." He was moving around like he had something in his pants. I said, "He's just standing there praying there isn't a close play at second base."

Ellie had to meet a plane, so today I was in charge of the bullpen. Guidry was warming up to start the game, and Art called on the phone and said, "When Gid's ready, just wave your hat." When Gid said he was ready, I started waving my hat, and as I did that, the umpire at second base saw me, and he started waving back at me. I couldn't believe it. I said to myself, "This guy's out there scared stiff, and he's saying, 'There's a friend out there. I see him. It's a friend. I don't know who it is, but I'm glad he's out there.'"

As for the umpires going on strike, they do deserve more money. Considering the number of calls they have to make in a game, they're right most of the time, and they're dependable for the most part. The biggest bitch the ballplayers have is that there isn't a system to get rid of the one or two bad apples. Ballplayers are rated every day, and if they don't measure up, they get sent down. It should be the same with umpires. But because they know how difficult it is for them to be booted out, there's no incentive to keep improving themselves.

When you come right down to it, we're only asking for one thing. Any ump can miss a pitch. A catcher can stand up or the ump could be anticipating one pitch and not get it. All we ask is for them always to try and make themselves better. The threat of their going down to the minors if they don't shape up will do that.

Reggie made headlines again today. He was quoted as saying how difficult it is to be Reggie Jackson, how unhappy he is here in New York, and how he's so misunderstood, that he really isn't the bad guy the press makes him out to be. He talks about how tough it is for him because of all the controversy. Well, since I've known the guy and played against him, he has always brought controversy upon himself. If anyone took the time to research his newspaper clippings from Oakland to Baltimore to the Yankees, you'd find the format exactly the same in each place. It's just different names and different people. He's always asking everyone, "Why is all this crap happening to me?" Hell, he creates it, plain and simple, and he always will, wherever he goes. If he kept his mouth shut, it would be much easier for him to just go out and play the Goddamn game.

Against the A's tonight Mickey hit two home runs and Reggie hit a grand slam to give Gid his eighteenth win. Even though Gid had struggled, he only allowed 'em five hits. Lem had gotten me up in the fifth with the score 1 to 1, and he had gotten me up in the sixth when it was still 1 to 1, and in the ninth with us leading 7 to 1, Art calls me up and tells me to pitch the ninth because Gid had thrown more than a hundred pitches. They hadn't put me in when it mattered, but now that the game was out of hand, they wanted me in there. I said to myself, "I'll be a son of a bitch. Here I go again, going in to mop up. Screw it, I'm not going."

I called back and Fowler answered the phone, and I said, "Art, you can tell Lemon to get somebody else. I'm not going in." There was a silence, and he said, "Ahhhhhhh, ahhhhhhhh, well, errrrrrr, OK," and he hung up. That sorta put Goose on the spot, I'm sorry to say. He had to go in. But I'm no mop-up man, during my entire career I've never been a mop-up man, and I'm not going to let them treat me like one.

I'll tell ya, I don't think Lemon's running this club anyway. I can't put my finger on it, but every now and then he bats guys in the lineup where they shouldn't be batting, and sometimes the moves he makes are just ridiculous, moves I don't think Lemon would make on his own. I'm not saying who's doing it, but it doesn't look right to me. It's like I knew damn well I wasn't gonna pitch this year no matter how well I did. It didn't matter because George couldn't afford to let me have a better year than Goose. And that's why most of the games I've been in are ones I can win, not save. I go into the tie games or the ones we're behind by a run or two. That's how I won all these games. George has it set up so that it looks like "Goddamn, now they have a great long relief man in there," meaning me. But they can stick that. I'm not gonna do it.

Even in the beginning of the season, when Goose was having trouble and I was pitching good, it didn't matter. I was still the first one out of the bullpen when they needed someone in the fifth and sixth innings. I kept telling Mary, "It doesn't matter how I do. As soon as Goose shows he's coming along, he's the one they're going to use." As he started throwing better and better, I became less and less important. So far this year, I have a grand total of seven saves. I got my fifth one in early May, which means that in four months, I've gotten exactly two. If we have a big lead or if we're losing, I come in. If the game is close or we have a lead, Goose comes in. But yet they want you to be loyal and faithful. Screw it. I can't.

Saturday, August 26   New York

Dirt wasn't too pleased about being taken out of the game with the score tied in the seventh, but it's better than going out one more inning and ending up with the loss. You can tell Lemon was a pitcher at one time. He knew just when to take him out. I went in, didn't have squat again, but ended up winning the game when Nettles hit one out in the eighth.

There was a sign hanging up in the upper deck in right field saying, "ALBANY LOVES NETTLES," or something like that, and before the game started, he said that during the game he was going to hit a home run right over that sign. And then he hit the dinger, and son of a bitch, he hit it right where the sign was. Babe Ruth couldn't have done it any better, except that Graig forgot to point.

When I got to work, just like in a restaurant, there was a brand-new hundred-cup coffee pot sitting in the clubhouse, which was real nice because it's nice to have coffee waiting for you when you want it. But during the game today, Lou struck out or popped up or something. I don't know which at-bat it was, and after making out he went into the clubhouse with his bat and waffled that hundred-cupper, really beat the hell out of it with his bat.

When I went into the clubhouse after the game, a tiny teapot with coffee in it was sitting on the table. It looked so funny because the hundred-cupper was about three feet high, and after seeing it, here was this little tiny teapot. Everybody was pissed off because everyone drinks coffee all day long.

The letter P made out of tape is still on the wall of the trainer's room, and I still don't know what it means.

Sunday, August 27   New York

Again Cat beat Oakland, and again Rico Carty hit a towering home run off him. Boy, I mean he hit the crap out of it. It went up into the third deck in left field. Goose and

I were sitting in the bullpen watching it go up, and Goose said, "I wonder why nobody hits them up there very often. There are a lot of them hit on the right side into the upper deck, but not on the left side." I didn't have to answer that.

Carty generates a lot of power. He loves to hit the fast-ball, which is why he's always yelling at you to challenge him. He doesn't like you to throw him curve balls and off-speed stuff 'cause he can't hit it. Yesterday I was pitching to him, and I threw him a slider that stayed up a little but moved just enough that he missed it. He took a big swing, and you could hear him grunt, "Ooooooooh, coneo." He was talking to the ball. But always he wants you to throw him that fastball. "You no challenge me," he'll say. "See if I can hit it." Christ, we know he can hit it. We aren't dummies out there.

Graig hit two more home runs today. After he hit the first one he said to Paul Blair, "Well, only one more to go." Blair said, "What do you mean?" Graig said, "I decided I'm going to hit two today." And son of a bitch, he did, and after Graig crossed the plate and came into the dugout after hitting the second one, Blair said to him, "I don't even want to listen to this bull. I don't want to hear about it at all."

Lemon told the clubhouse guy that he doesn't want the TV set on in the clubhouse during the game anymore. Guys were going in there and sitting in the clubhouse lounge and watching TV during the game. They were the guys pissed off because they weren't playing, and when Lem would need a pinch hitter, someone would have to run and get him from the TV room. If the game was televised, they'd be watching it, but if we weren't on, they'd be watching "Charley's Angels" or whatever.

Monday, August 28   New York

This is the first year that I can remember actually waiting for the Goddamn season to come to an end. I'm sick of all the bullshit too. Like the other day Cedric Tallis chewed

Art Fowler's ass out because Guidry didn't throw the first pitch of the game by eight o'clock. They called down and said, "Goddamn it, if the game is scheduled to start at eight, I want the son of a bitch throwing the first ball at eight." I think Gid was out there at eight oh three. These are things that just aggravate the hell out of you. For three minutes, who cares?

Nettles was talking about all the things that go on on this club. He said, "When you're a little kid, you dream about running away and joining the circus or you want to be a big-league ballplayer. Christ, here I have the best of both worlds. It's a circus, and I'm playing baseball."

We've been trying to win some games, concentrating on playing ball, but I don't think we can put it together. We're still seven and a half games behind Boston, and even though we have seven games left with them, hell, if we don't win six out of seven, we might as well pack it in. I don't honestly think we can do it. Figgie pitched a three-hitter today, beating Tanana 4 to 1 with Goose in relief, but the damn Red Sox scored three runs in the bottom of the ninth to beat Seattle 10 to 9, and yesterday they scored two in the bottom of the twelfth to beat the Angels. It's frustrating. If we could play like we played today every day, we'd be OK, but we can't seem to be able to put a winning streak together. We play well for three or four games and then we lose a couple. It would take a miracle for us to overcome Boston.

Tuesday, August 29 New York

Pitched tonight against the Angels. Relieved Beat after seven with the score tied. In the eighth Bucky walked and Randolph tripled him in. It looked like I'd get another win, but with two outs in the ninth Rudi hit a good pitch out to right field. I started walking off the mound, figuring Reggie would catch it, and Thurman was coming out to shake my hand, but the ball kept carrying, and it landed in the second row of seats for a home run to tie the game. I said, "Son of a bitch." Goose pitched the last two innings, and when Blair singled with the bases loaded in the bottom of the eleventh, he got his ninth win.

After the game, Lem came up to me and said, "What happened? Did you run out of gas?" I said, "No. Let's just say I ran out of everything."

What's happened to me this year is good in one small respect. It shows some of the guys I play with that I'm able to take it, and also that I can dish it out too 'cause I stand up for my rights every time I can. Some players who went through crap used to look at me like "You signed, and bang, you were a star from the first day you walked in and you've had it like that the whole time." Hell, it wasn't that way. Whenever I talked to guys who were dumped on and not pitching, they'd say, "Yeah, but you don't know what it's like." Now I do know, and I'm showing them that I can take it. I'm not pouting. I'm fighting the best I can. Most guys don't do anything. Their answer is "I have a wife and kids and a mortgage, and money's tight, and baseball is all I know." There's always the excuse for not sticking up for your rights. But you've got to realize that your career is short, and if you don't stick up for yourself, you're going to get buried. I'm thirty-four years old. I've been consistent throughout my career because I never believed that a relief pitcher should have a bad year after a good year, which is the way most relief pitchers think. And I've never had a bad year because I know exactly what I have to do in order to be effective, and that is that I have to pitch a lot.

The first thing that comes to people's minds when they see that I have only seven saves when they're used to my having 20 is "He can't get anybody out." They think I'm a bum because I'm not pitching well. I try to explain that I can't pitch well because I'm not being used right, but when it comes down to the nitty gritty, they don't believe me. When I pitch ten games in a row and pitch great, they say it's unbelievable. They've been talking about Sparky Lyle's bionic arm for fifteen years. But right now I'm not pitching enough, and all you hear is "He can't get anybody out." Because I'm thirty-four, people are saying, "He's losing it." Well, let me pitch enough, and you'll see how quickly it would come back. I absolutely refuse to let the way I'm being used cost me the four or five years I have left. I want to be able to play the game until I'm no longer able to, not to have them cut my career short because of a system that's been part of baseball for years.

Wednesday, August 30   Baltimore

Ken Singleton batted against Guidry in the eighth, swung and missed at a fastball, and the bat slipped out of Singleton's hands and headed straight for Gid, who looked like a pole vaulter going over the high bar. As the bat sailed toward him, Gid jumped horizontally in the air, tried to kick his back leg up, but got hit on the right ankle when the bat just did catch him. From the bullpen, I saw Gid hit the ground, sit up for a few seconds, and then lie back down. I thought, "Holy hell, the son of a bitch is out cold." His ankle hurt him so badly he was afraid it was broken.

Gid's got this bad ankle that snaps real loud every time he walks on it. If Gid's walking down the hall of a hotel, you can hear the *crack, crack, crack* from your room, it's so loud.

I hope to hell he's OK. We need him. The club's looking pretty good right now. Goose pitched the last two innings to save Gid's nineteenth win, our sixth win in a row. Chambliss and Nettles are hitting the hell out of the ball, and Reggie's finally starting to get some hits after a long time. I'll tell you, I didn't think we could pull this thing out. I still don't because so many things have to go right for us to even get close enough to make a move. Baltimore has to knock off Boston, and we have to win on the days Boston doesn't. If we win and they win, it won't do us any good. It goes without saying that when we go up to Boston next week, we gotta win three out of four. A split isn't going to be worth a damn. And, finally, Gid's ankle has to be all right. He seemed OK in the locker room after the game, but they're going to take X rays just to make sure.

When I got back to the hotel after the game Lemon called me on the phone and asked me to come see him. I went to his room and we had a long talk. He said that Ellie had told him that when he wanted me to pitch the ninth inning against Oakland the other night, I had refused. Lem said, "I can't believe this. All the time I've known you, and the way you pitched when I was here before, I just couldn't believe that would come out of your mouth. I told Ellie he was crazy." I said, "Ellie was telling the truth. I did say that." Then I told him why. I told him how hard it had been for me when Billy was here. I like Billy, yet all my trouble was over how Billy used me. I said, "I haven't had a chance to get a save except for maybe eleven times this entire year. When I go in, we're always behind. I'm tired of coming in and being the Goddamn mop-up man. I'm just not going to do it anymore. I'd rather not pitch at all." And I told him I was sick and tired of their waiting for me to make one mistake so they can bring Goose in. I said, "It's like they're sitting there just waiting for me to put a guy on so they can take me out."

I also told him I felt I was being shelved for no reason at all. Last year I won the Cy Young Award and had 26 saves. "I never had a chance to pitch myself out of the short-man job," I said. "When you're coming in once a week and the team's behind, it's hard to pitch well." I said, "You were a pitcher. You know that, and I'll be a son of a bitch if I'm going to put up with it." I told him I wanted to be traded to a team that would use me right.

Lemon was very nice about it. He told me that he hadn't realized what happened, and he said he was using me sometimes in long relief, sometimes not, bringing either me or Goose in depending who the next batter was after he took out the pitcher. He said that if it was a righty batter, he brought Goose in. If it was a lefty, I came in, which, after I thought about it, was exactly what he had been doing. I said, "I'll go along with that, but you know damn well you don't have to do it that way. Goose can get left-handers out, and I can get right-handers out." Lem listened and he told me he wanted me here at least for the other year he's going to manage. I said, "I'd like to, but I'd appreciate it if you'd do your best to get me away from here." He said he'd talk to me more about it later.

Thursday, August 31   Baltimore

Gid's OK, I'm glad to say. The X rays were negative. His
ankle's a little sore and he may miss a start, but nothing
worse than that.

My little talk with Lemon apparently did some good. I
relieved Tidrow in the seventh when we were actually
ahead, and I got my first save since June 15. It was save
number eight, and if I have to wait this long for the next
one, I hope the uniform on my back will say Texas on it.
Boston was idle. We're six and a half games back.

It was our last game of the year in Baltimore, and if I
never came back here, it wouldn't upset me. Yesterday
Reggie got hit on the head with something hard. He
thought it was a golf ball. I thought it was a quarter or a
half dollar or something like that because they couldn't find
anything lying on the field. Reggie has a knot on his head.
I mean a good one. That's horseshit. Last year Reggie
played with Baltimore. He was saying how bad the town
was and that he would never live there. It's downright
punishment for a ballplayer to have to play here. All the
years when they had Palmer and Brooks and Frank Robinson and Belanger and Grich, they didn't draw flies. Baltimore's a bad area for baseball. They ought to find another
city for that team to play in.

Friday, September 1   New York

Jay Johnstone and Cliff Johnson were messing around in
the outfield during infield practice, jumping on each other's
back while they tried to shag fly balls. After batting practice they came in and grabbed rakes and started raking
around home plate with the rest of the ground crew. Fowler got real serious and in his country twang, he said, "Wail,
I'll be Goddamned. Those two motherfuckers fanly found
a job that they can do right."

Cliff is ready to leave, like everyone else who's not
starting. What I said about having too much talent on a
club is falling into place. You get these guys who are used

to playing every day, and now they're sitting on the bench and watching guys playing in their places who maybe aren't hitting either, and that pisses them off even worse. I think Cliff's gonna get his wish to get outa here because his attitude isn't very good and everybody notices. Too many people notice him because he's such a big guy. He takes batting practice, but no one sees him do much else. He can win you some games by pinch-hitting late in the game, but the way his attitude rubs off on other players isn't good.

The Mariners beat us 3 to 0 behind some kid I never heard of. Catfish only allowed two earned runs, but you can't win when you don't score, and we didn't.

Saturday, September 2   New York

Figgie just keeps rolling along. He beat the Mariners 6 to 2 as Reggie and Chris hit home runs to help win his fourteenth. We've won eight out of nine, the Red Sox lost their third straight, and their lead is now five and a half and dropping. If the Sox aren't looking over their shoulders, they oughta be.

Sunday, September 3   New York

I read in the papers today that the Con Ed kids, who Con Ed brings to the games and sits in the bleachers behind the bullpen, voted Reggie the most popular Yankee.

Goose and I were kidding around. He said, "Jesus Christ, here we are, out here giving these kids balls and being nice to them and everything, and they go and vote Reggie the most popular." I said, "Man, we just didn't do our job." We laughed. Those kids are pretty rowdy, but deep down they're good kids. Yesterday was the last game they'll be at this year because the program's over. We hated to see them go, even though it's tough for us when they're here because they want your autograph all the time, and you can't do it. You just can't. One kid throws a glove down to be autographed, and you gotta throw it back without signing it 'cause if you sign the damn thing you're gonna get a barrage of gloves. I did that once, and it was *thud, thud, thud, thud,* with all these gloves being fired down at me. To them not signing probably seems unreasonable, but that's the only thing we can do.

Against Seattle today, I relieved Beattie in the ninth. We had a 4 to 2 lead, and the first guy up, Bochte, hit a high pop behind second base. I mean it was a rainmaker. When it fell in, Bochte was given a single. The next guy up hit a ball to Chris at first, and he went to backhand it, and it hit on the heel of his glove for another single, and that's what did me in. The next guy hit a double, a run scored, and it was 4 to 3 with men on second and third.

I've been in plenty of games like this when you pitch and have halfway decent stuff and this sort of crap happens, but it's especially frustrating because I've been lousy for so much of the year, and for the last two or three games I've had pretty good stuff. Lem brought Goose in.

I was in the clubhouse when Goose was out there, but after the games the other guys were saying that he was *bringing* it. He just blew them away—struck out the side on 11 pitches! The first guy was gone on three pitches. The next guy up, Bob Robertson, is a good fastball hitter, but Goose threw two balls right by him and then he threw him a little slider, and it was all over. Goose struck out Cruz on five pitches. He took the last one with his bat on his shoulder. I'm sorry I couldn't see it. Everyone said it was just something.

Monday, September 4   New York

Yesterday Beattie pitched a good game, and one of the papers had an article saying how Clyde King has come in here and saved the pitching staff. I don't believe that for a minute. All year long our pitching staff has been off and on, guys keep getting hurt. And he comes along just about the time when everyone starts to get healthy, and now he's telling everybody about how he did this, he did that. All Clyde ever does is attack the spread on the table in the clubhouse after the game. Since he's come along, I gotta run in from the bullpen to get there before he eats everything. That's how quick he attacks the spread. You've heard of Superman and Batman? Clyde is Spreadman. He said in the paper that there's a lot more stuff he knows, but he's not telling it all because he wants to use it when he becomes manager again. I'll tell you, if that's what he's waiting for, that information may never get out.

We split with Detroit today, Boston lost to Batlimore, their lead is down to five, but it should have been less.

Gid beat the Tigers 9 to 1 in the first game for his twentieth win. After we scored eight runs in the seventh, Lem wanted to take him out because his elbow has been acting up a bit. But Gid wanted to stay in because he wanted his twentieth to be a complete game, so Lem let him go and finish it. Gid's never asked to stay in a game before and they owed it to him. But still, I would have rather they took him out and saved him for Boston, which we play starting Thursday. I hope it doesn't hurt his chances for his next start. Even though Gid allowed only one run, it was his worst game. He was 3 and 2 on just about everyone, and everything was up in the strike zone. It was a struggle.

Since my talk with Lemon, he's been giving me the chance when it counts, and now it's up to me. I'm really trying hard to get my act together. Again I threw good tonight, but I got beat in the second game thanks to those walkie-talkies. They positioned Thomasson in right field too far toward center for Wockenfuss, and when Gary ended up having to dive for the ball and came up short, Wockenfuss had a double. I got a couple of guys out, and this kid shortstop Wagner hit a line drive to Thomasson. He was right there, but he lost the ball in the lights, the ball hit his glove, and Wockenfuss scored the run that beat us. Son of a bitch, we shouldn't have lost the game. If we had won both, that really would have put some hair up Boston's ass.

Tuesday, September 5   New York

Before tonight's game Catfish was getting on Piniella for some reason. Maybe it was because he hadn't done it in a while. Lou's been going through a period when he's been saying, "I don't know what's wrong with me. I just don't feel good." Cat was mimicking him. Cat was saying, "Here I am, Lou Piniella, and I just, I just don't feeeeeeeeeeeeeel goooooooooooooood." Catfish was getting on him, drawing out every syllable. "Damn, I don't feeeeeeeeeeeeeel goooooooooooooooood. I . . . JUST . . . DON'T . . . FEEL . . . GOOOOOOOOOOOOOOOOOOOOD. Ah. don't want to play every day. My legs are tired. I don't feeeeeeeeeeeeeel goooooooooooooooood. I'm not an everyday player. I'm hitting three-fifteen. I'm only supposed to hit against left-handers, but now they throw a right-hander, and I'm still playing." Cat's going on and on and everyone's cracking up, and Lou was pretending like he's pissed. Cat's saying, "How the hell am I going to keep hitting three-fifteen if I have to hit the right-handers?"

Finally Lou says, "I'll tell you one thing. I have a grandfather who's eighty-seven years old, and he hasn't had a hard-on for the last five years. If that Dr. Cowen can manipulate Catfish Hunter's arm and bring it back to life, I'm gonna have him play with my grandfather's dick."

Roy White played for the first time since early August, and he hit a three-run home run to help Tidrow beat the Tigers. That's the way we seem to be going. That's the way it was last year, too, when we started getting hot. Guys would come out of the woodwork, sometimes right off the disabled list, and they'd play great.

The scoreboard at the stadium was broken, so we didn't find out that the Red Sox lost again until after the game. We're creeping up on them. We're only four back, and everybody's getting hyped up about it. Nobody's jumping up and down, but everybody's really excited.

Tidrow's seven and nine, but he's pitched so well this year that he should be like 12 and 4, except that he's had bad luck. We don't normally get him runs until the eighth inning, and by that time somebody else is in there.

With one out in the ninth, I came in. We were leading 4 to 2 with a man on first, I walked a guy on four pitches, and Lem took me out.

After the game Lindblad said to me, "Did you pitch?" I said, "Yeah, I pitched." He said, "I went to take a piss, and I came out, and Gossage was pitching." I said, "That's about how fast it happened." I'm allowed eight warm-up pitches, but the most I ever take is five. I said, "Christ, if I'da known he was gonna take me out so quick, I'da taken all eight of my warm-up pitches so I coulda stayed out there a little longer."

Now that we're only four back, everybody's starting to say, "Jeez, if we hadn't lost this game or that game, we'd only be three out." Phil Rizzuto said on the radio, "Ah, Phil Rizzuto, holy Cow, if we hadn't lost that game where we got rained out in Baltimore, we'd only be three games out." Screw it, if we hadn't lost the first game of the season, we'd be three games out.

Wednesday, September 6   New York

I'm beginning to think that I was wrong about someone in the front office telling Lem how to run the team. Lately he's been doing all the things you should be doing with our club, playing the right guys, making the right moves. With this team, all you have to do is make the normal moves, and we'll play well. That's what he's been doing.

When he first got here sometimes he didn't use the right guy to pinch-hit or pinch-run. But now he knows the club better, and he hasn't been doing badly. We're four games behind Boston, with a four-game Series against them coming up starting tomorrow.

Figgie won his fifteenth today, and what's encouraging to me is that not only are we winning—we've won 12 of 14— but we're finally coming out of our batting slump. We're scoring runs in bunches again. In the last two games we've had three-run innings, and today we had a four-run inning. In the fifth, Dent singled, Rivers singled, Munson walked, Chambliss hit a sacrifice fly for a run, Nettles singled, and Piniella doubled. Reggie's been out with the flu, but with him or without him it won't matter, if we can continue like this we're gonna kick Boston's ass.

Thursday, September 7   Boston

I said last year that Mike Torrez wouldn't win 20 games
with Boston, and everybody thought I was crazy. I said it
on TV again last week. A reporter asked me to say whatever came into my mind about the Red Sox players, free
association, and he dropped the name Torrez on me, and I
said that we lost him in the free agent draft, but I didn't
think it was that big a loss. He pitched great down the
stretch last year, but in a lot of those games we scored
about eight runs. A guy with his stuff should never lose.
He should be more than a lifetime .500 pitcher. He throws
hard and has good stuff. He's just not a winner.

Torrez started today and didn't get through two innings,
as we scored five off him. It didn't matter who Boston put
in there, whether it was Torrez, Hassler, Drago, or Campbell. Whoever was in there got pounded. We scored 2 in
the first, 3 in the second, 2 in the third, and 5 in the fourth.
Every guy who started for us got at least one hit. Roy,
Willie, and Thurman each got three, and Lou and Reggie
hit homers. Every time we knocked one of their pitchers
out, it was "We owed him that for sticking it up our ass
earlier this season. We shoulda got more." To be thrown
for so long, and to have to hear about the unbeatable Red
Sox all year and how they're better than the 1927 Yankees
and all that crap, well, we beat them 15 to 3 and it was just
terrific.

Cat started, and he was ahead 12 to 0 in the third when
he pulled a groin muscle and had to leave the game. Thurm
got hurt too. Drago beaned him. He went down for a
minute, lying on the ground, not moving. But then he
pulled himself up, and we felt a lot better. After the game
I saw him in the clubhouse, and he said he was feeling
better.

Friday, September 8   Boston

We knew the Red Sox were hurting going into this Series, but this is ridiculous. Evans was beaned last week, and he's still dizzy, and because of it he dropped a long fly ball that cost them, and he had to leave the game. Fisk has cracked ribs, and he made two throwing errors. Burleson booted one, and so did Scott, and Burgmeier threw one away too. We won 13 to 2. We scored 2 in the first inning and 6 in the second, and that really helped because it took the pressure off Beattie right from the start. He was able to relax, and he pitched super. He would have had a shutout, except Heath dropped Fisk's foul pop with two outs in the ninth, and Fisk hit a two-run home run. Lem took Beat out, and this rookie, Bob Davis, got the last out.

Beat's a good competitor. He wants to win in the big leagues. He's trying real hard, and I'll tell you, he's improved a lot. Before, he'd have real good stuff but didn't win because he'd get behind the hitters all the time. Now he's throwing more strikes, and he keeps you in the game. He wants this pennant as bad as anybody.

We were sitting in the bullpen listening to the game on the radio, and as we were scoring all these runs, Ned Martin, the Boston announcer, was saying, "HERE THEY COME AGAIN." Late in the game, he was saying, "Here's Bucky Dent. This is the only man in the Yankee lineup who hasn't got a hit tonight. If he doesn't get a hit this time up, he'll probably get released." All of a sudden, boom, Dent singles to drive in another run, and Martin says, "Well, Dent got his hit."

Bill Lee, who hadn't pitched against us all year, pitched the last seven innings for Boston and gave up five runs. Lee wrote an article in the paper where he said the Yankees were a bunch of derelicts and has-beens and he called Steinbrenner a Hitler and said Billy Martin was Hermann Göring and called the Yankees their storm troopers. Billy hated Lee for what he said and had a dead mackerel hung in Lee's locker. George was pissed off too. George hung the article on the wall of the clubhouse, but that didn't mean anything to us. What did we care what he said? All we wanted was for him to pitch again so we could kick his ass.

Everybody talks about Lee being flaky, but I respect his judgment. At the beginning of this year the Red Sox traded Bernie Carbo, and Lee was so mad he walked off the team. He told me he did that because during spring training the management said, "We're going to be a family. Nobody's going anywhere, 'cause that's the best way to play." Lee said, "They give you all this rigamarole and then they traded Carbo to Cleveland." He said he told them, "I wouldn't trade my cousin to Cleveland." He wanted people to know it wasn't right, so he walked off the club. He felt he had to bring some attention to the situation, and I respect that.

Everybody's been talking about all the injuries the Red Sox have. "This one's hurt. That one's hurt. Blah. Blah. Blah." But two months ago nobody would accept injuries as 90 percent of the reason we were 14 games behind. Randolph was hurt, and Dent and Rivers and Cat and Gullett and Messersmith—those two guys are still out—and Clay and Roy and Reggie. The Red Sox now are going through the same thing we did, only they're going through it at the worst possible time. Who would have guessed we could have gotten as hot as they were, and they could have gotten as cold as we were? Nobody could have possibly foreseen that, but it is happening, and we're only two games away from them.

Saturday, September 9   Boston

We were kidding Heath before today's game about the pop-up he dropped yesterday. Guys were standing around the outfield, throwing the ball way up in the air, running around in circles, and letting it hit the glove and drop. They'd say, "Player quiz. Who's this?" and they kept doing it to him. At the beginning he was laughing, but after a while, it started to bother him a little.

* * *

Gid pitched a shutout, a rare thing for a left-handed pitcher in Fenway, and won 7 to 0. He's now 21 and 2 and is as unbeatable as any pitcher who ever lived. The invincible, all-powerful Red Sox popped him for two big ones. In the first, Burleson hit a liner past him up the middle, and later Bucky bobbled a Rice bouncer that was ruled a hit but was really an error. With a little luck, Gid would have had a no-hitter.

For the third time in three games, we batted around against the Sox. Here's the fourth inning: there were two outs when Chris doubled and Nettles was walked on purpose. Piniella doubled for a run. White was walked intentionally. Dent singled to center for another run and went to second when Yaz bent over and booted the ball. Mickey singled for two more runs, and Mickey went to second when Yaz threw home late. Randolph walked. Thurma singled for another run. Burgmeier replaced Eckersl Randolph came home on a wild pitch. Reggie walk Chris flied out for the third out.

Are you ready for this?

BOSTON	86	55	.610	—
NEW YORK	85	56	.603	1

Sunday, September 10   Boston

It's very hard to believe what's going on. For the fourth game in a row, we came out and started kicking ass and scored runs and hit the ball like I couldn't believe. Today we had 18 hits. We were ahead 5 to 0 in the second inning, and there was no way they were going to beat Figgie, and Goose, who pitched the last three innings. To sit there and watch it was really something. For five years I played with the Red Sox, and I've never seen a team come in and do that to the Sox. I think we even surprised ourselves. I mean, we came into Boston loaded for bear. We'd been hoping to win three out of four, and we got 67 hits and 42 runs, and they started making errors, and our pitching was solid, and after it was over, we were almost feeling sorry for them. Almost. Before we got here their momentum had been taken away, and we completely destroyed them. In every game by the time we scored the third or fourth run, they'd be standing around in the field with their gloves off, their heads down, as if to say, "Oh, Goddamn, I hope we get a little luck and get out of this inning giving them only five runs."

I was talking with Piniella tonight, and he was saying how he's started to hit with his legs instead of with his hands and how much it's helped him. Evidently, it must be because he's hitting the hell out of the ball. They'll throw him a live fastball or a good pitch down and away, and boy, he'll hit the dogshit out of it, which is how he gets when he's hot. And he's been hitting like that for the last two weeks. In the four games against the Red Sox, he had ten hits, scored eight runs, had five RBIs, and had two doubles, a triple, and a home run.

Piniella doesn't get nearly the money he should be getting. Every year they tell him he's getting too old to play full time, and they tell him they're not going to raise his salary because he's only going to play against left-handers, but every year Lou starts hitting, and he'd be in there every day to where Lou would start saying, "Goddamn, they don't want to pay me for playing every day, but now they want me in there every day." But the way Lou is, he ends up saying to himself, "Screw it, what's another five thou? It ain't gonna make that much difference anyhow."

When Goose got the last out, it wasn't like winning the pennant. It was more like "We've struggled all year, and here we're tied for first place where nobody thought we'd be, even us." I don't think any of us really thought we could overtake the Red Sox, but we never gave up. We always felt that if we got close to them, we'd have an outside shot at it. That was the best we were hoping for. But once we got within seven of them, we started thinking, "We just might have a chance at this. *If* we could keep on playing good ball. *If* this. *If* that, *If*, *if*, *if*. But all the ifs happened.

The past four days we weren't playing over our heads, even though it may have seemed that way scoring seven, eight runs in the first couple of innings every game. That was phenomenal. But this ball club is capable of doing that if everybody's healthy and has his act together, which is exactly what we have. Even the bench guys have gotten into winning this thing. They stopped talking about leaving. Winning solves a lot of problems.

For four days we had everything together to where you couldn't have planned it any better. If you had made a wish and said, "I wish such-and-such for these four games," you couldn't have had it any better.

No one is celebrating because we know we have our work cut out for us. We could very easily be three games back in three days, so everybody's keeping his mouth shut, and we're going to go out and play good baseball and not get too gung ho. Even though we just blew Boston away, it's not over. We can't be screwing around like we have a five-game lead.

Everyone's talking about how Boston's been so together all year, and now that we've kicked their ass and tied them for first, now all you hear about is the controversy on the Red Sox that the players think George Scott is too fat and hasn't been trying, and stuff like that, that Zimmer is a lousy manager, and how Fred Lynn is jealous of Jim Rice and that Rice is angry because the Sox brought Lynn up before him. Crap like that. Ordinarily, you won't see dissension on a winning club.

Monday, September 11   Detroit

Even though he's no longer our manager, it's amazing just how strong Billy Martin's influence has been on us. When we'd get a team on the ropes, Billy would turn us on doing things, stealing, hitting and running, bunting, whatever, taking a lot of chances, and often we just blew the other team away. That's how we started scoring nine, ten runs an inning. He'd walk up and down the dugout telling us why he was doing what he was doing, and he'd also be ripping you if you made a mistake out there. He would be agitating us and turning our club on.

Now, even though Billy's no longer with us, we're veteran

enough that we can do that by ourselves because he taught us how. Now we turn ourselves on when we get the other team on the ropes. After two years with Billy, he's taught us how to win. And see, Lemon knows that with this club, he didn't have to do much. And he didn't do much, but because he was the complete opposite of Billy, he had a positive effect on some of the players. For instance, Lem has probably made Reggie and Micky better because their minds are most at ease. There isn't any crap going on. Our team was coming when Lem got here, and he was smart enough to just let it keep coming.

In spring training Goose was talking about the Pirates and how they could mash. I said, "I'll tell you what, before the year is over, and it won't be till late in the year, you'll forget about Pittsburgh because you've never seen a team that can turn it on like this one." I said, "Just wait till you see what we do to teams. It's unbelievable." And now Goose knows exactly what I was talking about. When you think that these guys were so far down that they were looking up and that now they're all of a sudden, bam, tied for first, it's incredible.

We know we're awesome as hell when we get it together. When the other batters see a couple of guys starting to hit, they'll start talking and say, "Boy, Nettles and Chambliss are hot, and you know what that means." And pretty soon Rivers and Reggie start hitting, and I'll tell you, you get three or four guys hot, and all of a sudden the guys hitting eighth and ninth starting getting pitches to hit, where before they weren't getting anything to hit because they were at the bottom of the lineup, and if the pitcher didn't get them, they'd get the guys at the top. But now the pitchers have to be careful with them, and they start hitting too, and it becomes an awesome thing to watch.

Tuesday, September 12　　Detroit

The Tigers knocked Tidrow out in the third, and Lemon brought Lindblad in, and in the top of the ninth losing 7 to 4, he brought Ron Davis in. When Davis couldn't get the last two outs, I had to come in. After the game the writers were asking me if it pissed me off that Lem used Davis in the ninth before me. Well, that didn't piss me off at all. I don't want to be in games where we're so far behind it doesn't even matter. Those are the games I've been in all this year. It didn't piss me off at all. The only thing that pissed me off were the writers asking their stupid questions.

We got this guy Davis in the Holtzman trade, and the only thing anyone notices about him is how much he eats all the time. He makes sandwiches two feet high and stuffs them in his mouth. You give him half a hot dog so he can take a bite, and he shoves the whole thing into his mouth. And after the game, he charges the spread like he has no concern for anyone else. The guy's a pig, plain and simple. And what really pissed me off about him is that he keeps calling Lindblad an old man. All the time. He better hope he'll get enough time in for some fresh rookie to be calling him an old man 'cause right now all he's got is the two weeks when the minor leaguers are called up at the end of the season. Maybe I'm wrong, but I don't think he should be calling Lindblad an old man. He hasn't done anything to be able to call him that. This Davis has the stuff to be a halfway decent pitcher, but I can't see that he'll set the world on fire unless he calms down, and I don't know whether he'll do that.

There was an article in a magazine called *The Baseball Bulletin,* saying that the Yankees would be going for a youth movement at the end of the year and giving a list of trades, which were ridiculous. One trade had me, Munson, and Roy going to Pittsburgh for Dave Parker, Bruce Kison, and a minor leaguer. We were all laughing at the trades in there. There were nine of us traded who can't be traded without our permission, so what good are they? I'm sure as hell not going to give my permission to go to Pittsburgh. I don't want to go to the National League. I want to stay in the American League so just one time I can come back and haunt George. All I'm looking for is a chance to beat his club out of something once. If I can do that, then I don't care where I go. They can send me anywhere—even Cleveland. But I promise you, I'm going to come back and haunt him. I won't rest till I do.

George is almost positive I'm washed up right now, but he's not absolutely positive and he doesn't want to take the chance of being ridiculed like the Boston management was when they got rid of me. That's why George wants me out of the American League. But guess what? He can't trade me without my permission, and the only place I'm going is to an American League team that'll let me play.

Before the game, George was sitting right behind the dugout. I saw him there, so I went back in the clubhouse and got *The Baseball Bulletin,* and I said, "George," and he looked up, and I slid it across the roof of the dugout to him. I said, "Here, read these trades." And I ran off into the outfield.

Wednesday, September 13   Detroit

NEW YORK   87   57   .604   —
RED SOX   87   58   .600   ½

We got 14 hits and seven runs and beat the Tigers 7–3 with Goose finishing up. Since the All-Star break, Goose has five wins, two losses, and 11 saves. I have three wins two losses, and one save.

I was kidding around with Nettles today about how I'm being used, or rather not used, how I have suddenly disappeared, and he says, "I guess you're right. You've gone from Cy Young to Sayonara."

For the second night in a row Boston made three errors and lost.

A writer asked me whether I didn't think I should have pitched today instead of Goose. I told him no. I said, "Last year they went with me every game, and that's why I had such a good year. You have to go with the guy who's doing the job, and right now that's Goose. You gotta go with him. The man's pitching tremendously, and you can't just stick me in there after I haven't pitched for fifteen days. You can't do it. You have to go with Goose and not even worry about pitching me at this point."

But what I don't understand is, had they traded me, Goose would have had an even better year than he's having now. He'd be getting even more work, which would have made him even sharper, and he wouldn't have this Sparky Lyle thing on his mind. Mark my words. If they trade me at the end of the season, next year both of us will have sensational years.

Thursday, September 14   Detroit

We were ahead 4 to 0 when Goose came in for Figgie in the eighth, and gave up two hits, a walk, and two runs. He got one out. Lem brought me in, and I got out of it and got the save, my ninth save of the season, my first since August 31. Some kind of stats, huh?

I was so happy because it had been so Goddamn long since I had a chance to pitch in a situation where the game was on the line. I didn't throw very well because I haven't pitched much, but I was really glad to be in a game where there was some excitement for me. While I was out there, I wasn't thinking about our lead over the Red Sox or the save or anything else. All I was thinking was that it was exciting to be on the mound again. It wasn't important whether I got out of it or not. Just being out there when it counted was what was important.

Nettles hit two home runs and a double to beat Slaton, and when people start talking about the Most Valuable Player, they talk about Gid and Rice and Carew, but as far as I'm concerned over the past few years the Most Valuable Player has been Nettles. Graig doesn't get the credit he deserves because he only hits .240 or .250, but now he's at .280, and I would think he'll have a shot at MVP if Gid doesn't win it. He's a great hitter, gets lots of home runs, and his play at third is super every day. It is a privilege to watch him.

The Red Sox lost—again. We're a game and a half up with just 16 to play.

Friday, September 15   New York

We opened a three-game Series with Boston at the stadium tonight, and Gid was phenomenal, boy, I'll tell you. He threw *another* two-hitter, and shut out the Red Sox, 4 to 0. I've never seen anyone like this guy. Even on the days when he doesn't have his good stuff he only gives up six hits.

Chambliss and Nettles hit back-to-back home runs off Luis Tiant, and Nettles made a play I couldn't believe was possible, except that he does these things all the time. Bob Bailey hit a hard ground ball that Graig had to dive for— his entire body was stretched out off the ground, and after he reached out and caught it, he jumped up real quick and threw Beiley out by two steps. The 50,000 people in the stands almost fainted. I wouldn't trade him for any other third baseman in the majors. In fact, I wouldn't trade him for any other player in the majors.

Just like at Fenway, Fisk hit a high pop-up behind the plate that Heath got under and dropped. When it fell, I was saying to myself that I hoped it wasn't because of all the ribbing everyone was giving him after he dropped the first one. That time Fisk hit a home run. This time, we got Fisk out anyway.

I don't know where this "Boston Sucks" thing started, but when you see a ten-year-old kid running around with a shirt that says "BOSTON SUCKS" on it, somebody's parents ought to have their ass kicked. It's ridiculous to see that crap. For little kids to holler "Boston Sucks" or in Fenway "Yankees suck," even if they don't know what it means, who in the hell wants to go to a ball game and hear that sort of thing? The sound of it should not be ringing from a ball park. Boo, throw beer, OK, but "Boston Sucks" does not fit in. I don't know whether it started here or up in Boston 'cause there are just as many "YANKEES SUCK" shirts up there. Wherever it started, I think it's horseshit.

It's too damn bad we gotta take abuse like that. The American League office writes letters to the players: "Don't use foul language on the fans." When you're talking about fans, you're not talking about the people who come with their families. You're talking about the idiots who pay their $2.50 to sit in the stands and throw things at you.

Those are the people who should be hit hard. I'd like to drag them onto the field and kick their ass 'cause eventually some player's gonna get hurt real bad, and there's not gonna be a damn thing done about it. Nothing. I don't see any letters going out to the fans saying, "Don't use abusive language on the players and don't throw stuff at them." But we get fined if we drop a "motherfucker" on somebody after they spend five minutes calling you an asshole.

Saturday, September 16   New York

Mickey Rivers led off against Torrez in the bottom of the ninth with the score tied at 2 to 2, and from the bullpen I saw where the Boston outfielders were playing him, and I couldn't believe it. Yaz and Lynn looked like they were playing deep infield, and I said to Goose, "Goddamn, Mickey has some power. They're making a mistake playing him so close." No sooner had I said that than bang, Rivers hit that son of a bitch over their heads for a triple. When Thurman hit a bullet that Rice had to make a diving catch for, Mickey could have crawled home. Cat got his tenth win, and now we're three and a half ahead. Maybe they were playing him so the balls he just slaps for base hits wouldn't fall in. Maybe they were just trying to keep him off the base paths. Or they could have been playing, "Screw it, if he hits it over our heads, he hits it over our heads." Someone said Yaz was playing in because he's used to playing that way in Fenway. No way. Yaz has been playing too long to make mistakes. Evidently they must have had a scouting report, but that report wasn't right and it cost them the game.

Reggie's been hitting. He went 3 for 4 today and drove in a couple of runs. Late in the game he was kneeling in the on-deck circle when he got his thumb mashed trying stupidly to barehand a hard-hit bouncer fouled toward him by Munson. Took his nail right off. It was ugly. After the game all the reporters were standing around him, and Reggie was saying that he had tried to stop the ball because before the game he had noticed a bunch of little kids sitting behind him and he was afraid the ball was going to go into the stands and hurt them. Can you believe that?

Eddie Lucas, who despite being blind does radio shows on baseball, came up to me after the game and told me a great joke. He said, "One guys says to the other guy, 'Do you talk to your wife when you're having sex?' The other guy says, 'Only when I'm near a phone.'"

Sunday, September 17   New York

Before the game Reggie sat down next to Lemon in the middle of the clubhouse and they started talking about something, and a lot of cameramen started taking their picture together. Reggie said to Lem, "If I hang around you, you'll get your picture in the paper." Lem laughed. He said, "I might even get a candy bar named after me."

The reporters were asking Reggie how he felt having to DH because his thumb hurt him too much to field. Reggie was going on about how it really doesn't matter to him whether he fields or not because he's on the team to hit and he's a bad fielder anyway so it really doesn't matter at all. I was listening to this, and I said to myself, "If he doesn't care whether he fields or not, why did he make it so Goddamn tough for Billy when Billy wanted to DH him?" Even now Reggie hasn't stopped giving it to Billy. Reggie was telling the writers how much better it is since Billy left and how relaxed he is and how he's a different person. Well, let me tell you, Reggie's no different than he ever was.

With Reggie DHing, Piniella is playing right. Everyone always says that Lou is a lousy outfielder because he doesn't run real good or have a great arm, but Goddamn, he catches every ball he can get to. I've always said I'd rather have him out there than most guys, including Reggie. He's the best slow outfielder in baseball.

Mop-up Man Lyle got into the game today and stunk out the joint. Eckersley was beating us 3–1 in the eighth

when I came in, walked Fisk, and gave up a single to
Frank Duffy on an 0 and 2 count. George Scott got up and
tried to bunt twice. He was 0 for 35 and figured it was
the only way he was going to get on, but he missed both
times. Again on 0 and 2, Scotty was forced to swing away,
and he hit a double for another run. Lem took me out and
brought Clay in. I didn't do the job, and that's frustrating
no matter who it's against, but it was worse because it was
the Red Sox and we're in pennant contention. I'm trying
to do a job that I love to do, but that's hard for me to do
because of the way I'm being used. I feel like I'm going
out there and getting my ass kicked for no reason at all.

I could accept it if I was getting my ass kicked because
I don't have it anymore, but that's not what's happening.
If I could pitch right, I'd be kicking their ass. It gets so
frustrating, you get on edge, and you start hearing things
that are said to you from the stands like, "You're washed
up, ya bum." After a while that gets to you, especially
when you know how you're pitching is out of your control.
I've found myself hollering back at people in the stands,
something I've never done before. I won't take it anymore.
I won't take anybody's bull. If I hear somebody, I'll turn
around and air them out good right away.

It's been tougher for me and for everybody because there
are so many reporters around you can't do or say anything
or else you'll see it in the papers the next day. Like today,
a guy was standing right in the doorway of the lounge listening, right beside the sign that says "PLAYERS ONLY." I
wanted to yank the son of a bitch by the back of the neck
and throw him out of the clubhouse. But you can't do that
because he's not breaking any rules. Then they wonder
why Thurman gets pissed off.

Monday, September 18   New York

Figgie went all the way tonight, beating the Brewers 4 to 3
for his eighteenth win. Figgie's been pitching really well,
he's something like 11 and 2 since the All-Star break, which
just goes to show that for a pitcher to win, the whole team
has to be playing well behind him. Figgie had been pitching well all year long, but he was something like 7 and 7

at the All-Star break because we weren't getting him any runs. Now the club's got its stuff together, and he'll end up with a great record.

Tuesday, September 19   New York

Lou has a habit of grabbing the ends of his hair with the tips of his fingers, twirling them into a strand, running his fingertips along the strand, and then after dropping the strand, he smells his fingers. It's a compulsion with him. He can't stand not to do it.

Before the game, Lou was getting on Cat real good. He said, "When I take my wife out to dinner, I take her in my Cadillac. When you take your wife, you take her in a John Deere tractor."

Cat said, "Oh yeah, well why don't you go smell your hair." Lou didn't know what to say. He said, "What? Huh? What did you say?" Then Cat and Graig and a couple of other guys put their fingers up to their nose the way Lou does and started smelling them. Afterward, Lou was grabbing the ends of his hair, twirling them like he always does, but he wouldn't drop the strand unless he was sure no one was watching him. He waited and waited, and when he thought no one was watching, real nonchalantly he sniffed his fingers.

Mike Caldwell of the Brewers gave up four hits, and he won his twentieth game. In the clubhouse after the game, Piniella was saying to the writers, "Caldwell is a Goddamn cheater. The son of a bitch was cheating. That's all there was to it. He was cheating." Piniella was pissed because Caldwell was throwing a spitter, and a spitball is not only illegal but, worse for Lou, it's hard to hit. It comes up to the plate and drops like a son of a bitch. But Jeez, he still had to get it over the plate just like a curve ball or a fast-ball. And hell, the guy didn't throw a hundred spitballs in the game. But Lou, he gets so frustrated when any pitcher gets him out, he can't stand it. Yeah, the guy throws a spit-ball, big deal, but it was too tough for him to take, especially since we were on the losing end of the son of a bitch.

Wednesday, September 20   Toronto

Gid started the first game and really got his ass kicked. He gave up five runs in an inning and a third. It was only his third loss against 22 wins. He'd have been all right, but a couple of guys were on when he fielded a bunt and threw· the ball past Nettles into left for a couple of runs. I guess it's just as well they got him out of there in a hurry because this way he has a chance to rest and come back strong.

Lemon brought in Larry McCall in the second inning, and he pitched the rest of the way. McCall's a pretty good kid, has good stuff, throws hard, is a good competitor, and he has an idea of what he's doing out there. He's got everything it takes. All he needs is a chance.

Toronto pitched two lefties, Willis and Underwood, against us. They did OK because they changed speeds pretty well, which is a good way to get our hitters out. When you don't see a guy a lot, and he's changing speeds, it's pretty tough to hit him. I think these teams bring lefties up from the minors specifically to pitch against us. I'll tell you what, if Toronto tries pitching these two guys again when they come back to the stadium, they're gonna get their asses kicked bad 'cause our hitters will remember what they throw and be ready for them.

Willis beat us 8 to 1 in the first game, and we were losing to Underwood 2 to 0 in the ninth inning of the second game. Even so, I wasn't worried, because the Red Sox were losing their game, and even if we had lost them both we would still have been a game and a half ahead.

We were sitting out in the bullpen hoping we could tie it. Willie Randolph led off with a single, and Underwood walked Reggie, and this pitcher Cruz was brought in in relief. Piniella swung and hit the ball right off the end of his bat, and if it hadn't been for the Astroturf, the ball never would have gone through. You couldn't have taken the ball and rolled it any better than where he hit it, and that's what set off the inning right there. Chambliss hit a two-hopper up the middle and almost took Cruz's head off and we had our tie. Then Nettles hit a bullet for a third run, Goose got his tenth win, and we ended up gaining a half game, and now we're two up on the Sox.

Ralph Houk announced his retirement from baseball today, and that surprised me. Maybe Ralph isn't feeling good, because Ralph loves baseball too much to stop managing. He had an open-ended contract, and he loves kids, and in another year or so the Tigers are gonna be a really respectable team. I just can't understand Ralph leaving before he has a chance to see the team blossom. I'm sorry to see him go, and I'm grateful for having had the chance to play for him. He was without a doubt the best manager I ever played for.

Thursday, September 21   Toronto

Catfish left in the sixth with a 3 to 0 lead, and it would have been a great game for me to have pitched in, to have tried to get myself together. But Lem put Goose in again, and he got the save. I can kinda understand that. Lemon figures that if he puts me in the game and I pitch the way I have been—every time I've pitched lately I've given up a run—he'd be taking the chance that I'd give up a couple of runs right off the bat and have a guy on second and third and nobody out. Then he'd have to take me out and bring Goose in, and Goose has been a little wild lately, and there'd be a question whether Goose would walk a couple of guys before getting out of the inning. So Lem just figured, "Screw it, I'll go with Goose from the beginning." OK, I understand that, yet Goddamn, give me a fucking chance. If he wants to take me out after one guy gets on, I don't care, but Christ, at least let me try.

I'm through, through for the year. I'm not pissed off or nothing anymore. I'm just waiting. I'm gonna contribute as much as I can, which I don't think will be much because they know I'm not pitching good, so I'll just wait for the season to be over. I'll resign myself to that. I can't do a thing about it. I've tried all year not to let them bury me. I've talked to them, walked out of games, got pissed off, tried everything I could think of. But none of it worked, so here I am. Yeah, I got some more money out of George, but money doesn't mean anything to me compared to what it means to be able to be pitching. Screw it, I'd take less money to be able to pitch every day.

Friday, September 22   Cleveland

We opened the Cleveland Series with an awful 8–7 loss. Andre Thornton hit a three-run home run off Figgie in the first inning, and this new guy, Cage, hit one right after his. Before the game Larry McCall went to Figgie and told him that Cage will hit anything low, breaking balls, anything. He said that Cage had kept him from becoming a 20-game winner in the minors. He told Figgie to pitch the guy up and in. Well, Figgie didn't pay any attention to him, and when Cage got up, Figgie threw him a low fastball, and he hit it out, and the next time up Figgie got ahead of him and tried to throw a fastball low and away, and Cage smoked it down the left-field line for a double. Figgie hadn't thrown him a pitch up yet.

The Indians might have a pretty good team if they had a couple more decent pitchers, and if they get another manager. The manager they got now, Genius Torborg, is nothing but a showboat. He's always saying, "We're going to be the spoilers and beat the Yankees." That's 'cause the only thing he has to look forward to by the All-Star break is beating the Yankees. By that time their season is already over. He makes this big deal about beating the Yankees, and when he plays us, he has his bullpen up before "The Star Spangled Banner." The first sign of trouble, those sons of bitches are up. I mean they throw their asses off when they play us. And during the game he makes that trip to the mound four or five times, and each time he walks out there real slow to show he's controlling the game. He's always coming out to talk to his pitchers, telling them to do this or do that, and then sometimes he'll sprint out of the dugout and say something and run real quick back in.

We're always screaming at him from the dugout, "What are you going to tell him now, Stylemaster?" That's what we call him, Stylemaster. When he walks off the field he takes tiny little steps so he doesn't step on the foul line.

He probably saw that in an old William Bendix movie. It's a pain in the ass watching him walk in and out to the mound. He doesn't say anything to the pitchers anyhow. Today Nettles hollered at him, "Hey, Stylemaster, you have a hair out of place."

Today he almost lost that damn game for them. The Indians were ahead 7 to 4 with the bases loaded and one out, and he took Jim Kern out and brought in Monge to pitch to Reggie Jackson. Kern was throwing 200 miles an hour, and, yeah, he was a little wild, but I'll tell you, when you see Monge come in with that garbage he throws and you see Kern walking off the mound, you have to be happy about that. Torborg said, "The book says that the last four times Jackson faced Monge, he got him out, twice striking him out, and that's why I brought him in." Well, Monge sure as hell wasn't throwing the same way today as he had been when that book was made up. Monge walked Reggie to drive in a run, and then Piniella drove in two more runs with a single to put us ahead 7 to 6, and we shouldn't have even come close. His great maneuvering almost lost it for them.

Thurm isn't talking about it, but he's been playing with a dislocated shoulder. He hurt it up in Boston. The shoulder is so loose you can take it and move it. Even though he insists on playing with it, his body is hurting so badly that he isn't able to stop some balls he normally can. Lemon tried catching Heath for a few games, but Heath just doesn't hit. With Thurm hurting, Heath is a better catcher, but I don't know if they can afford to catch Heath and DH Thurm 'cause Thurm doesn't hit as well when he's DHing. He's just not into the game as much.

When I relieved Lindblad in the eighth, Kuiper singled and Thurm allowed a passed ball because his shoulder was killing him and he wasn't able to reach it. The runner then scored on a single to tie it up. Goose ended up losing it 7 to 6 in the tenth. But that's just the kind of luck we've been having this year. The Red Sox also lost. Toronto scored two runs in the bottom of the ninth to beat them, so we're still two games ahead with eight games left in the season.

Saturday, September 23   Cleveland

Beat was wild and Tidrow was hit hard, and we were getting beat 7–1 with two outs in the fourth when Lem
brought this kid Rajsich in to pitch, which really pissed
Mickey Rivers off. Mickey was saying, "Damn it, I don't
care if Lyle's getting his ass kicked, bring the man in.
Even if he doesn't have good stuff, he's got a better chance
than this guy." Mickey really gets mad when he sees the
manager make a move he doesn't like, and when the
manager brings in less than who he thinks is the best reliever just because we're behind, he goes crazy. He says,
"What are we playing, givers away? Are we playing givers
away? Bring the right man in."

Mickey has this rap that he doesn't hustle. There are
times he doesn't, but this is one of the reasons why. He
feels, "If the manager won't try his hardest, why should
I?" In the seventh, Mickey jogged after a long fly ball and
didn't catch up to it. He was still pissed about Lem's
bringing Rajsich in.

Tiant beat Toronto, and our lead is down to one game.

Sunday, September 24   Cleveland

Guidry's in a terrible rut. He pitched another two-hit shutout and beat Cleveland 4 to 0 for his twenty-third win.
Just think, if Gid is only throwing six hitters next year,
winning four to three, George will be on his ass for not
pitching well. George did that to Gid once. He called Gid
into his office and said, "What the hell is going on here?
You're not striking out enough batters. You have to get
more strikeouts." George then told Gid he didn't have guts
and that he'd never be a major leaguer. That's what Gid
told me. Gid just laughed. But George, he was serious.

In the fourth, Reggie slid into third, and when Nettles
got hung up between first and second, everybody was yelling for Reggie to score. Had Reggie slid in, come up, and

took off, he would have scored, but he slid in and just sat on the ground dusting himself off, showboating the way he does. It didn't cost us because he scored anyway, but that's the type of thing that really pisses everybody off. Hey, Reggie's hustling, hitting the ball good now, but what's the sense of losing your head for that one minute and maybe costing us a run? If Piniella hadn't gotten a hit, Reggie wouldn't have scored, and that might have been the difference in the ball game.

Reggie knows when he screws up. I'm convinced of that, and yet he does it in a way that he always has a reason— "I didn't realize Nettles was hung up" or "I jammed my knee when I came into third"—the sort of answer where you can't pin him down. Maybe these things did happen. Except that they happen so often.

After the game I was in the clubhouse getting a cup of coffee, and Lou comes over and said, "Count, I admit I shouldn't have thrown my helmet. That was the wrong thing to do, and I'm gonna try not to do it anymore. But he shouldn't have called me a fucking asshole. I play hard for the guy. Why should he call me a fucking asshole?"

I'm going, "Jeez, I don't know, Lou." I mean, I didn't even know who he was talking about, what happened, or nothing.

Later, Nettles told me Lou got robbed of a hit by Very-zer, the Cleveland shortstop, and when Lou came back to the dugout he whizzed his batting helmet right by Lemon's head. When that happened, Nettles said, Lemon got pissed and said, "Goddamn it, there's no reason to throw your helmet. It doesn't do any good. I'm getting tired of watching helmets flying by my head." And Puff said there was a short pause, almost an afterthought, and Lem said, "You fucking asshole." The good thing about Lem: when he gets mad, he lets you know about it right there so you don't do it again.

After the game, we had a closed-door meeting. Lem got mad because Mickey wasn't in the on-deck circle when he should have been, and Lem took him out of the game. Mickey was getting a drink of water. You gotta be in the on-deck circle in case a guy is scoring so you can tell him whether to slide or not. In the meeting Lem said, "If there's anyone who doesn't want to play, just let me know because there are plenty of guys on the bench who want to play. I'm not gonna put up with that crap, I don't give a damn who you are." I guess, to Lem, Mickey's not being in the on-deck circle indicated to him that Mickey wasn't playing heads-up ball, that his mind wasn't where it was supposed to be. So he aired us out for about three minutes and he said, "You know who you are, and I'm telling you, I'm not putting up with it." Mickey doesn't give a damn anyhow. To him being on deck doesn't mean squat. He's there to hit and run and catch the ball.

After Lem chewed our ass out, he said, "That's all I gotta say," and he started walking back to his office. He got about halfway there, and you could hear the murmuring in the clubhouse, and all of a sudden he turned around and said, "And one more thing. I don't want to see any more of them helmets whizzing by my head." And he turned back and walked away. Everybody started to laugh, and you could see him laugh, and that was it.

It's always fun to watch the writers come into the clubhouse after the door's been locked. They're like a swarm of bees. They start saying, "Did he say 'This'?" "No." "Did he say 'THIS'?" "No." "Give me a hint. Was it 'this'?" These guys aren't dumb. In thirty seconds somebody comes over and tells you everything that happened word for word. It's amazing. What the hell is the sense of locking the door if some son of a bitch is gonna tell? Maybe we ought to just tape the meeting for them and give them the tape. It would save them a lot of trouble.

Tuesday, September 26   New York

George is mad at me. He says I've been popping off again by asking to be traded. Christ, I haven't said any more about being traded other than what I said three months ago. The writers come up and ask me, "Do you still feel the same as you did in July?" And I say, "Yeah, I do." And then the writers go ahead and write whatever they want. I don't know why that should make George mad.

He's also mad at me because of my throwing *The Base-*

ball Bulletin with all those trades in it to him the other day in Detroit. I was doing it as a joke, and now I find out he's pissed off because of that. He says I tried to embarrass him in front of his friends. Why would he think that? Why shouldn't he take it as being a little funny, as I intended?

Tidrow was telling me he heard that Billy would be managing Texas next year, and Dirt doesn't usually talk about stuff like that unless there's truth to it. He said that he and I are both going to Texas for Toby Harrah because George wants Harrah to play shortstop. I guess George has never seen Harrah play shortstop. He may be a better hitter than Bucky or Chicken, but we don't need that on our club. I have a feeling George thought Bucky was going to hit better. Also, Bucky wants to be traded because they keep pinch-hitting for him in the late innings. Bucky didn't come over here to be platooned. Bucky's a good defensive shortstop, and he can hit the long ball every once in a while. What more do you want? Why the hell does George need a number nine hitter to be hitting .270? Somebody has to be the last out.

If they traded me to Texas, that would be fine with me. I think there was something going on between us and Texas when we got Lindblad. He was one of the guys mentioned in a trade early this spring along with my name, so maybe the Yankees feel they now have their left-handed long man in Lindblad. And this young kid, Rajsich, maybe can take over as the left-handed short man. He's just about ready for the major leagues. He throws the ball pretty good. Maybe they'll take a chance on him and that way they won't have to listen to me bitch and holler. They'll use him about the way they've been using me this year, and Goose'll be able to take over, which will be good for Goose. The only thing is, if Goose gets tired and they're in the heat of things and have to use this other kid, they only have a fifty-fifty chance. They don't know if this kid can get guys out consistently in the big leagues. He could be a tremendous pitcher, but who knows? But I still think they're going to take the gamble because I'm sure George figures Goose can pull them through. And with Goose there, it's not that big a gamble.

*   *   *

Cliff's really pissed. He was upset because Lemon held a workout yesterday on our day off, and Lem asked him to come out and hit, and he hit all day, and today he comes to the ball park and he wasn't in the lineup, which really burned his ass. Cliff said to me, "I came out and hit extra, and it screwed up my off day, and I'm not even in the lineup. What the hell is going on?" Who am I to answer that question? I'm down deeper than he is. I mean, I'm looking up at him.

Cliff is just waiting for the season to get over too. That's what has happened to all of the guys on the bench. They're just waiting. Cliff and Spencer and Johnstone and Thomasson. But I'll tell you what, if George is thinking of getting rid of all these guys and going with a youth movement, I have no idea where he's gonna get the youth from because our prospects in our minor league system are few and far between. We have these two kid infielders Garcia and Ramos. They start at Tacoma. Ramos can't hit and he can't cover any ground. Garcia's a good athlete, he can play the game, but nobody's taught him the game, which is somebody's fault, I'll tell you that. It's like what Piniella was saying to me the other day. He said, "I can't believe Garcia hits with his hands way in the air. Ya can't hit like that. I can't believe they'll let a kid go like that and not teach him how to hit. What the hell are they doing down there?" But they don't teach them because they don't have anybody to teach them. That's one reason the Yankees have to make so many trades. We really don't have anybody in our farm system except pitchers. But with all the free agent pitchers George signs, where's he gonna put these kids?

Figgie was leading 4 to 1 in the ninth, and Lem brought Goose in to save Figgie's nineteenth win. Lem should have brought in Goose. With six games left and a one-game lead, it's a touch-and-go situation where we have to win every day. They can't afford to take the chance again that I'd give up a run or two, so they'd rather bring Goose in. He's been pitching great, has 20-odd saves, and I can't blame them a bit for that. I'd do the same thing if I was the manager. I wouldn't want to see my ass out there either.

After the game Nettles said to me, "Did they actually have Rajsich throwing with Goose instead of you?" I said, "Yeah." He said, "I can't really believe that. I don't know what they're doing to you or why, but I just can't believe it. We're trying to win and they're thinking of bringing some damn rookie in?" He went on and on. I figure at this point I've gone as far down as I can go. I just told him, "Screw it all." If I didn't think this would be my last World Series, I'd quit right now and go home so I could have some peace of mind for the rest of the season.

Phil Pepe of the *Daily News,* who's covering the Yankees for one of the strike papers, asked Nettles who he thought should win the Comeback Player of the Year. Nettles said, "Hell, Thurman had that won the first day of the season." Pepe said, "Why?" Puff said, "Thurman said he was never coming back, and he came back, so he's gotta win it." Then Puff said, "I know who's gonna win it next year." Pepe said, "Who?" Puff said, "Lyle. He's so far down this year, he's my choice for next year already." I told Pepe, "I just might quit and ruin his prediction."

Lem wore a batting helmet tonight while he sat on the bench. I guess he was protecting himself from Piniella.

For the first time, women are now allowed in the clubhouse after the game. This woman judge made a ruling they couldn't be kept out, so a whole flock of these women reporters came strolling in before and after the game. This one woman reporter walked up to Goose, who was wearing only boxer shorts, and Fowler snuck up behind him and pulled his shorts down.

Wednesday, September 27 New York

Catfish pitched another beautiful game tonight, gave Toronto six hits, and won, 5 to 1. I've never seen a pitcher like Cat. Throws 'em in and out, up and down. Changes speeds. Guidry I can understand because he's so damn fast. But Cat, he's just amazing.

Lou was teasing Cat, ribbing him because he gives up

about 40 home runs every year. "That's right," Cat said, "and I'll probably give up two hundred and forty more before I retire. 'Cause I'll throw the damn ball in there every time. I'm going to make them hit it. They gotta hit it out. And I don't care if they do. I'll keep throwing it in there, and I'll keep getting most of them out." And that's the way you have to pitch, of course. How many years in a row did Cat win 20 games throwing them in there? Five. This year, pitching half a season, he's 12 and 5. Who's to say he won't win 20 again next year?

We're a game ahead of Boston and have to win our last five games to clinch the Division title. Gid is starting tomorrow with three days rest so he'll be ready Monday in case there's a play-off, and that has me worried. Evidently Gid told them he could do it, but I don't know what's gonna happen. I tell you, I'd start Gossage. Let Goose blow them away for five or six innings, and run in there whoever you want to. I was thinking of talking to Lem about it, but I decided not to. Lem knows what he wants to do right now, and I wouldn't want to go in there and say something and put doubt in his mind.

Thursday, September 28   New York

Roy White made another of his spectacular catches tonight, running to the stands and jumping up to catch Otto Velez's dinger before it went into the stands. I don't know why George doesn't like Roy. It's ridiculous. He's a steady, reliable ballplayer, and if you look back, he's always been instrumental in the big games we win. I've seen him make catches like that a lot of times since I've been here. That man can play.

Since Reggie hurt his thumb and has been DHing, Roy's been in left, Lou in right, and both are playing the field tremendously.

I shouldn't have been worried about Gid, meanwhile. He didn't have his usual stuff because he was working with three days' rest, but with less than his best he allowed four hits, one run, and he struck out nine. He won his twenty-fourth, 3 to 1. We have to hope the Red Sox lose

tomorrow 'cause Beattie's starting for us tomorrow against
the Indians, and the last time out he just didn't have it. We
can't afford to have that happen again because if they got
four runs off him right away, the way Torborg manages,
we would face nine different pitchers just so we couldn't
catch up. We have got to score first if we're going to
beat Cleveland these next three games. Boston has won
its last five in a row and seems to be back on the track.

Friday, September 29   New York

I shouldn't have worried about Beat either. Beat was tough,
allowed four hits, and beat the Indians 3 to 1, but even
though we won, we could be in trouble. Willie Randolph
pulled a hamstring real bad running out a ball, and he's
finished for the year. Without Willie in there, we're a whole
different team. Willie's the perfect number two guy in the
batting order, he can hit and run, bunt, hit behind the
runner, and he hits .280, plus he's the best second baseman
in the major leagues. Brian Doyle has an excellent glove,
but he doesn't hit much. Without Willie, we're not nearly
as good a team. I just hope we'll be able to win our last
two games so we won't have to play the Red Sox in a play-
off.

When I got to the ball park today, I got dressed, and
while I was sitting in my locker, this woman reporter came
over and asked me what I thought of women being able
to come into the Yankee clubhouse for the first time. I
was honest with her. I said that if everybody stays within
their regular routines, everyone'll get along just fine, but
once someone starts going outside of those routines, there'll
be trouble. I told her I felt very sorry for the older men,
like the coaches, who are embarrassed by it. They don't
want to be running around naked with women in there.
"I've always walked from my locker to the shower and
back with nothing on," I told her, "and I'm not going to
change now. I don't give a damn. I'm not changing my
routine."

I mean, I'm not going to run around and throw my

dick in their faces, but I'm just not going to change my ways. It's a damn shame, though, that some guys have to get dressed in the shower room or have to take their clothes into the trainer's room to get dressed.

Saturday, September 30   New York

In the second inning Mickey singled, Thurman singled, Reggie walked, Nettles singled for a run, Chris doubled for two more, and Roy singled for two more, and Figgie finally got his twentieth win, a five-hit shutout over the Indians. I'm really glad because we won't have to listen to all the crap about whether Figgie's gonna be the first native-born Puerto Rican to win 20 games anymore. A couple of years ago he should have won 20, but I messed up a couple of games for him, and he only won 19. I told him, "I'll never go to your hometown, not after this."

As Figgie was surrounded by reporters and TV cameras, Reggie stuck his head in there and said to Figgie, " 'Bout time you won twenty, you cunny thumper." Anybody else could have done that, me or Nettles or Tidrow, and nobody would have said, "Look at Lyle jumping in and trying to get in front of the cameras." But when Reggie does it, even when he's trying to be nice, it's "Look at that son of a bitch horning in. He has to be in the center of things."

Reggie wears two big crosses around his neck, and today he was talking about how everything is in God's hands. When Reggie says that stuff, it sounds like such garbage. Hey, I believe in God. I might even feel that way sometimes, but I would never say that to a reporter, not because I would be ashamed to but because I don't feel it's in place. Lately, he's been talking a lot about how everything's in God's hands. Maybe it is, but you don't have to keep repeating it, repeating it over and over and over again. Reggie's gone from "If Reggie doesn't hit, the Yankees don't win" to "It's in God's hands." It's like what George Carlin says: "How do you know His hands are better than yours?"

* * *

We were out in the bullpen today, and this kid Brian Doyle was playing shortstop. I was watching him, and on every pitch Doyle would wipe his mouth on his left sleeve, wipe his mouth on his right sleeve, and then he'd grab the bill of his cap and straighten it. He did this after every pitch, like clockwork. The pitch would come in, he'd take a crow hop, get right back, and wipe, wipe, straighten. Bang, bang, bang. It's something Joe Garagiola could put to music on his pregame TV show.

I love to watch routines of guys. A few years ago, we had this kid, Rick Sawyer, who was a pitcher. He had a cup of coffee with the Yankees. Every day he'd come to the clubhuose after the game, get a towel, and fold it a certain way every time and hang it on the rack. Then he'd take a shower. When he came out, he'd always take the towel, flip it over, and dry himself.

One day, when Sawyer went into the shower, I unfolded the towel, pasted it with shoe polish, and folded it back up. Walt Williams was in the whirlpool, and he was watching me, and he said, "What the hell are you doing, man?" I said, "Just watch." He said, "It's never gonna work." I said, "Yeah, it is." So Sawyer came out of the shower, unfolded his towel as usual, and started drying away. Pretty soon he had shoe polish all over him. I mean *all* over him, it worked so well. It worked so easily it was unbelievable. Williams was laughing so hard he almost drowned in the whirlpool.

Alex Johnson was another guy whose habits I watched. He used to lie in his locker and read an electronics book. Every single day that he was with us he read this electronics book. He'd go over to our candy supply, take a handful of candies, and lie down in his locker and read.

One day I went to a joke shop and bought this awful-tasting candy that has garlic and peppers in it and tastes like shit. Plus it gets hotter'n hell. This stuff, I'll tell you, tastes like a pair of dirty sweatsocks—that's what's so great about it. I bought five pieces. They looked like the little white candies that have little fruit things in them. They're kinda nice and chewy. I put my candies in our candy box, and remember there were only five of them among all this candy, and as I was waiting for someone to come over and take a piece, Alex comes over and picks out all five of them! Which I never expected. I was going crazy!

He went back to his locker, lay down with the candy next to him, and started reading. He took one of my candies and unwrapped it. They have sugar coating on them so when you first put them into your mouth, they taste good. Then all of a sudden the sugar's gone, and it's *el churcho*. He put the first one in his mouth, and just as quickly spat it back out. He looked at it, made a face, and wrapped it back in the cellophane and threw it away. He must have been thinking, "Screw it, I got a bad one." So he took another one! He put it in his mouth and right away started chewing vigorously. Well, boy, now this hit him. You could see that he had the Chinese army in his mouth, and the thing is, when you chew it, it gets so sticky inside your mouth that you can't get it out. I looked over, and Alex was trying to pull the goo out of his mouth with his fingers. Oh, man, it was funny! Boy, that was great, I'll tell you, it was really a good one.

After the game, there must have been 30 women reporters in the locker room because every newspaper and TV station decided it would be great to send a woman to cover the Yankees. The women who had sued to get in here, their assignments have been few and far between. Half these women don't know the first thing about baseball, but the media decided to make it a circus, so they sent the first woman they could find, and this is what's going to cause trouble.

After the game, I took one of my sanitary socks, the white thin tube socks that go under our stirrups, and instead of putting a towel around me, I put my dick and balls into the sani, and I walked to the shower with my sani hanging down between my legs. I said, "Nobody'll know whether it's big or little." On the way back, I wrapped the towel around the top of me, not quite covering everything. It got a few laughs, and I don't think it pissed anyone off. It didn't matter if it did. It's still my clubhouse.

Jay Johnstone had a big sign above his locker: "U.S. JUDGE CONSTANCE MOTLEY SUCKS RATSHIT!!" He's really pissed about the women in the locker room. He yelled at this one reporter, "Why don't you go back to the kitchen?"

Now if you want to sit in your locker on your stool with no clothes on and eat something, you can't. I suppose you can, but some of the women will get very offended. Even if that's what you did every day, they'd figure you were doing that just to piss them off. It's things like that that are causing the uneasy feelings.

I ran into George today and he said, "Go down to the bullpen and get yourself ready to pitch 'cause you're going to be very important to us in the big games." I told him I've been going out to the park early and throwing, trying to get my act together. I said it's coming around a little bit, but I know damn well it won't get any better unless I pitched in the games.

Tomorrow's the final game of the season. We're up by one and Cat's pitching. Here's hoping.

Sunday, October 1   New York

There are trade rumors going around that the Yankees have traded Paul Blair to Texas for Juan Beniquez, their center fielder. This time the rumor looks like it's true, and if George did that, he might be making a mistake. They used to talk about Brooks Robinson being a clutch hitter. He was hitting .220, but you didn't want him up there with men on base. I'll bet in the last two years for the number of times he's gotten up, Blair has more game-winning hits than anybody. For the small amount of time he plays, he always ends up getting on base or getting the winning hit in a key situation. I can't believe they're going to trade him. I guess George figures he's thirty-four years old, and paying him a hundred grand to be Mickey's caddy is too much. Beniquez is another guy who'll play when he wants to. He can't carry Paul Blair's jockstrap, and not only that, Beniquez isn't going to hit. He'll be another guy who'll hit like a house afire for a while, and that'll be it. He's not going to fit into this ball club.

George doesn't learn, and before long he ain't gonna be

winning either. Every year he gets rid of people who have helped him win the year before, and he gets somebody who's never been through a pennant race before, a guy who was never on a winner. And if he isn't careful, he's gonna have a whole club of these guys. He'll have gotten rid of all his winners, and he'll be left with a team of good ballplayers who have never been on winners. He'll have a hell of a second-place ball club. He'll end up having a club like Boston, a team that wins 99 games but no bananas.

I'm anxious to see what trades George is going to make this winter because this time I think he might make a few mistakes. He doesn't have Gabe anymore, and it was Gabe who talked him out of trading Gid. I don't know whether Rosen knows talent, and I don't know whether Rosen will be able to argue with George and make George see when a trade he wants to make is a bad mistake, like Gabe did.

I bought a cake from a bakery in Manhattan and brought it into the clubhouse for anyone who wanted to eat it. It was in the shape of a dick, about two feet long and six inches wide, and I put a sign on it, "FOR WOMEN REPORTERS ONLY." One of the guys saw that cake and he went and go some cream-colored shampoo and squirted it on a strategic part of the cake. One girl reporter got real upset. She walked over and saw it and said, "Who did this? I don't think this is very nice." She asked Nettles if he brought it in. He said, "No. I just modeled for it." She stormed out of the clubhouse. Another reporter saw it and she thought it was funny. She took it in good humor, which was all it was meant to be for. But the other took offense to it, just because she's a woman. Some people can't take a joke.

We're gonna have to play Boston in a play-off tomorrow. The Red Sox shut out Toronto, and Cleveland's Rick Waits beat us on a five-hitter. Clubs are starting to bring the lefty phenoms in to pitch against us. They might have brought him up from the Egyptian League for all I know. Catfish gave up two home runs to Cage and Alexander and didn't get through the second inning. After Cat got knocked out, Lem brought in Tidrow, and then Rajsich, and McCall, and finally Lindblad, and I was sitting out there thinking,

"Well, Goddamn, why are all these guys pitching? Rajsich and McCall aren't even eligible for the play-offs."

Nothing fazes me anymore. I've seen stuff going on all summer and I don't even bat an eye anymore. You can't do it any other way or else you'll drive yourself batty. I've been throwing every day to keep in shape and get my act together. It doesn't do any good because if I go in and give up a hit or two—even when I'm throwing good—that's it, I'm out of the game, unless the game is out of hand, in which case they'll leave me out there to mop up. I guess I'm along for the ride this year. Last year I did my part. This year someone else is doing it.

When we learned that the Red Sox had won, everyone was saying, "This is the way it should be." I feel that way. It's the way the season should end. They were ahead of us by 14 games in July, and we caught them because we played good and they played poorly. That's how they got 14 games ahead: they played good and we played poorly. It's evened out. I think a one-game sudden death is the one true way of determining the winner this year, and whoever wins, nobody's going to second-guess anybody. Boston won the last eight games in a row to get where they got. You can't say that Boston choked.

Monday, October 2   Boston

It was strange, but for a game that was so important to both teams, there was very little tension. Last night a bunch of us went out and had a few drinks, and we were sitting at the hotel bar, and the general consensus was "We're gonna win tomorrow." We just knew we were going to win. And the Red Sox weren't tight because they had just had the Division championship taken away from them, and now they were getting a second chance. So they played as good a game as they could play because they felt they had absolutely nothing to lose.

It was a tremendous day, I'll tell you, it really was. It was like being in the seventh game of the World Series. Gid started and he didn't really have his good stuff 'cause he was going with only three days' rest again, but he was still good enough to hold them to two runs in six and a third, quite an accomplishment for a lefthander in Fenway. In the second Yaz got up, and he knew Gid was going to try to pump a fastball by him, and Gid got the ball up, and Yaz has such power in his hands, he just turned those wrists over and *boom* that ball was gone.

They scored again in the sixth when Rice singled Burleson home. Everything was real quiet in our bullpen, and I said to Tidrow, "We're just teasing them. In the ninth inning, we're gonna win this son of a bitch three to two and go home." Dirt said, "I think we're gonna win eight to two." We were both wrong—the score was actually 5 to 4 —but we just knew, we had a feeling out there, that we were going to win. We had all those goose eggs up there on the scoreboard, but the way the game was going, Torrez had been lucky, and there was no way he was going to shut us out. And there wasn't.

In our half of the seventh Chambliss singled and Roy singled and Bucky Dent got up. Because Willie Randolph's still out, Fred Stanley went in to play second when Lem pinch-hit for Doyle, so they didn't pinch-hit for Bucky like they usually do. Torrez threw Bucky a slider, Bucky swung, and he hit the ball off his ankle. Bucky went down, and when he dragged himself back up, he hobbled over to third-base coach Dick Howser, and he said, "If that son of a bitch comes in there again with that pitch, I'm going to take him into the net." And Torrez threw it in there again, and *bang* there it went. Bucky hit it into the net for a three-run homer.

In the bullpen we were laughing because our shortstops have devastated Torrez. In June, Stanley hit that grand slam off him, and now Bucky hit this three-runner. Seven RBI's in two swings. Torrez just can't get our shortstops out! Then Rivers walked and stole second, and he scored when Thurman doubled off reliever Bob Stanley.

When Reggie got up in the eighth, Mr. October, as he likes to call himself, hit another home run to make it 5 to 2. Despite the fact that Reggie at times can be hard to take, there's no question that in the big games, he can get way up and hit the hell out of the ball. No one's ever denied him that. I can't figure out why he does it, but he does it. I think that in the big games a pitcher has a tendency to be finer around the plate, and that makes the hitter more selective. If Reggie could concentrate all year long like he does in the play-offs and the Series games, his records would be unbelievable. Reggie's so strong, and he has so much power that a pitcher can't fool with him. If he makes a mistake, and Reggie gets his bat on it, Reggie swings such a heavy bat it's gone.

Goose relieved Gid in the seventh and got the last two outs, but in their half of the eighth, the Red Sox came back with two runs against him. Remy doubled, Yaz singled to drive him in, Fisk singled, and Lynn singled for their fourth run.

They got us out in the top of the ninth, so the score was still 5–4 ours when Boston batted in the bottom of the inning. Goose walked Burleson with one out. Remy then hit a line drive to Piniella in right. Lou lost it in the sun, which was beating right in his eyes, but he pretended he was going to catch it, pounding his glove, so Burleson had to hold up and could only go to second when the ball bounced in front of him. That won the game for us, 'cause Rice fiied out, and had Burleson been on third, he would have tagged and scored and tied up the game. With Burleson on second, though, it was just a harmless fly ball.

Now there were two outs in the bottom of the ninth. The Red Sox were down to their last batter: Carl Yastrzemski. I had seen the way the game was going, and I was heating up pretty good in the bullpen cause I thought to myself, "Goddamn, the way this is going, I'm going to face Yaz if he comes up in the ninth." Even Tidrow had said, "They're gonna be using you. Stay ready." I guess he figured Yaz is left-handed and they'd bring me in to face the lefty.

If I could have gone in there and gotten him out and saved the game, that one out would have let me be part of something. Just one fucking out, which is all it would have been. I've always been able to get Yaz out, and if ever there was a time to bring me in this was it.

I stood out in the bullpen waiting for Lemon to come out of the dugout and get Goose. Lemon, however, never left the bench. He left Goose in to pitch to Yaz. I said, "Screw it," and I stopped warming up.

I suppose I should have been annoyed, pissed off, angry,

but I wasn't any of those things. You gotta look at it from Lem's way too. When you have a reliever like Goose—just like I was last year—you gotta go with the guy all the way. You can't be making too many moves.

Yaz stepped in, Goose fired the ball in there, and Yaz sent a high pop behind third. When Graig settled under the ball and caught it and the game was over, suddenly I felt a tremendous surge of happiness come over me. Even though I had hardly contributed at all, for the first time since the spring I really felt part of this team. I was proud of what we did, and all the records the team set. I was happy for Guidry, who won his twenty-fifth, and I felt happy for Goose, who got his twenty-seventh save. I was thinking about how we came from 14 games back in July, and how no other team in the entire history of baseball had ever done that. The events were rushing through my mind. There were so many things that happened to this team this year, I'll probably remember this season more than any other season of my baseball career.

We were celebrating in the clubhouse, and I was feeling excited and happy, when I started thinking about what Steinbrenner had said to me during midseason: "I want you to know that just as much as you were responsible for getting us into the play-offs last year, you're just as responsible for our having to struggle so much this year. If you had pitched halfway the way you can, we would have run away with it."

Well, I'll be out of here by Christmas, I guarantee you that, and next year I'll come back and I'll get even with him. I'm going to miss the guys. I have no bitch with them. No team could have as great a bunch of guys as this team. But when I come back to Yankee Stadium, and I'm sitting in the opposite dugout, I'm going to break that man's heart, just like he broke mine. And that's a promise.

Epilogue

We were dead tired after our sudden-death win over the Red Sox, but because we went right to Kansas City without getting a day off, we didn't have time to suffer a let-

down before the start of the Championship Series. We beat
the Royals in the first game in their ball park and lost the
second, which was all we were looking to do, and when
we came back home, we kicked their ass and won two in a
row to knock them off for the third year in a row.

I hope to hell they realign the Divisions like they're talking about and put Kansas City with us because it would be
the last play-off spot they ever seen. If they had been in
the East this year, they would have been fourth, behind us,
Boston, and Milwaukee.

When we returned to the Stadium after going out to
Kansas City, Gene Monahan and Herman Schneider, the
two trainers, were in the trainer's room talking to George.
They were pointing to the mysterious *P* taped on the wall,
and Gene said to George, "Now that we've won the East,
can we take that down?" George said they could. Later I
asked Gene what they were talking about. It turns out the
P stood for *probation*. Right after the All-Star break when
Gullett and Catfish and Dent and Randolph and Rivers
and Messersmith got hurt, George called the trainers up to
his office and said, "These injuries have to cease. One
more thing happens and you two guys are gone. Fired.
You're on probation right now. One more injury and it's
see ya." So they put the *P* up on the wall to remind them
of their status. I know it sounds absolutely insane, George
blaming them for all the injuries, but after that, the injuries stopped.

I only pitched a couple of innings in the play-offs, mop-
ping up and pitching poorly in the second game, but I felt
just as much involved as I had been last year because I was
able to do it through Goose. I just couldn't help myself.
During the games I was telling him, "You're going to be
up soon. I can tell by the way things are going. You're
about to get the call." He'd say, "Yeah, yeah, I know." It's
a great feeling to be going into a game at a crucial time,
and I was having that experience through him, especially
after he won the fourth game and saved the clincher.
Maybe he thought I was goofy in what I was saying, but
that was my way of being in the play-offs. I knew I wasn't
going to pitch, but that didn't mean I couldn't be involved.

* * *

Damn my luck.

I wouldn't have been able to pitch in the first couple of Series games even if they had asked me. I have a varicose vein under my nuts that acts up sometimes. It hurts like somebody's hit you in the nuts with a hammer, coming up from inside. I've had it before, and always it goes away.

We were out in L.A., and before the first game, I almost passed out, it hurt so much. During the national anthem I was lucky to get through. Afterward I made my way to the bullpen, and I was turning white. Tidrow said, "You're really hurting." I said, "Yeah." He said, "If you don't go into the clubhouse, I'm calling them." So I went in and lay down. A couple of days later the pain left.

What pissed me off was that when Lem made the announcement, he said, "Sparky's having trouble with his balls." All the writers laughed. They were thinking, "Oh, he's pissed off about something" or "It's something else he must have, like the clap." They made a big joke about it. Made it sound like I was jaking.

Lem didn't help my disposition. On the flight back from L.A. after we lost the first two games, Lem was talking with Mary. He said, "Sparky's just given up." And that really pissed me off. Him of all people. I know Rosen thinks I lost my confidence on the mound. Hell, that'll never happen. Mary told Lem, "No, he didn't. He never gave up. That's one thing he didn't do."

Then when we got back to New York, the Dodgers really pissed us all off. In those first couple of games in L.A., the only games they won, Lopes was hitting home runs and circling the bases with his finger pointing in the air, as if to say, "We're number one." How bush is that? Our guys kept saying, "We don't want to just beat them. We want to really kick their ass." And we did. We swept the next four in a row, and people like Bucky and Doyle hit like they never hit before, and Graig made about seven of the greatest plays you ever saw, and Rivers and Roy and Thurman and Reggie hit the crap out of the ball. Then as soon as we started winning, they started crying. They were such crybabies. They have about zero class. They kept making excuses like "If only the ball hadn't taken a bad hop." "If only Nettles hadn't made those great plays." Sheeit. When Russell said, "If you play in New York long enough, you're bound to be an asshole," that was the last straw. Then he started bitching about how lousy our field was. He should talk about lousy. He was lousy. He couldn't have caught a ground ball with a shovel. Hell, their field was as different for us as ours was for them. You didn't see us complaining. And I'd like to see the Dodgers play that fucking Series without Garvey and Lopes like we did without Randolph and Chambliss. There would have been no contest. Except that whoever played in Garvey's place would have hit better than he did. I mean, hell, anybody can go 2 for 20, even me.

The Dodgers weren't even the second-best team in baseball. There's no doubt whatsoever that Boston is a lot better team than they are, in every way.

On November 10, 1978, Sparky Lyle was traded to the Texas Rangers along with catcher Mike Heath, pitchers Larry McCall and Dave Rajsich, and infielder Domingo Ramos. In return, Texas sent outfielder Juan Beniquez, and minor league pitchers Dave Righetti, Paul Mirabella, and Mike Griffin, and minor league outfielder Greg Jemison to New York. Steinbrenner also paid Texas $400,000 in cash.

The next day Lyle met with Texas owner Brad Corbett and signed a three-year contract that will bring him about a million dollars. When he retires, Lyle will get another half million to broadcast Ranger games on TV. More important, Lyle has been promised a chance to pitch again. He has a lot to prove.

Dell Bestsellers

- [ ] **TO LOVE AGAIN** by Danielle Steel $2.50 (18631-5)
- [ ] **SECOND GENERATION** by Howard Fast $2.75 (17892-4)
- [ ] **EVERGREEN** by Belva Plain $2.75 (13294-0)
- [ ] **AMERICAN CAESAR** by William Manchester . . . $3.50 (10413-0)
- [ ] **THERE SHOULD HAVE BEEN CASTLES**
  by Herman Raucher $2.75 (18500-9)
- [ ] **THE FAR ARENA** by Richard Ben Sapir $2.75 (12671-1)
- [ ] **THE SAVIOR** by Marvin Werlin and Mark Werlin . $2.75 (17748-0)
- [ ] **SUMMER'S END** by Danielle Steel $2.50 (18418-5)
- [ ] **SHARKY'S MACHINE** by William Diehl $2.50 (18292-1)
- [ ] **DOWNRIVER** by Peter Collier $2.75 (11830-1)
- [ ] **CRY FOR THE STRANGERS** by John Saul $2.50 (11869-7)
- [ ] **BITTER EDEN** by Sharon Salvato $2.75 (10771-7)
- [ ] **WILD TIMES** by Brian Garfield $2.50 (19457-1)
- [ ] **1407 BROADWAY** by Joel Gross $2.50 (12819-6)
- [ ] **A SPARROW FALLS** by Wilbur Smith $2.75 (17707-3)
- [ ] **FOR LOVE AND HONOR** by Antonia Van-Loon . . $2.50 (12574-X)
- [ ] **COLD IS THE SEA** by Edward L. Beach $2.50 (11045-9)
- [ ] **TROCADERO** by Leslie Waller $2.50 (18613-7)
- [ ] **THE BURNING LAND** by Emma Drummond $2.50 (10274-X)
- [ ] **HOUSE OF GOD** by Samuel Shem, M.D. $2.50 (13371-8)
- [ ] **SMALL TOWN** by Sloan Wilson $2.50 (17474-0)

At your local bookstore or use this handy coupon for ordering:

DELL BOOKS
P.O. BOX 1000, PINEBROOK, N.J. 07058

Please send me the books I have checked above. I am enclosing $ _____
(please add 75¢ per copy to cover postage and handling). Send check or money
order—no cash or C.O.D.'s. Please allow up to 8 weeks for shipment.

Mr/Mrs/Miss _____

Address _____

City _____ State/Zip _____